Free to
LEARN

Free to
LEARN

---·✳·---

*Why Unleashing the Instinct to Play Will
Make Our Children Happier, More Self-Reliant,
and Better Students for Life*

Peter Gray

BASIC BOOKS

New York

Copyright © 2013 by Peter Gray

Published by Basic Books,
A Member of the Perseus Books Group

All rights reserved. Printed in the United States of America. No part of this book may be reproduced in any manner whatsoever without written permission except in the case of brief quotations embodied in critical articles and reviews. For information, address Basic Books, 250 West 57th Street, 15th Floor, New York, NY 10107-1307.

Books published by Basic Books are available at special discounts for bulk purchases in the United States by corporations, institutions, and other organizations. For more information, please contact the Special Markets Department at the Perseus Books Group, 2300 Chestnut Street, Suite 200, Philadelphia, PA 19103, or call (800) 810-4145, ext. 5000, or e-mail special.markets@perseusbooks.com.

Typeset in 11.5 point Minion Pro Std by the Perseus Books Group

Library of Congress Cataloging-in-Publication Data

Gray, Peter.
  Free to learn : why unleashing the instinct to play will make our children happier, more self-reliant, and better students for life / Peter Gray.
      p.   cm
  Includes bibliographical references and index.
  ISBN 978-0-465-02599-2 (hbk.)—978-0-465-03791-9 (ebk.)
  1. Play—Psychological aspects. 2. Developmental psychology.
  I. Title.
  BF717.G73 2013
  155.4'18—dc23
                        2012040660

10 9 8 7 6 5 4 3 2 1

*To Scott, who inspired it,
and Diane, who made it possible.*

CONTENTS

PROLOGUE

"GO TO HELL."

The words hit me hard. I had on occasion been damned to hell before, but never so seriously. A colleague, frustrated by my thickheaded lack of agreement with an obvious truth, or a friend, responding to some idiotic thing I had said. But in those cases "go to hell" was just a way to break the tension, to end an argument that was going nowhere. This time it was serious. This time I felt, maybe, I really would go to hell. Not the afterlife hell of fire and brimstone, which I don't believe in, but the hell that can accompany life in this world when you are burned by the knowledge that you have failed someone you love, who needs you, who depends on you.

The words were spoken by my nine-year-old son, Scott, in the principal's office of the public elementary school. They were addressed not only to me but to all seven of us big, smart adults who were lined up against him—the principal, Scott's two classroom teachers, the school's guidance counselor, a child psychologist who worked for the school system, his mother (my late wife), and me. We were there to present a united front, to tell Scott in no uncertain terms that he *must* attend school and *must* do there whatever he was told by his teachers to do. We each sternly said our piece, and then Scott, looking squarely at us all, said the words that stopped me in my tracks.

I immediately began to cry. I knew at that instant that I had to be on Scott's side, not against him. I looked through my tears to my wife and saw that she, too, was crying, and through her tears I could see that she was thinking and feeling exactly as I was. We both knew then that we had to do what Scott had long wanted us to do—remove him not just from that school but from anything that was anything like that school. To him, school was prison, and he had done nothing to deserve imprisonment.

That meeting in the principal's office was the culmination of years of meetings and conferences at the school, at which my wife and I would hear the latest accounts of our son's misbehavior. His misbehavior was particularly disturbing to the school personnel because it was not the usual kind of naughtiness that teachers have come to expect from exuberant boys confined against their will. It was more like planned rebellion. He would systematically and deliberately behave in ways contrary to the teachers' directions. When the teacher instructed students to solve arithmetic problems in a particular way, he would invent a different way to solve them. When it came time to learn about punctuation and capital letters, he would write like the poet e. e. cummings, putting capitals and punctuation wherever he wanted to or not using them at all. When an assignment seemed pointless to him, he would say so and refuse to do it. Sometimes—and this had become increasingly frequent—he would, without permission, leave the classroom and, if not forcibly restrained, walk home.

We eventually found a school for Scott that worked. A school as unlike "school" as you can imagine. A little later I will tell you about it and the worldwide educational movement it has inspired. But this book is not primarily about a particular school. It is about the human nature of education.

Children come into the world burning to learn and genetically programmed with extraordinary capacities for learning. They are little learning machines. Within their first four years or so they absorb an unfathomable amount of information and skills without any instruction. They learn to walk, run, jump, and climb. They learn to understand and speak the language of the culture into which they are born, and with that they learn to assert their will, argue, amuse, annoy, befriend, and ask questions. They acquire an incredible amount of knowledge about the physical and social world around them. All of this is driven by their inborn instincts and drives, their innate playfulness and curiosity. Nature does not turn off this enormous desire and capacity to learn when children turn five or six. We turn it off with our coercive system of schooling. The biggest, most enduring lesson of school is that learning is work, to be avoided when possible.

My son's words in the principal's office changed the direction of my professional life as well as my personal life. I am, and was then, a professor of biopsychology, a researcher interested in the biological foundations of mammalian drives and emotions. I had been studying the roles of certain hormones in modulating fear in rats and mice, and I had recently begun looking into the brain mechanisms of maternal behavior in rats. That day in the principal's office triggered a series of events that gradually changed the focus of my research. I began to study education from a biological perspective. At first my study was motivated primarily by concern for my son. I wanted to make sure we weren't making a mistake by allowing him to follow his own educational path rather than a path dictated by professionals. But gradually, as I became convinced that Scott's self-directed education was going beautifully, my interest turned to children in general and to the human biological underpinnings of education.

What is it about our species that makes us the cultural animal? In other words, what aspects of human nature cause each new generation of human beings, everywhere, to acquire and build upon the skills, knowledge, beliefs, theories, and values of the previous generation? This question led me to examine education in settings outside of the standard school system, for example, at the remarkable non-school my son was attending. Later I looked into the growing, worldwide "unschooling" movement to understand how the children in those families become educated. I read the anthropological literature and surveyed anthropologists to learn everything I could about children's lives and learning in hunter-gatherer cultures—the kinds of cultures that characterized our species for 99 percent of our evolutionary history. I reviewed the entire body of psychological and anthropological research on children's play, and my students and I conducted new research aimed at understanding how children learn through play.

Such work led me to understand how children's strong drives to play and explore serve the function of education, not only in hunter-gatherer cultures but in our culture as well. It led to new insights concerning the environmental conditions that optimize children's abilities to educate themselves through their own playful means. It led me to see how, if we had the will, we could free children from coercive schooling and provide learning centers that would maximize their ability to educate themselves without depriving them of the rightful joys of childhood.

This book is about all of that.

1

WHAT HAVE WE DONE TO CHILDHOOD?

I'VE LEARNED FROM HUNDREDS of great teachers over the course of my life, but if I had to pick the single greatest it would be Ruby Lou. I met her the summer I was five and she was six. My family had just moved to a new town and, at my mother's suggestion, I had gone door to door, by myself, up and down both sides of the street, knocking and inquiring, "Do any children about my age live here?" That's how I found her, right across the street. Within a few minutes we were best friends, and we remained so for the two years that I lived in that town. Ruby Lou was older, smarter, and bolder than I, but not too much so, and that's why she was such a great teacher for me.

In the mid-1980s Robert Fulghum published a wildly popular collection of essays, *All I Really Need to Know I Learned in Kindergarten*. I didn't go to kindergarten. The little town we moved to when I was five didn't have one. But I think even Fulghum, if pushed, might agree that most of the important lessons anyone learns in life are not learned in kindergarten or anywhere else in school. They are learned from life itself.

During that first summer, Ruby Lou and I played together almost every day, often all day, sometimes just the two of us and sometimes with other kids in the neighborhood. Then she started first grade and I did not, but we continued to play together after school and on weekends.

I've sometimes thought of writing a book titled *All I Really Need to Know I Learned from Ruby Lou*. The first thing I remember Ruby Lou teaching me was how to ride a bicycle. I didn't have one, but she did, and she let me use it. It was a girl's bike, which meant it was easier to learn on because you didn't have to swing your leg up over a horizontal bar to get on or off. The street we lived on ran down a small hill, and Ruby Lou showed me that if I got on the bike at the top of the hill and gave myself a little push-off with my foot, I would immediately pick up enough speed, even without pedaling, to remain upright. That way I could learn to balance independently of learning to pedal. She instructed me to start pedaling as I reached the bottom of the hill and to try to go as far as possible each time before toppling over or putting my feet to the ground to stop. I got a couple of skinned knees and dinged a neighbor's parked car on my early trials, but Ruby Lou told me not to worry, that I was getting better and would soon be riding "forever" without falling. Within a couple of days I indeed could ride forever. When my parents saw that, they bought me a clunker of a used bike. It was too big for me ("so you won't outgrow it too quickly") and had a boy's bar so high that it was hard to mount. But I could ride it. It was my first set of wheels, and it gave me a freedom, at age five, that I had never before known.

Once I had my own bike, Ruby Lou and I began going on bike rides all over the village and into the nearby countryside. They seemed like huge adventures, though I imagine we never went more than two or three miles from home. I wasn't allowed to take such trips alone, but I could take them with Ruby Lou. My mother could see that Ruby Lou, at six, was mature and responsible and knew her way around. She would keep me out of trouble. On every adventure we learned something new about the world in which we lived and we met new people. Even today, my favorite way to get around is by bike, and I sometimes think of Ruby Lou as I pedal along to work or to wherever I'm going.

Ruby Lou also helped me climb trees. There was an amazing pine tree in my front yard. My guess is that to an adult it was an average-sized pine, but to me, then, it seemed huge, its top in heaven, built by God for climbing. I was not the boldest or most agile kid around, so I had to work hard, for weeks and months, at climbing ever higher. The tree called out to Ruby Lou as much as it did to me, and she was always a more advanced climber. Each time she made it up to a higher, never previously achieved branch, I knew that I could, too. What a thrill to climb toward heaven and then look down at earth, so far below. Maybe it was fifteen feet below, maybe twenty, but it was enough to fill my five-year-old self with the thrill of danger and the even greater thrill of confidence that I could embrace danger and, through my own efforts, come out alive, a confidence that has served me well throughout my life.

And then, one scorching summer day, Ruby Lou gave me my first lesson about death. I was playing outdoors with my blowup plastic pool, running and leaping into it, sliding on my butt through the water. Ruby Lou walked into the yard and I expected her to leap into the pool as she usually did, but she didn't. She simply sat down on the grass a distance away and didn't say anything. I tried to get her to laugh, by performing some silly tricks, but nothing worked. I had never seen anyone act like that before. Finally I walked over and sat down next to her. She told me then that her grandfather, who had been living with her, had died during the night. It was my first experience with death and my first attempt at consoling a person who had lost someone she loved. I failed, of course, and what I learned, eventually, is that you always fail at that. All you can do is be there, as a friend, and let time do the healing. Fortunately, time works quickly when you are six and every day has the power of two weeks. Not much of the summer slipped by before Ruby Lou and I were playing and laughing together again.

I'm not the only person who looks back at childhood and regrets that today's children have less freedom than we did. Ask almost anyone of middle age or older about their childhood and they'll start to reminisce about time spent in adventures with other children, well away from adults. Here's an excerpt from an essay by former First Lady and then US Secretary of State Hillary Rodham Clinton about her childhood in Park Ridge, Illinois:

> We had a well-organized kids' society and we had all kinds of games, playing hard every day after school, every weekend, and from dawn until our parents made us come in at dark in the summertime. One game was called chase and run, which was a kind of complex team-based hide-and-seek and tag combination. We would make up teams and disperse throughout the entire neighborhood for maybe a two- or three-block area, designating safe places that you could get to if somebody was chasing you. There were also ways of breaking the hold of a tag so that you could get back in the game. As with all of our games, the rules were elaborate and they were hammered out in long consultations on street corners. It was how we spent countless hours. . . .
> We were so independent, we were given so much freedom. But now it's impossible to imagine giving that to a child today. It's one of the great losses as a society.[1]

Regardless of which side of the political fence you are on, you will agree that Hillary grew up to be an extraordinarily competent, confident, and socially adept adult. When I think of Secretary Clinton hammering out agreements among world leaders, I imagine next to her a little girl hammering out agreements with neighborhood kids about the rules for chase and run.

"WE WERE SO INDEPENDENT, we were given so much freedom. But now it's impossible to imagine giving that to a child today. It's one of the great losses as a society." It's not just a great loss; it's a tragic and cruel loss. Children are designed, by nature, to play and explore on their own, independently of adults. They need freedom in order to develop; without it they suffer. The drive to play freely is a basic, biological drive. Lack of free play may not kill the physical body, as would lack of food, air, or water, but it kills the spirit and stunts mental growth. Free play is the means by which children learn to make friends, overcome their fears, solve their own problems, and generally take control of their own lives. It is also the primary means by which children practice and acquire the physical and intellectual skills that are essential for success in the culture in which they are growing. Nothing that we do, no amount of toys we buy or "quality time" or special training we give our children, can compensate for the freedom we take away. The things that children learn through their own initiatives, in free play, cannot be taught in other ways.

We are pushing the limits of children's adaptability. We have pushed children into an abnormal environment, where they are expected to spend ever greater portions of their day under adult direction, sitting at desks, listening to and reading about things that don't interest them, and answering questions that are not their own and are not, to them, real questions. We leave them ever less time and freedom to play, explore, and pursue their own interests.

I'm an evolutionary developmental psychologist. That means that I study child development from a Darwinian perspective. I'm particularly interested in those aspects of children's nature that equip them to learn, on their own initiatives, what they must in order to survive and do well in the culture into which they are born. Stated differently, I am interested in the biological foundations of education. To this end, I have studied education as it occurred in the original kinds of human societies, hunter-gatherer societies, where there was nothing like schools, and children always took charge of their own learning. I have also studied education as it currently occurs at a remarkable alternative school near my home in Massachusetts, where hundreds of children and adolescents have educated themselves successfully through self-directed activities, with no adult-imposed curriculum or testing. In addition, I have looked at education in families that practice a version of homeschooling called "unschooling," and I have looked deeply into and contributed to the biological and psychological research on the functions of play.

All of this work tells a remarkably consistent and surprising story, a story that defies modern, mainstream beliefs about education. Children are biologically predisposed to take charge of their own education. When they are provided with the freedom and means to pursue their own interests, in safe settings, they bloom and develop along diverse and unpredictable paths, and they acquire the skills and confidence required to meet life's challenges. In such an environment, children ask for any help they may need from adults. There is no need for forced lessons, lectures, assignments, tests, grades, segregation by age into classrooms, or any of the other trappings of our standard, compulsory system of schooling. All of these, in fact, interfere with children's natural ways of learning.

This is a book about children's natural instincts to educate themselves, about the environmental conditions required for those instincts to operate optimally, and about how we, as a society, can provide those conditions at far less expense than what we currently spend on schools. The drive to play is a huge part of children's natural means for self-education, so a portion of this book is about the power of play. In this first chapter, however, I assess the damage we are causing through our present treatment of children. Over the past half century or more we have seen a continuous erosion of children's freedom to play and, corresponding with that, a continuous decline in young people's mental and physical health. If this trend continues, we are in serious danger of producing generations of future adults who cannot find their own way in life.

A Half Century of Decline[2]

It used to be that you could walk through almost any neighborhood in America—after school, or on weekends, or during the summer—and see children playing outside, without adult supervision. Now if you see them outside at all they are likely to be wearing uniforms and following the directions of adult coaches, while their parents look on and dutifully cheer their every move.

In an authoritative book on the history of children's play in America, Howard Chudacoff refers to the early to mid-twentieth century as "the golden age of children's unstructured play."[3] By "unstructured play," Chudacoff does not mean play that lacks structure. He recognizes that play is never random activity; it always has structure. By "unstructured" he really means structured by the players themselves rather than by an outside authority. I refer to this as *free play,* defined as play in which the players themselves decide what and how to play and are free to modify the goals and rules as they go along. Pickup baseball is free play; a Little League game is not. Free play is how children learn to structure their own behavior.

It is reasonable, if somewhat oversimplified, to say that over time in postcolonial America children's opportunities to play freely have been determined by two trends. One is the gradual decline in need for child labor, which allowed children more time for play. This explains the general rise in play up to the early to mid-twentieth century. The other trend is the gradual increase in adult control of children's lives outside the world of labor, which has reduced children's opportunities for free play. This trend began to accelerate around the middle of the twentieth century and explains the continuous decline in play since then.

One significant reason for this increase in adult control over children's lives is the ever-increasing weight of compulsory schooling. Children start school at ever younger ages. We now have not only kindergarten, but prekindergarten in some districts. And preschools, which precede kindergarten or prekindergarten, are structured more and more like elementary schools—with adult-assigned tasks replacing play. The school year has grown longer, as has the school day, and opportunities for free play within the school day have largely been eliminated. When I was an elementary school student in the 1950s we had half-hour recesses each morning and afternoon, and at noon we had an hour for lunch. During these periods (which occupied a third of the six-hour school day) we were free to do whatever we wished, even leave the school grounds. In third grade my friends and I would spend nearly the entire lunch hour wrestling on the grass, or in the snow, on a hill not far from the school. We also played games with jackknives and had major snowball wars in winter. I don't remember any teacher or other adult observing us in such play. If they did, they certainly didn't interfere. Such behavior would not be allowed today at any of the elementary schools I've observed. We were trusted then, in ways that children are not trusted today.

Not only has the school day grown longer and less playful, but school has intruded ever more into home and family life. Assigned homework has increased, eating into time that would otherwise be available for play. Parents are now expected to be teachers' aides. They're supposed to keep track of all the homework and special projects assigned to their kids and to coax, nag, or bribe them to complete those assignments. When kids blow off their homework or perform poorly on it, parents are often made to feel guilty, as if they had failed. Parents no longer dare to schedule family vacations that will keep their child out of school for even a day or two, or allow their child to miss school for activities at home that might, in truth, produce more useful learning than what would have occurred during that time in school.

But school has taken over children's lives in an even more insidious way. The school system has directly and indirectly, often unintentionally, fostered an attitude in society that children learn and progress primarily by doing tasks that are directed and evaluated by adults, and that children's own activities are wasted time. This attitude is seldom explicitly articulated, although when the superintendent of schools in Atlanta, Georgia, decided to end the tradition of free play at recesses, he declared, "Rather than give children 30 minutes to while away the time as they please, it makes more sense to teach them a skill, like dancing or gymnastics."[4] The same superintendent also said that children don't need free play to get exercise, because they get that in physical education classes. Few educators would voice such an anti-play attitude so baldly. Most at least give lip service to the value of free play. Yet, at a level that controls adults' actual behavior toward children, the anti-play attitude grows more pervasive with every passing decade and has seeped through the school walls to infect society everywhere. Children are increasingly encouraged or required to take adult-directed lessons and engage in adult-directed sports even out of school, rather than to play freely.

Related to this anti-play attitude is an ever-increasing focus on children's *performance*, which can be measured, and decreasing concern for true learning, which is difficult or impossible to measure. What matters in today's educational world is performance that can be scored and compared across students, across schools, and even across nations to see who is better and who is worse. Knowledge that is not part of the school curriculum, even deep knowledge, doesn't count. By "true learning" and "deep knowledge," I mean children's incorporation of ideas and information into lasting ways of understanding and responding to the world around them (more on this in later chapters). This is very different from superficial knowledge that is acquired solely for the purpose of passing a test and is forgotten shortly after the test is over.

Parents, teachers, schools, and whole school districts—not just the children themselves—are evaluated these days on the basis of the children's test performance. Children are pawns in a competitive game in which the adults around them are trying to squeeze the highest possible scores out of them on standardized tests. Anything that increases performance short of outright cheating is considered "education" in this high-stakes game. Thus, drills that enhance short-term memory of information they will be tested on are considered legitimate education, even though such drills produce no increase at all in understanding.

This focus on performance has moved beyond the classroom to all sorts of extracurricular and out-of-school activities. In the eyes of many parents and educators today, childhood is not so much a time for learning as a time for résumé building. School grades and standardized-test performance "count," as do formal, adult-directed activities outside of school, especially those that produce trophies, honors, or other forms of positive evaluation by adults. In this way, children and adolescents are coaxed and guided, if not pushed, into adult-organized sports, out-of-school lessons, and adult-directed volunteer activities. Even young children, whose activities won't realistically go on paper, are directed onto stepping-stones toward later, more explicit résumé building. Free play doesn't count because it's *just play*; there's no place for it on a college application.

The increased weight of schooling and the perceived need to build résumés are not the only reasons free play has declined over the past half century. Equally influential is the continuous rise in adults' belief that unsupervised play is dangerous. Today, if a playing child is abducted, molested, or murdered by a stranger anywhere in the developed world, the media swarm to cover it, so the fears are exaggerated beyond reason. The actual rate of such cases is low and has declined in recent years.[5] In a recent large-scale multinational survey, the most often cited fear that led parents to restrict their children's outdoor play was, "They may be in danger of child predators" (cited by 49 percent of parents).[6] Other prominent fears expressed in the survey that may be more realistic are fears of road traffic and of bullies. In another, smaller survey conducted in the UK, 78 percent of parents cited fear of molestation by strangers as a reason they restricted their children's outdoor play, while 52 percent cited dangers from traffic.[7]

In yet another survey—of 830 mothers from a representative sample of geographical areas in the United States—85 percent agreed that their child or children played outdoors less often than they themselves did when they were children.[8] When asked about the obstacles to their own children's outdoor play, 82 percent of the mothers cited safety concerns and crime. Surprisingly, the rates of these fears were little affected by geographic region; they were as prominent in rural areas and small villages as they were in cities. If we want to increase children's opportunities for free outdoor play, we must strengthen neighborhoods in ways that allow parents to perceive them as safe. What kind of a society do we live in if our children cannot play safely and freely outdoors?

Statistical evidence for the decline in play comes also from diary studies in which parents were asked to keep records of their children's activities on randomly chosen days. In a long-term study of this sort, sociologist Sandra Hofferth and her colleagues compared the amount of time that representative samples of children spent daily on various activities in 1997 with the time that similar samples spent at the same activities in 1981.[9] Among other things, the study revealed that children age six to eight spent 18 percent more time in school, 145 percent more time doing schoolwork at home, 168 percent more time shopping with parents, 55 percent *less* time conversing with others at home, 19 percent *less* time watching television, and 25 percent *less* time playing in 1997 than they did in 1981. All this in a sixteen-year period, roughly half a generation. In this study the "play" category included indoor play, such as board games and computer games, as well as outdoor play. We can only assume that the amount of outdoor play decreased even more than 25 percent, as the amount of indoor computer play must have increased during this period (it would have been essentially zero in 1981). The total amount of time that the average child in this age group spent at play (including computer play) in 1997 was slightly over eleven hours per week. In a follow-up study, using the same methods, Hofferth and her colleagues found a continued increase (of 32 percent) in time spent at homework and a slight further decrease (of 7 percent) in time spent playing for this age group over the six-year period from 1997 to 2003.[10]

When parents are asked why their children don't play outside more, they often cite their children's own preferences as well as safety concerns. In particular, they often refer to the seductive qualities of television and computer games.[11] However, in a large-scale study in which children themselves were asked about their play preferences, outdoor play with friends came out on top. In paired comparisons with specific other activities, 89 percent said they preferred outdoor play with friends to watching television, and 86 percent said they preferred it to computer play.[12] Perhaps kids today play on the computer as much as they do partly because that is one place where they can play freely, without adult intervention and direction. Many are not allowed to play freely outdoors, and even if they are, they are unlikely to find others to play with, so they play indoors instead. Of course that's not the only reason for the popularity of computer play. Such play is great fun, and kids do learn a lot from it. But for physical fitness and learning about the real world and how to get along with peers, outdoor play with friends has no equal.

The Rise of Psychological Disorders in Young People

The decline of free play and the careerist approach to childhood have exacted a heavy toll. A not-atypical kid you might find in any middle-class neighborhood today is someone I'll call Evan. He's eleven years old. On weekdays his mom drags him from bed at 6:30 A.M. so he can dress and grab something to eat in time for the school bus. He's not allowed to walk to school, even though walking would take less time, be more fun, and give him some exercise; it's too dangerous. At school he spends most of the day sitting still, listening to teachers, taking tests, reading what he's told to read, writing what he's told to write, all the while daydreaming about what he would really like to be doing. The school has even done away with the half-hour recess it used to have, to prevent injuries and lawsuits and to create more time to prepare children for the statewide exams. After school, Evan's life is scheduled in a way designed (primarily by his parents) to give him a balanced set of skills and keep him out of trouble. He's got soccer on Monday, piano on Tuesday, Karate on Wednesday, Spanish on Thursday. In the evening, after watching TV or playing a video game, he spends a couple of hours on homework. His mother has to sign his homework sheets each night as evidence that she has monitored his doing them. On weekends he's got a league game, Sunday school, and maybe a little free time to hang out with friends in the safety of one of their homes. His parents like to boast about his many activities, always explaining that it's "his own choice" and that "he likes to keep busy." They see him as preparing himself for admission to the prestigious college that they hope he'll get into seven years hence. Evan has a strong constitution, but at times he admits to feeling a bit "burned out."

Evan is one of the successes. Down the street is Hank, diagnosed with attention-deficit/hyperactivity disorder, who takes Adderall because without it he can't sit still all day at school. With it, he manages to do well enough to pass, but the drug takes away his appetite, keeps him awake at night, and generally makes him feel "weird." He says he doesn't feel like himself when he takes it, and his parents admit that he's not as playful, funny, or happy when he's on the drug as when he's off it. But they don't see a choice; he has to make passing grades at school or they fear he will fall hopelessly behind.

Of course, not all kids today suffer to such a degree as Evan or Hank. But the reality is that altogether too many kids do suffer from problems like theirs, and many feel burned out by the time they graduate from high school, if not before. Here's a quotation, clipped from an article in my local newspaper, from an eighteen-year-old high school graduate, who could be Evan seven years older: "I was consumed with doing well and didn't sleep a lot the last two years. I would have five or six hours of homework almost every night. The last thing I wanted to do was more school." In the same article, another eighteen-year-old, who had been accepted to Harvard, described his stressful last year of high school. Among other things, he had juggled six Advanced Placement courses while wrestling competitively, playing the viola, and taking classes in Chinese black-and-white portraiture. He, too, felt burned out, in need of at least a year off before going on to college.

Representing the other end of the school-age spectrum, here's a comment that was posted on a blog I write for *Psychology Today* magazine: "Here in NYC, the kids start Kindergarten at 4. My best friend's son started this past September. About 2 weeks into the school year, he was getting letters home from the teacher that he was 'falling behind academically.' Since then, he's gotten letter after letter, and meeting after meeting with the teacher. My friend has been trying to deal with the problem by drilling his son at home in the evenings. The poor kid begs to be allowed to go to bed. The both of them are discouraged and feel like failures."[13] Comments such as these are depressingly easy to find.

Impressions, prototypes, and selected quotations are one thing, but hard evidence is another. How does young people's mental health today compare, statistically, to that of decades past?

RATES OF STRESS-RELATED MENTAL DISORDERS in young people have skyrocketed over the past fifty years. These increases are not simply the result of greater awareness of such disorders and greater likelihood that they will be detected and treated. They represent real increases in incidences of the disorders. Psychologists and psychiatrists have developed standard questionnaires to assess mental problems and disorders, some of which have been used with large samples of young people for several decades. Therefore, it is possible to look at changes in the rates of certain mental disorders over time using the very same, unchanged measures.

For example, Taylor's Manifest Anxiety Scale has been used to assess anxiety levels in college students since 1952, and a version of this test for children has been used with elementary school students since 1956. Another questionnaire, the Minnesota Multiphasic Personality Inventory (MMPI), has been given to college students since 1938, and a version for adolescents (the MMPI-A) has been used with high school students since 1951. The MMPI and MMPI-A are designed to assess levels of a number of psychological problems and disorders, including depression. All of these questionnaires consist of statements about the self, to which the person must agree or disagree. For example, Taylor's Manifest Anxiety Scale includes such statements as "I often worry that something bad will happen" and "Most of the time I feel pleasant." A "yes" to the first statement would add to the anxiety score and a "yes" to the second would subtract from it. An example of a question on the MMPI for which a "yes" adds to the depression score is "The future seems hopeless to me."

Jean Twenge, a psychology professor at San Diego State University in California, has conducted extensive analyses of changes in young people's scores on these tests over time. The results are truly disheartening. By these measures, anxiety and depression have increased continuously, linearly, and dramatically in children, adolescents, and college students over the decades since the tests were first developed. In fact, the increases are so great, for both anxiety and depression, that approximately 85 percent of young people today have scores greater than the average for the same age group in the 1950s. Looked at in another way, *five to eight times* as many young people today have scores above the cutoff for likely diagnosis of a clinically significant anxiety disorder or major depression than fifty or more years ago. These increases are at least as great, if not greater, for elementary and high school students as for college students.[14]

In work conducted independently of Twenge and her colleagues, psychologist Cassandra Newsom and her colleagues analyzed MMPI and MMPI-A scores collected from adolescents age fourteen to sixteen between 1948 and 1989.[15] Their results were comparable to Twenge's, and their article includes tables showing how the adolescents responded to specific questionnaire items in 1948 and in 1989—years when large normative samples were tested. Here, for illustration, are the results for five items that were among those showing the largest changes.[16]

	1948	1989
"I wake up fresh and rested most mornings."	74.6%	31.3%
"I work under a great deal of tension."	16.2%	41.6%
"Life is a strain for me much of the time."	9.5%	35.0%
"I have certainly had more than my share of things to worry about."	22.6%	55.2%
"I am afraid of losing my mind."	4.1%	23.4%

An even more sobering index of decline in young people's mental health is found in suicide rates. Since 1950, the US suicide rate for children under age fifteen has quadrupled, and that for people age fifteen to twenty-four has more than doubled. During this same period, the suicide rate for adults age twenty-five to forty rose only slightly and that for adults over age forty actually declined.[17]

These increases seem to have nothing to do with realistic dangers and uncertainties in the larger world. The changes do not correlate with economic cycles, wars, or any of the other kinds of national or world events that people often talk about as affecting young people's mental states. Rates of anxiety and depression among children and adolescents were far lower during the Great Depression, during World War II, during the Cold War, and during the turbulent 1960s and early '70s than they are today. The changes seem to have much more to do with the way young people view the world than with the way the world actually is.

ONE THING WE KNOW for sure about anxiety and depression is that they correlate strongly with people's sense of control or lack of control over their own lives. Those who believe they are in charge of their own fate are much less likely to become anxious or depressed than are those who believe they are victims of circumstances beyond their control. You might think that the sense of personal control would have increased over the past several decades. Real progress has occurred in our ability to prevent and treat diseases; the old prejudices that limited people's options because of race, gender, or sexual orientation have diminished; and the average person is wealthier today than in decades past. Yet, the data indicate that young people's sense of control over their own destinies has declined continuously.

The standard measure of sense of control is a questionnaire called the Internal-External Locus of Control Scale, developed by psychologist Julien Rotter in the late 1950s. The questionnaire consists of twenty-three pairs of statements. One statement in each pair represents belief in an *internal locus of control* (control by the person) and the other represents belief in an *external locus of control* (control by circumstances outside of the person). For each pair, the person taking the test must decide which of the two statements is truer. One pair, for example, is the following: (a) *I have found that what is going to happen will happen.* (b) *Trusting to fate has never turned out as well for me as making a decision to take a definite course of action.* In this case, choice (a) represents an external locus of control and (b) represents an internal locus of control.

Twenge and her colleagues analyzed the results of many studies that had used Rotter's scale with groups of college students and of children (age nine to fourteen) from 1960 through 2002. They found for both age groups that over this period, average scores shifted dramatically, away from the internal toward the external end of the scale, so much so, in fact, that the average young person in 2002 was more external (more prone to claim lack of personal control) than were 80 percent of young people in the 1960s. The rise in externality over this forty-two-year period showed the same linear trend as did the rise in depression and anxiety.[18]

There is good reason to believe that the rise of external locus of control is causally linked to the rise in anxiety and depression. Clinical researchers have shown repeatedly, with children and adolescents as well as with adults, that the helpless feelings associated with an external locus of control predispose people to anxiety and depression.[19] When people believe they have little or no control over their fate, they become anxious. "Something terrible can happen to me at any time and I will be unable to do anything about it." When the anxiety and sense of helplessness become too great, people become depressed. "There is no use trying; I'm doomed." Research has also shown that those with an external locus of control are less likely to take responsibility for their own health, their own futures, and their communities than are those with an internal locus.[20]

The Decline of Children's Freedom and the Rise of Psychological Disorders

As any good scientist will tell you, correlation does not prove causation. The observation that anxiety, depression, sense of helplessness, and various other disorders have all increased in young people as play has declined does not by itself prove that the latter causes the former. However, a strong logical case can be built for such causation.

Free play is nature's means of teaching children that they are not helpless. In play, away from adults, children really do have control and can practice asserting it. In free play, children learn to make their own decisions, solve their own problems, create and abide by rules, and get along with others as equals rather than as obedient or rebellious subordinates. In vigorous outdoor play, children deliberately dose them-selves with moderate amounts of fear—as they swing, slide, or twirl on playground equipment, climb on monkey bars or trees, or skateboard down banisters—and they thereby learn how to control not only their bodies, but also their fear. In social play children learn how to negotiate with others, how to please others, and how to modulate and overcome the anger that can arise from conflicts. Free play is also nature's means of helping children discover what they love. In their play children try out many activities and discover where their talents and predilections lie. None of these lessons can be taught through verbal means; they can be learned only through experience, which free play provides. The predominant emotions of play are interest and joy.

In school, in contrast, children cannot make their own decisions; their job is to do as they are told. In school, children learn that what matters are test scores. Even outside of school, children spend increasing amounts of their time in settings where they are directed, protected, catered to, ranked, judged, criticized, praised, and rewarded by adults. In a series of research studies conducted in wealthy suburban neigh-borhoods in the northeastern United States, psychologist Suniya Luthar and her colleagues found that those children who felt most pressured by their parents to achieve in school and were most frequently shuttled from one extracurricular activity to another were the most likely to feel anxious or depressed.[21] Every time we reduce children's opportu-nities for free play by increasing their time at school or at other adult-directed activities, we reduce further their opportunities to learn to control their own lives, to learn that they are not simply victims of cir-cumstances and powerful others.

A few years ago, research psychologists Mihaly Csikszentmihalyi and Jeremy Hunter conducted a study of happiness and unhappiness in public school students, in 6th through 12th grades. More than 800 participants, from 33 different schools in 12 different communities across the country, wore special wristwatches for a week, which were programmed to provide signals at random times between 7:30 A.M. and 10:30 P.M. Whenever the signal went off participants filled out a questionnaire indicating where they were, what they were doing, and how happy or unhappy they were at the moment. The lowest levels of happiness, by far, occurred when children were at school, and the highest levels occurred when they were out of school and conversing or playing with friends. Time spent with parents fell in the middle of the happiness-unhappiness range. Average happiness increased on weekends, but then plummeted from late Sunday afternoon through the evening, in anticipation of the coming school week.[22] How did we come to the conclusion that the best way to educate students is to force them into a setting where they are bored, unhappy, and anxious?

WE HAVE HERE A TERRIBLE IRONY. In the name of education, we have increasingly deprived children of the time and freedom they need to educate themselves through their own means. And in the name of safety, we have deprived children of the freedom they need to develop the understanding, courage, and confidence required to face life's dangers and challenges with equanimity. We are in a crisis that continues to grow more serious with every passing year. We have lost sight of the natural way to raise children. We have, not only in the United States but also throughout the developed world, lost sight of children's competence. We have created a world in which children must suppress their natural instincts to take charge of their own education and, instead, mindlessly follow paths to nowhere laid out for them by adults. We have created a world that is literally driving many young people crazy and leaving many others unable to develop the confidence and skills required for adult responsibility.

And yet, the hue and cry that we hear from pundits and politicians today is for more restrictive schooling, not less. They want more standardized tests, more homework, more supervision, longer school days, longer school years, more sanctions against children's taking off a day or two for a family vacation. This is one realm in which politicians from both of the major parties, at every level of government, seem to agree. More schooling and more testing are better than less schooling and less testing.

It is time for people who know better to stand up and move against this terrible tide. Children do not need more schooling. They need less schooling and more freedom. They also need safe enough environments in which to play and explore, and they need free access to the tools, ideas, and people (including playmates) that can help them along their own chosen paths.

This book is not one of complaint; it is a book about hope and a path to improvement. It's a book for people who have an internal locus of control, who want to do something to make the world better, not throw up their hands and say, "That's the way it is and we might as well accept it." As I'll show in the next chapters, natural selection endowed human children with powerful instincts to educate themselves, and we are foolish to deprive children of the conditions necessary for them to exercise those instincts.

2

THE PLAY-FILLED LIVES OF HUNTER-GATHERER CHILDREN

HALFWAY AROUND THE WORLD, and far removed from the educational pressures that act on Evan and Hank, we find Kwi, also eleven, who is growing up in a culture that trusts children's instincts and judgment. Kwi lives in a hunting-and-gathering band in Africa's Kalahari Desert, part of a cultural group called the Ju/'hoansi. He has no school and no fixed schedule. He gets up when he is fully awake, and he spends his days as he likes, playing and exploring with his age-mixed group of friends, sometimes in camp, sometimes well away from camp, without adult direction. He has been doing this since he was four, the age when, according to Ju/'hoan adults, children can reason and control themselves and no longer need to stay close to adults. Every day brings new adventures, new opportunities for learning.

At their own initiative, because they want to grow up to be effective adults, Kwi and his friends play at, and thereby practice, all of the activities that are crucial to the life of the band. They play endlessly at tracking and hunting. With bows and arrows, they stalk and shoot at butterflies, birds, rodents, and sometimes at larger game. They build huts and tools that resemble those the adults construct. With great delight they mimic, in exaggerated fashion, the sounds and actions of the kudu, wildebeest, lion, and dozens of other animal species whose habits they must learn to become effective hunters and defenders against predators; and they play games in which different players take the parts of different animals. They also, with great humor, caricaturize the speech and actions of the adults of their band and of visiting bands, whom they study carefully. Sometimes they venture far away into the bush to find secret, hidden places. They run, chase, leap, climb, throw, and dance, and in doing so they develop fit and coordinated bodies. They make musical instruments and play the familiar Ju/'hoan songs and create new ones. They do all this because they want to. Nobody tells them they must. Nobody tests them. No adults try to direct their play, though sometimes adults, especially the younger ones, join in for fun, and sometimes Kwi and his friends join games and dances initiated by adults. Their guide is their own free will.

This is childhood as nature designed it.

GENETICALLY, WE ARE ALL HUNTER-GATHERERS. Natural selection shaped us, over hundreds of thousands of years, for that mode of existence. Anthropologists have aptly described hunter-gatherer existence as the only stable way of life our species has ever known.[1] Agriculture first appeared in western Asia's Fertile Crescent a mere 10,000 years ago, and in various other parts of the world considerably later.[2] That invention set off an ever-growing whirlwind of changes in the ways humans lived, changes that far outpaced the rate of natural selection, changes to which we have had to adapt, as best we can, with the biological machinery that evolved to meet our needs as hunter-gatherers.

If we take, arbitrarily, a million years ago as the beginning of human history, then for 99 percent of that history we were all hunter-gatherers.[3]

The pure hunter-gatherer way of life is now nearly extinct, pushed out by intrusions from agriculture, industry, and modern ways of life generally, but as recently as the 1970s and '80s, and to some extent even later, anthropologists could trek into hard-to-reach parts of the globe and find groups of hunting and gathering peoples who had been almost unaffected by development in the rest of the world. Indeed, at the time I am writing this, anthropologists are still studying hunter-gatherer groups that carry on many of the traditions and maintain the values of their ancestors, even though they are involved in trading networks with non-hunter-gatherers. These hunting and gathering people are, of course, not our ancestors, but we can be confident that their cultures are much closer to those of our preagricultural ancestors than to the culture you and I experience daily.

Hunter-gatherer societies found throughout the world differ from one another in many ways. (Note: In describing hunter-gatherer practices throughout this chapter, I use what anthropologists call the *ethnographic present,* that is, the present tense referring to the time when the studies were conducted, even in cases where those practices don't exist today.) They have different physical habitats, languages, ceremonies, and art forms. Yet, despite those differences—whether they are found in Africa, Asia, South America, or elsewhere—they are remarkably similar in certain basic ways. They have similar social structures, similar values, and similar ways of raising children. Such similarity permits researchers to refer to "hunter-gatherer culture" in the singular, and it adds confidence to the view that these societies represent, in basic ways, the kinds of societies that predominated before the onset of agriculture.[4] Among the most fully studied of these societies are the Ju/'hoansi (also called the !Kung, of Africa's Kalahari Desert), Hazda (of Tanzanian rain forests), Mbuti and Efé (of Congo's Ituri Forest), Aka (of rain forests in Central African Republic and Congo), Batek (of Peninsular Malaysia), Agta (of Luzon, Philippines), Nayaka (of south India), Aché (of eastern

Paraguay), Parakana (of Brazil's Amazon basin), and Yiwara (of the Australian desert).

This chapter is about the lives and education of children in hunter-gatherer cultures, but along the way I will also talk about the unifying characteristics of the cultures themselves. *Education,* by my definition, *is cultural transmission.* It is the set of processes by which each new generation of human beings, in any social group, acquires and builds upon the skills, knowledge, lore, and values—that is, the culture—of previous generations in that group. To understand hunter-gatherers' approach to child-rearing and education, it is necessary to know something about their cultural values.

Autonomy, Sharing, and Equality[5]

Hunter-gatherers live in small bands (typically twenty to fifty persons, including children) that move from place to place within large but circumscribed territories to follow the available game and vegetation. Their core social values, as described by nearly all researchers who have studied them, are *autonomy* (personal freedom), *sharing,* and *equality.*[6] We, in modern democratic cultures, generally hold these values as well, but hunter-gatherers' understanding of and emphasis on them go way beyond ours.

Hunter-gatherers' sense of autonomy is so strong that they refrain from telling one another what to do. They even refrain from offering unsolicited advice to one another, so as to avoid the appearance of interfering with the other's freedom. Each person, including each child, is free every day to make his or her own choices, as long as those choices don't interfere with others' freedoms or violate a social taboo. Their autonomy, however, does not include the right to accumulate private property or to make others indebted to them, as that would run counter to their second great value—sharing.

From an economic point of view, sharing is the purpose of the hunter-gatherer band. People share their skills and efforts freely as they cooperate in obtaining food, defending against predators, and caring for children. They share food and material goods with everyone in the band and even with members of other bands. Such ready sharing apparently is what allowed hunter-gatherers to survive for so long in such challenging conditions. The hunter-gatherer concept of sharing is different from our Western understanding. For us, sharing is a praiseworthy act of generosity, for which a thank-you is due and some form of repayment may be expected in the future. For hunter-gatherers, sharing is neither a generous act nor an implicit bargain, but a duty. It is taken for granted that you will share if you have more than others; failure to do so would invite ridicule and scorn.[7]

Intimately tied to hunter-gatherers' sense of autonomy and expectation of sharing is what anthropologist Richard Lee has called their "fierce egalitarianism."[8] Their egalitarianism goes far beyond our modern, Western notion of equal opportunity. It means that everyone's needs are equally important, that no one is considered superior to others, and that no one possesses more material goods than anyone else. Such equality is part and parcel of their sense of autonomy, as inequalities could lead those who have more, or who believe themselves to be superior, to dominate those who have less.

Hunter-gatherers, of course, recognize that some people are better hunters or gatherers than others, some are better negotiators, some better dancers, and so on, and they value such skills. However, they strongly disapprove of any flaunting of abilities or overt expressions of superiority. The weapons they most commonly use to combat boasting, or failure to share, or other tabooed actions, are ridicule and shunning.[9] As a first step, people make fun of the violator for behaving in such an inappropriate way. They might make up a song about how so-and-so thinks he is such a "big man" and "great hunter." If the behavior persists, the next step is to act as if the violator does not exist. Such measures are highly effective in bringing around the transgressor. It is hard to act like a big shot if everyone ridicules you for it, and it is not worth hoarding food if the price is being treated as if you don't exist.

Consistent with their high valuation of individual autonomy and equality, hunter-gatherer bands do not have "big men," or chiefs, of the sort commonly found in primitive agricultural societies (and in collector societies—see endnote 4), who make decisions for the whole group. Some hunter-gatherer bands have no regular leader at all. Others have a nominal leader who speaks for the band in dealing with other bands, but who has no more formal decision-making power than anyone else. Decisions that affect the whole band, such as when to move from one campsite to another, are made by group discussions, which might go on for hours or days before consensus is reached and action is taken. Women as well as men take part in these discussions, and even children may voice their opinions. Within any given band some people are known to be wiser than others and are therefore more influential, but any power they exert comes from their abilities to persuade and to find compromises that take everyone's desires into account.[10]

Trustful Parenting

A term often used by researchers to describe adults' general treatment of children in hunter-gatherer cultures is *indulgent,* but perhaps a better term is *trustful.* The spirit of egalitarianism and autonomy that pervades hunter-gatherer social relationships applies to adults' interactions with children, just as it applies to adults' interactions with one another. The central tenet of their parenting and educational philosophy seems to be that children's instincts can be trusted, that children who are allowed to follow their own wills will learn what they need to learn and will naturally begin to contribute to the band's economy when they have the skills and maturity to do so. This trustful attitude is well illustrated by researchers' comments, such as the following (each from a different observer concerning a different hunter-gatherer culture):

- "Aborigine children [of Australia] are indulged to an extreme degree, and sometimes continue to suckle until they are four or five years old. Physical punishment for a child is almost unheard of."[11]

- "Hunter-gatherers do not give orders to their children; for example, no adult announces bedtime. At night, children remain around adults until they feel tired and fall asleep. . . . Parakana adults [of Brazil] do not interfere with their children's lives. They never beat, scold, or behave aggressively with them, physically or verbally, nor do they offer praise or keep track of their development."[12]

- "The idea that this is 'my child' or 'your child' does not exist [among the Yequana of Venezuela]. Deciding what another person should do, no matter what his age, is outside the Yequana vocabulary of behaviors. There is great interest in what everyone does, but no impulse to influence—let alone coerce—anyone. The child's will is his motive force."[13]

- "Infants and young children [among Inuit hunter-gatherers of the Hudson Bay area] are allowed to explore their environments to the limits of their physical capabilities and with minimal interference from adults. Thus if a child picks up a hazardous object, parents generally leave it to explore the dangers on its own. The child is presumed to know what it is doing."[14]

- "Ju/'hoan children very rarely cried, probably because they had little to cry about. No child was ever yelled at or slapped or physically punished, and few were even scolded. Most never heard a discouraging word until they were approaching adolescence, and even then the reprimand, if it really was a reprimand, was delivered in a soft voice."[15]

Most people in our culture would consider such indulgence to be a recipe for producing spoiled, demanding kids who grow up to be spoiled, demanding adults. But, at least within the context of the hunter-gatherer way of life, nothing could be further from the truth. Here is how Elizabeth Marshall Thomas, one of the earliest observers of the Ju/'hoansi, responded to the question of spoiling: "We are sometimes told that children who are treated so kindly become spoiled, but this is because those who hold that opinion have no idea how successful such measures can be. Free from frustration or anxiety, sunny and cooperative, . . . the Ju/'hoan children were every parent's dream. No culture can ever have raised better, more intelligent, more likable, more confident children."[16]

Given this indulgent, trustful attitude, it is not surprising that children in hunter-gatherer societies are allowed to spend most of their time playing and exploring freely. The general belief among hunter-gatherer adults, borne out by centuries of experience, is that children educate themselves through their self-directed play and exploration.[17] To learn more about the lives of hunter-gatherer children, my then–graduate student Jonathan Ogas and I conducted a survey of ten prominent researchers who had studied various hunter-gatherer cultures.[18] To our question, "How much free time did children in the group you studied have for play?," all of the researchers said, essentially, that the children were free to play nearly from dawn to dusk every day. Here are three typical responses:

- "Both girls and boys had almost all day every day free to play" (Alan Brainard, concerning the Nharo, of southern Africa).
- "Children were free to play nearly all the time; no one expected children to do serious work until they were in their late teens" (Karen Endicott, concerning the Batek of Malaysia).
- "Boys were free to play nearly all the time until age 15–17; for girls most of the day, in between a few errands and some babysitting, was spent in play" (Robert Bailey, concerning the Efé, of central Africa).

These responses are consistent with published reports. In a formal study of Ju/'hoan children's activities, anthropologist Patricia Draper concluded, "Girls are around 14 years old before they begin regular food gathering and water- and wood-collecting. . . . Boys are 16 years old or over before they begin serious hunting. . . . Children do amazingly little work."[19] The Hazda (of the Tanzanian rain forests in Africa) are sometimes cited as an exception to the rule that hunter-gatherer children engage in little productive work. Hazda children forage for a good portion of their own food. However, a study of Hazda children, ages five to fifteen, revealed that they spent only about two hours per day foraging, in the rich vegetative areas near camp, and that even while foraging they continued to play.[20]

Although adults in hunter-gatherer cultures do not attempt to control, direct, or motivate children's education, they assist children's self-education by responding to their wishes.[21] They allow children to play with adult tools, even potentially dangerous ones, such as knives and axes, because they understand that children need to play with such objects to become skilled at using them. They trust children to have enough sense not to hurt themselves. There are some limits, however. Poison-tipped darts or arrows are kept well out of small children's reach.[22] Adults also make scaled-down bows and arrows, digging sticks, baskets, and other such instruments for young children, even toddlers, to play with. They allow children to watch and participate in essentially all adult activities, as they please. Children often crowd around adults, and young ones climb onto adults' laps, to watch or "help" them cook, or play musical instruments, or make hunting weapons or other tools, and the adults rarely shoo them away. Draper describes a typical scene:

> One afternoon I watched for 2 hours while a [Ju/'hoan] father hammered and shaped the metal for several arrow points. During the period his son and grandson (both under 4 years old) jostled him, sat on his legs, and attempted to pull the arrowheads from under the hammer. When the boys' fingers came close to the point of impact, he merely waited until the small hands were a little farther away before he resumed hammering. Although the man remonstrated with the boys, he did not become cross or chase the boys off; and they did not heed his warnings to quit interfering. Eventually, perhaps 50 minutes later, the boys moved off a few steps to join some teenagers lying in the shade.[23]

When children ask adults to show them how to do something or to help them do it, the adults oblige. As one group of hunter-gatherer researchers put it, "Sharing and giving are core forager values, so what an individual knows is open and available to everyone; if a child wants to learn something, others are obliged to share the knowledge or skill."[24] Hunter-gatherers also impart knowledge by telling stories—about their foraging and hunting adventures, their visits to other bands, and significant events in the past. Thomas notes that women in their sixties and seventies, in the groups that she observed, were especially great storytellers about the past.[25] The stories are not directed specifically to children, but the children listen and absorb the meanings. Hunter-gatherer children control and direct their own education, but all of the adults in the band, as well as other children, are resources.

Technical Skills and Knowledge

It would be a mistake to assume that because hunter-gatherer cultures are "simpler" than ours, children in those cultures have less to learn than do our children. The hunting-and-gathering way of life is extraordinarily knowledge- and skill-intensive, and because of the relative absence of occupational specialization, each child has to acquire essentially the whole culture, or at least that part of it appropriate to his or her gender.

Hunting itself requires enormous knowledge and skill. Unlike such carnivorous animals as lions, tigers, and wolves, we humans are not adapted for capturing game by speed and force; instead we rely on wit and craft. Hunter-gatherer men—and women, too, in those cultures where women also hunt—have a vast knowledge of the habits of the two hundred to three hundred different mammals and birds they hunt. They can identify each animal by its sounds and tracks as well as by sight. Some years ago, Louis Liebenberg wrote an entire book about the sophisticated scientific reasoning that underlies hunter-gatherers' abilities to track game.[26] Hunters use the marks they see in the sand, mud, or foliage as clues, which they combine with their accumulated knowledge from past experience, to develop and test hypotheses about such matters as the size, sex, physical condition, speed of movement, and time of passage of the animal they are tracking. Such tracking is essential not only for finding game and getting close enough to shoot, but also for pursuing game that has been shot. Hunter-gatherers typically hunt with small arrows or darts treated with poison, which take time to act. Sometimes a large animal must be tracked for days before it dies and can be brought back to camp.

In describing the tracking abilities of the Ju/'hoansi, anthropologist Alf Wannenburgh wrote, "Everything is noticed, considered, and discussed. The kink in a trodden grass blade, the direction of the pull that broke a twig from a bush, the depth, size, shape, and disposition of the tracks themselves, all reveal information about the condition of the animal, the direction it is moving in, the rate of travel, and what its future movements are likely to be."[27] Concerning the same issue, Thomas wrote, "To recognize the tracks of [the specific kudu that had been shot], who is traveling with six or seven other kudus, all about the same size, is a feat that must be seen to be appreciated, especially because none of the tracks are clear footprints. They are dents in the sand among many other scuffed dents made by other kudus. . . . Even the tiniest sign, such as the tracks of a beetle superimposed upon a footprint of the victim, would have meaning to the hunters, especially if the beetle was of a type that moved about after the day had reached a certain temperature."[28]

The tools of hunting—which might include bows and arrows (with or without poisoned tips), blow pipes and poisoned darts, spears, snares, and nets—must be crafted to perfection, with great skill. And great skill is needed, too, in the use of the tools. No anthropologist has reported an ability to hunt at even close to that of the hunter-gatherers he or she studied, using their tools.[29] Most speak with awe of the abilities they observed. Quantitative studies of hunting success have shown that the best hunters are not the men in their twenties, even though they have reached their peak physical condition, but those in their thirties, forties, and above. It takes that long to acquire the knowledge and skill needed to be a superlative hunter.[30]

It is no surprise that children growing up in a culture where hunting is so greatly valued, so much talked about, and known to be so difficult, would play and explore in ways that help them to become skilled hunters. All of the respondents to our survey said that the boys in the culture they studied spent enormous amounts of time at playful tracking and hunting. The two respondents who studied the Agta—a culture where women as well as men hunt—observed that girls as well as boys in that culture engaged in much playful hunting.

Hunter-gatherer children as young as three years old track and stalk small animals and one another in their play.[31] With their little bows and arrows they shoot at stationary targets, or at butterflies and toads. By age eight or nine they are already killing some small edible creatures, which they might tie to a stick and carry back to camp, mimicking the way their fathers transport large animals. By age ten, they sometimes contribute small amounts of meat to the camp's daily food supply. By the time they are in their early teens, they might be allowed to join adults on real big-game hunting expeditions, so they can learn by watching, and by age sixteen or so they might be full participants in such expeditions, still in the spirit of play.

The gathering of plant-based foodstuffs likewise requires great knowledge and skill. Humans are not adapted to graze on readily available foliage, as our ape relatives are. Rather, we depend on nutrient-rich plant matter that must be sought out, extracted, and processed. Hunter-gatherer women—and men, too—have to know which of the countless roots, tubers, nuts, seeds, fruits, and greens in their area are edible and nutritious, when and where to find them, how to dig them up or extract the edible portions efficiently, and in some cases how to process them to make them edible or more nutritious than they otherwise would be.[32] These abilities include physical skills, honed by years of practice, as well as the capacity to remember, use, add to, and modify an enormous store of culturally shared verbal knowledge about the food materials. Research has shown that the efficiency of hunter-gatherer women in gathering and processing foods increases up to the age of about forty, just as the men's skill at hunting does.[33]

Hunter-gatherer children learn about plant-based foods in the same general way that they learn to hunt. They hear stories. They join their mothers and other adults on gathering trips. They watch adults processing foods in camp and "help" when they can. Entirely on their own initiative, they play with digging sticks and with mortars and pestles, and they devise games that involve finding and identifying varieties of plants. They sometimes also seek and receive verbal instruction from adults. In interviews, Aka women described how, when they were young, their mothers had placed varieties of mushrooms or wild yams in front of them and explained the differences between those that were edible and those that were not.[34]

As is true in all cultures, boys and girls in hunter-gatherer cultures segregate themselves by sex for some, although not all, of their play. Boys, more often than girls, play at hunting and other predominantly men's activities. Girls, more often than boys, play at gathering, food processing, birthing, infant care, and other predominantly women's activities. Boys and girls play together at the many activities engaged in regularly by both men and women. All of their play is in age-mixed groups, of children ranging from about four on up to the mid-teens. In their play, the younger children learn skills from the older ones, and the older children practice leadership and nurturance through their care for the younger ones. Although children learn much from adults, their more usual teachers are the children with whom they play.

The researchers who responded to our survey noted that hunter-gatherer children mimic many valued adult activities in their play, beyond hunting and gathering, including caring for infants, climbing trees, building vine ladders, building huts, making tools, building rafts, making fires, cooking, defending against attacks from make-believe predators, imitating animals (a means of identifying animals and learning their habits), making music, dancing, storytelling, and arguing. Hunter-gatherer groups have rich traditions of music, dance, and stories, so it comes as no surprise that the children make and play musical instruments, sing, dance, and tell stories in their play. Depending on the culture, they might also create beaded designs or other visual artwork.

The outdoor lives of hunter-gatherers, including the need to flee from or fend off predators, require that people of all ages and both sexes maintain fit and agile bodies. In agricultural and industrial societies, boys generally engage in considerably more vigorous physical play than do girls, but in hunter-gatherer societies both sexes engage, nearly equally, in a great amount of such play.[35] They chase one another around and, depending on geography, climb and swing on trees, leap, swim, carry heavy objects, and perform all sorts of acrobatics. They also practice graceful, coordinated movements in their dances. Dancing and dance-like games are popular forms of play in nearly all hunter-gatherer cultures; they are exercises in cooperation as well as fluid movement.

Social Skills and Values

By allowing their children unlimited time to play with one another, hunter-gatherer adults allow their children unlimited practice of the social skills and values that are most central to their way of life. Social play (that is, all play that involves more than one player) is, by its very nature, a continuous exercise in cooperation, attention to one another's needs, and consensual decision-making.

Play is not something one *has* to do; players are always free to quit. In social play, each player knows that anyone who feels unhappy will quit, and if too many quit, the game ends. To keep the game going, players must satisfy not only their own desires but also those of the other players. The intense drive that children have to play with other children, therefore, is a powerful force for them to learn how to attend to others' wishes and negotiate differences. Research in our culture has shown repeatedly that even preschool children engage in enormous amounts of negotiation and compromise in the context of play (more on this in Chapter 8). One of the great evolutionary purposes of social play is to help children learn how to treat one another respectfully, as equals, in ways that meet everyone's needs and desires, despite differences in size, strength, and ability. These skills are crucial for survival in hunter-gatherer societies, but are valuable in every human society.

We all need the help and support of others, and to obtain that we need to know how to help and support others.

As I noted before, hunter-gatherer children always play in groups that encompass a wide range of ages. Even if they wanted to play only with age-mates, they would not be able to. Hunter-gatherer bands are small, and births are widely spread, so it is rare to find more than two or three children within a year or two in age. Research in our culture (discussed in Chapter 9) shows that age-mixed play is qualitatively different from same-age play.[36] It is less competitive and more nurturing. In age-mixed play, each child tries to do his or her best, but has little or no concern for beating others. When playmates differ greatly in age, size, and strength, there is little point in trying to prove oneself better than another. The age-mixed nature of the play, coupled with the egalitarian ethos of the cultures, ensures that the play of hunter-gatherer children is highly cooperative and noncompetitive.

In a worldwide cross-cultural comparison of games conducted in the 1950s and '60s, John Roberts and his colleagues concluded that the only cultures that seemed to have no competitive games at all were hunter-gatherer cultures.[37] Consistent with that conclusion, all of the respondents to our survey stressed the noncompetitive nature of the play they observed. For example, anthropologist P. Bion Griffin commented that the only consistent rule of play that he observed among Agta children was that "no one should win and beat another in a visible fashion." In the most extensive descriptive account of the play and games of any hunter-gatherer group, Lorna Marshall pointed out that most Ju/'hoan play is informal and noncompetitive and that even their formal games, which have explicit rules and could be played competitively, are played noncompetitively.[38] For instance, Ju/'hoan children of ages five to fifteen, of both sexes, often play a game of throwing the zeni. The zeni consists of a leather thong, about seven inches long, with a small weight fastened at one end and a feather at the other. The player hurls it into the air as high as possible with a stick, then tries to catch it with the stick when it comes fluttering down, and from that position hurls it again. The game is played with great skill by many, and it could easily be played competitively—for instance, by seeing who can hurl it the highest or catch it the most times in succession—but, according to Marshall, it is not played that way. Players try to do their best, but comparisons between players are not made.

Many hunter-gatherer games involve close coordination of each player's movements with those of the other players. This is true of all of their dancing and dance-like games, but it is also true of other games. For example, in playful hunting with nets, the net-handlers and bush-beaters must coordinate their actions just as adults do in real net hunting. Another example is a tree-swinging game, in which children coordinate their actions to bend a sapling to the ground and then all but one releases it, so that the one who didn't let go swings wildly in the treetop or is catapulted through the air.[39] Such games apparently not only help children learn to work together as a team, but also help bind them together emotionally as a community.

Collin Turnbull, who studied the Mbuti of central Africa, described ceremonial tug-of-war games played by the entire band each year as part of their celebration of the honey season. Men and boys take one side of the vine rope, women and girls take the other, and they sing in antiphony as they pull. In Turnbull's words, when the men and boys start to win, "one of them will abandon his side and join the women, pulling up his bark-cloth and adjusting it in the fashion of women, shouting encouragement to them in a falsetto, ridiculing womanhood by the very exaggeration of his mime." Then, when the women and girls start to win, "one of them adjusts her bark clothing, letting it down, and strides over to the men's side and joins their shouting in a deep bass voice, similarly gently mocking manhood." Turnbull continued: "Each person crossing over tries to outdo the ridicule of the last, causing more and more laughter, until when the contestants are laughing so hard they cannot sing or pull any more, they let go of the vine rope and fall to the ground in near hysteria. Although both youth and adults cross sides, it is primarily the youth who really enact the ridicule. . . . The ridicule is performed without hostility, rather with a sense of at least partial identification and empathy. It is in this way that the violence and aggressivity of either sex 'winning' is avoided, and the stupidity of competitiveness is demonstrated."[40]

Several researchers have commented on the games of give-and-take played by hunter-gatherer infants with older children or adults.[41] Infants as young as twelve months old, or even younger, happily give an object to the older playmate, then receive it, give it again, and so on. The joy of such giving seems to lie in the instincts of all normal human infants. In a series of little-known experiments conducted in the United States, nearly every one of more than one hundred infants, ages twelve to eighteen months, spontaneously gave toys to an adult during brief sessions in a laboratory room.[42] In our culture, such behavior is not much commented upon, but in some hunter-gatherer cultures it is celebrated. Among the Ju/'hoansi, such giving by infants is deliberately cultivated. Grandmothers, in particular, initiate infants into the culture of sharing and giving by guiding infants' hands in the giving of beads to others.[43] This is the one example of systematic, deliberate adult influence on children's play that I have found in researchers' descriptions of hunter-gatherer practices. No human trait is more important to the hunter-gatherer way of life than the willingness to give or share.

To be a successful adult hunter-gatherer, one must not only be able to share and cooperate with others, but also be able to assert one's own needs and wishes effectively, without antagonizing others. Practice at such self-assertion occurs in social play everywhere, as players negotiate the rules and decide who gets to play what part. In addition, hunter-gatherer children practice such assertion quite deliberately as they mimic adults' arguments. For example, Turnbull described, as follows, how Mbuti children, from age nine on up, playfully rehashed and tried to improve upon the arguments they had heard among adults:

It may start through imitation of a real dispute the children witnessed in the main camp, perhaps the night before. They all take roles and imitate the adults. It is almost a form of judgment for if the adults talked their way out of the dispute the children, having performed their imitation once, are likely to drop it. If the children detect any room for improvement, however, they will explore that, and if the adult argument was inept and everyone went to sleep that night in a bad temper, then the children try and show that they can do better, and if they cannot, then they revert to ridicule which they play out until they are all rolling on the ground in near hysterics. That happens to be the way many of the most potentially violent and dangerous disputes are settled in adult life.[44]

Self-Control

Researchers who study hunter-gatherers often comment on their extraordinary cheerfulness and stoicism. Anthropologist Richard Gould, after quoting another researcher on hunter-gatherers' cheerfulness, wrote, "Often I have had cause to notice this same good cheer and readiness to laugh and joke among the people of the Gibson Desert [hunter-gatherers in Australia], even when they are plagued by boils and heat, pestered by flies, and short of food. This cheerfulness seems to be part of a disciplined acceptance of frequent hardships which complaints would only aggravate."[45]

Hunter-gatherers seem to accept the twists and turns of fate and make the best of them, rather than complain. Their attitude toward what we would call hardship is nicely illustrated by Jean Liedloff in her now-classic book *The Continuum Concept*. As a young, adventurous woman, Liedloff had joined two Italian explorers on a diamond-hunting expedition in a Venezuelan rain forest. At one point on this trip, she, the two Italians, and several native South Americans of the Tauripan culture, whom they had hired as helpers, were struggling to portage their heavy, awkward dugout canoe over treacherous, sun-baked rocks. As an excuse to take a moment off from this torturous work, she stepped back to photograph the scene, and this is her report on what she saw from that relatively detached perspective:

> Here before me were several men engaged in a single task. Two, the Italians, were tense, frowning, losing their tempers at every-thing, and cursing nonstop in the distinctive manner of the Tus-can. The rest [the Tauripans] were having a fine time. They were laughing at the unwieldiness of the canoe, making a game of the battle, relaxed between pushes, laughing at their own scrapes, and especially amused when the canoe, as it wobbled forward, pinned one, then another, underneath it. The fellow held bare-backed against the scorched granite, when he could breathe again, invariably laughed the loudest, enjoying his relief. . . . As I finished photographing and rejoined the team, I opted out of the civilized choice and enjoyed, quite genuinely, the rest of the portage.[46]

Later, Liedloff spent time living among the Tauripans and two other native South American groups in Venezuela, and she was most im-pressed by their playfulness, their relaxed attitude toward life, and their pleasant ways of interacting with one another, even in times of hardship. At the time that Liedloff observed them, these groups were not fully hunter-gatherers, as they had small gardens to supplement what they obtained from hunting and gathering, but they had apparently retained the values and attitudes that characterize the hunting and gathering way of life.

Hunter-gatherers' capacity for cheerfulness in the face of hardship is so surprising, to we soft complainers, that I feel compelled to present one more example of it. In her book about the Ju/'hoansi, Elizabeth Marshall Thomas recounts the story of a girl who had been walking far from her band's campsite and stepped into a hidden trap that had been set by a wildlife biologist for a hyena. The trap's steel teeth had gone through the girl's foot, and the trap was anchored solidly to the ground, so all she could do was stand on the other foot and wait. Hours later, her uncle, who was hunting in the area, saw her from afar, went to see what was wrong, and then, when he couldn't open the trap, went back to the camp for help. Here is Thomas's comment on the incident:

> I will always remember her calmness as we brought her to the encampment and dressed the wound. She had been alone, helpless, and in pain for many hours in a place frequented by hyenas, yet she acted as if nothing had happened, nothing at all. Instead, she chatted about this and that in an offhand manner. To me, such composure in such circumstances did not seem possible, and I remember wondering if the nervous systems of the [Ju/'hoansi] were not superior to ours. But of course their nervous systems were the same as ours. It was their self-control that was superior. . . . The value of this is firmly from the Old Way. Nothing would be more attractive to a predator than a weeping, struggling creature, alone and unable to run away.[47]

To survive, it is sometimes better to play that nothing is wrong than to fret, whine, and look like a weakling not only to hyenas but also to your companions, who may need your strength. On occasions when life is especially difficult, such composure can keep things from getting worse. It can allow one to find humor, and therefore even pleasure, in adversity.

How do hunter-gatherers develop their remarkable capacity for self-control? Nobody really knows, and as far as I can tell nobody before has even speculated on this issue. My theory is that they develop the capacity at least partly through their extensive play. In the 1930s the great Russian psychologist Lev Vygotsky argued convincingly that free play with other children is the primary means by which children learn to control their impulses and emotions. Children's drive to play leads them to ignore discomforts and suppress impulses so they can continue abiding by the rules of the game, and such abilities gradually transfer to their lives outside of play. More recently, research with animals (discussed in Chapter 8) suggests that play is essential to development of those parts of the brain that are crucial for controlling fear and anger and for behaving effectively in stressful situations. It may be no coincidence, therefore, that the same cultures that allow their children the greatest freedom to play also produce people who, apparently, have the greatest capacity for self-control.

"WELL," I HEAR SOME OF YOU CRY, "all this may be well and good for hunter-gatherers, but what relevance does it have for the education of our children, in our culture?"

Good question. Our children may not need to learn more than what hunter-gatherer children learn, but they do need to learn much that is different from what hunter-gatherer children learn. For starters, reading, writing, and arithmetic are absent from hunter-gatherer cultures. Moreover, our culture is far more diverse than a hunter-gatherer culture is, and no child can see it all. It's by no means obvious that the learning instincts that evolved to meet the educational needs of hunter-gatherers are sufficient for education in our culture today.

But read on. The chapters to come present compelling evidence that children's natural, hunter-gatherer ways of learning *are* sufficient for education in our culture, if we provide conditions that are equivalent, for our culture, to those that hunter-gatherer adults provide for their children. Such provision requires effort, but not as much effort as that required by our present, coercive system of schooling.

First, however, a little history, aimed at understanding the origin of our modern schools.

3

WHY SCHOOLS ARE WHAT THEY ARE: A BRIEF HISTORY OF EDUCATION

HOW DID WE GET FROM KWI TO EVAN? How did we go from conditions in which learning was self-directed and joyful to conditions in which learning is forced on children in ways that make so many of them feel helpless, anxious, and depressed?

When we see that children today are required by law to go to school, that almost all schools are structured in the same way, and that our society goes to a great deal of trouble and expense to provide such schools, we naturally assume that there must be some good, logical reason for all of this. Perhaps if we didn't force children to go to school, or if schools operated differently, children would grow up to be incompetent in our modern world. Perhaps educational experts have figured all this out, or perhaps alternative methods of allowing children to develop have been tested and have failed.

The reality, as I will show later, is that alternative ways have been tested and *have succeeded*. Children's instincts for self-directed learning can work today as well as they ever did. When provided with freedom and opportunity, children can and *do* educate themselves marvelously for our modern world. The schools that we see around us are not products of science and logic; they are products of history. History is not logical; it is not directed toward any planned ends; and it does not necessarily produce progress in the sense of improved human conditions. Yet, to understand why things are as they are today, we must know something about the history that created them.

For hundreds of thousands of years humans lived under relatively stable conditions as hunter-gatherers. Our instincts were adapted to that way of life. Then along came agriculture. According to archaeologists, crop cultivation appeared about 10,000 to 11,000 years ago in the Fertile Crescent of Southwest Asia, about 9,000 to 10,000 years ago in eastern China, about 5,000 to 6,000 years ago in South America and Mexico, and about 3,000 to 4,000 years ago in North America.[1] We don't know exactly how agriculture was developed in each place, but it must have been gradual. Resourceful human beings discovered that they could exert a degree of control over nature's food supply, by such means as clearing brush to make more room for edible plants or digging irrigation ditches to nurse plants through dry spells. Eventually such practices led to the harvesting and replanting of seeds or roots and the domestication of animals—full-blown farming.

Agriculture, once established, kicked off an ever-accelerating whirlwind of changes in our ways of living, and those changes dramatically altered our ways of thinking about and rearing children. Here is a brief tour of that shift, as it occurred in the Western world.

How Agriculture Changed the Goals of Parenting

Agriculture offered many improvements to people's lives. It provided a steadier food supply and thereby reduced, at least initially, the threat of starvation. It eliminated the need to keep moving in search of food and allowed people to settle down and build sturdy houses to protect themselves from predators and storms. But agriculture also came with a big price tag, which could not have been foreseen by those who took the first, irreversible steps away from hunting and gathering. It altered the conditions of human life in ways that led to the decline of freedom, equality, sharing, and play. When we bit the apple of agriculture, as it were, we left the Garden of Eden and entered a world in which we had to do the gardening ourselves, in which toil, not play, was king.

The hunter-gatherer way of life was knowledge-intensive and skill-intensive, but not labor-intensive. To be effective hunters and gatherers, people had to acquire deep knowledge of the plants and animals on which they depended and the landscapes within which they foraged. They had to develop great skill in crafting and using the tools of hunting and gathering. They had to be creative in finding food, tracking game, and defending against predators. But they did not have to work long hours. In fact, long hours of hunting and gathering would have been counterproductive, as they would have led to the harvesting of nature's food supply faster than nature could regenerate it. Moreover, the work of hunting and gathering was exciting and joyful, partly because it was so knowledge-intensive and skill-intensive. Anthropologists report that hunter-gatherers did not distinguish work from play as we do. They grew up playing at hunting and gathering and moved on gradually to the real thing, still in the spirit of play. They had no concept of work as toil.

Anthropologist Marshall Sahlins famously referred to hunter-gatherer societies, collectively, as "the original affluent society."[2] They were afflu-ent not because they had so much, but because their needs were so few.

They could satisfy those needs with relatively little work, and were therefore left with abundant free time, which they spent at such activities as "singing and composing songs, playing musical instruments, sewing intricate bead designs, telling stories, playing games, visiting other bands, or lying around and resting."[3] These are exactly the kinds of activities that we would expect of happy, relaxed people anywhere.

Agriculture gradually changed all that. With a steady food supply, people were able to have more children. Agriculture also allowed—or forced—people to live in permanent dwellings near their crops, rather than live as nomads. But these changes came at a great cost in labor. While hunter-gatherers skillfully harvested what nature had grown, farmers had to plow, plant, cultivate, tend their flocks, and so on. Successful farming required long hours of relatively unskilled, repetitive labor, much of which could be done by children. With larger families, children had to work in the fields to help feed their younger siblings, or at home to help care for those siblings. Children's lives changed gradually from the free pursuit of their own interests to increasingly more time spent at work that was required to serve the rest of the family.

Agriculture also provided the conditions that led to private property and class differences, and to the breakdown of the equality among individuals that pervaded hunter-gatherer societies. Because hunter-gatherers had to keep moving to follow the available game and edible plants, there was no economic value in owning a plot of land or material goods beyond what one could carry. In contrast, farm families had to stake claims to and defend their land. Having gone to the trouble of plowing, planting, and cultivating, farmers could not afford to have others walk in and collect the harvest. Because of their sedentary lifestyle, they could store food and accumulate other material goods. All that provided a basis for status differences to emerge. The more land and goods a farm family owned, the better off they were. They could feed more children, and those children gained more inherited wealth and higher status, which served them well in attracting mates and in staking out their own farms.

Thus, agriculture fostered values that were negatives among hunter-gatherers: toil, child labor, private ownership, greed, status, and competition.

Perhaps the clearest evidence that a change from hunting and gathering to farming increases work and decreases play is found in comparisons of hunter-gatherers with their close relatives and neighbors who had recently taken up farming. In the 1960s, anthropologist James Woodburn noted that Hazda hunter-gatherers, despite being surrounded by farmers and being urged by government authorities to do so, refused to take up farming themselves on the grounds that it required too much work.[4] In a formal comparative study, Patricia Draper found that sedentary Ju/'hoansi, who had recently taken up gardening and animal raising, had a higher material standard of living than did the neighboring nomadic Ju/'hoansi, but had much less free time.[5] Children in the sedentary group had more chores and less time to play than did those in the nomadic group, and new distinctions emerged in the treatment of girls and boys. Girls helped with child care and domestic chores, supervised closely by their mothers or other adult women, while boys helped with animal herding, which took them far from home where they could continue to explore and play, away from adult interference. In a study of peoples with mixed hunter-gatherer and agricultural subsistence, in Botswana, John Bock and Sarah Johnson found that the more a family was involved in hunting and gathering, the more time children had for play.[6]

Many of the so-called primitive cultures described by anthropologists are primitive farming cultures, not hunter-gatherer cultures, and they show a wide range of departures in social structure and values from those of hunter-gatherers. One much publicized example is that of the Yanomami of the Amazon rain forest, made famous by Napoleon Chagnon in his book subtitled *The Fierce People*. Although Chagnon portrayed this culture as similar to that in which our ancient ancestors would have evolved, the Yanomami were in fact not true hunter-gatherers and hadn't been for centuries. They did some hunting and gathering, but got most of their nourishment from their crops, chiefly bananas and plantains. Farming allowed their population density to grow to two or three times what a purely hunter-gatherer way of life could sustain.[7] It also promoted the establishment of relatively permanent villages and the accumulation of property. Chagnon reported that these people had sharp hierarchies of power, in which "big men" exerted authority over others and men brutally dominated women. He also found them to be quite warlike, with frequent raids and murders between neighboring villages. Although they valued play, they afforded their children, especially their daughters, less time for it than did hunter-gatherers. Girls were expected to do the work of adult women by the age of about ten.[8]

Another example of reduced play in a primitive agricultural society is that of the Baining, of Papua New Guinea. According to Jane Fajans, who lived among them and studied them for several years, the core value of the Baining culture was that of work, which they saw as the opposite of play.[9] A common Baining saying was, "We are human because we work." In their view, to not work is to be an animal. The tasks that made them human were those of turning natural products (plants, animals, babies) into human products (crops, livestock, and civilized human beings) through effortful work (cultivation, domestication, and disciplined child-rearing). The adults devalued childhood play and, according to some of their claims, even punished children for it, not just because it took time away from work, but also because they considered it to be shameful—shameful *because* it was natural and therefore appropriate to animals, not to humans. They believed that children learn what they need to know through work, not play. When Fajans asked adults to talk about their own childhoods, they often talked about their struggles to embrace work and overcome their childish desires to play. The Baining lived by a philosophy that seems to be deliberately the opposite of that of hunter-gatherers: the rejection of nature.

All work and no play make Jack a dull boy, so it is no surprise that the Baining have the reputation of being perhaps the dullest culture that anthropologists have ever turned up. The famous anthropologist Gregory Bateson tried to study them early in his career, for fourteen months in the late 1920s, but found them so uninteresting that he abandoned that study and wrote later that they lived a "drab and colorless existence."[10] They seemed to him, and to some observers after him, to be lacking in curiosity, imagination, and playfulness in adulthood and, unlike most cultures, they had no tradition of storytelling. Their conversation was almost entirely about work and the necessities of daily life.

The fierce Yanomami and the reportedly dreary Baining are two extreme examples of variations in culture that followed on the heels of agriculture. Not all primitive agricultural societies differed so dramatically in values from hunter-gatherers as these. Yet, apparently everywhere, the onset of agriculture tended to reduce children's freedom and promote punitive methods of child-rearing. In a classic study conducted in the 1950s, Herbert Barry, Irvin Child, and Margaret Bacon used anthropological documents to rank primitive societies according to their child-rearing philosophies and methods.[11] At one end were cultures that stressed obedience and commonly used corporal punishment to achieve that end. At the other end were cultures that valued children's assertiveness and rarely or never used corporal punishment. They found that this ranking correlated strongly with a culture's means of subsistence. The more a culture depended on agriculture and the less it depended on hunting and gathering, the more likely it was to value obedience, devalue self-assertion, and use harsh means to discipline children. Subsequent studies have produced similar results.[12]

As a number of researchers have pointed out, this cultural difference in child-rearing makes sense when we consider the character traits of the ideal farmer compared to those of the ideal hunter-gatherer.[13] Success in farming generally depends on adhering to tried-and-true methods. Creativity is very risky; if a crop fails, a whole year's food supply may be lost. Farmers, unlike hunter-gatherers, don't regularly share food, so a family that loses its crop may starve. Moreover, farming societies are generally structured hierarchically, so obedience to those higher in wealth, rank, and power is essential to social and economic success.

Thus, the ideal farmer is obedient, rule abiding, and conservative; farmers' strict discipline of children seems designed to cultivate those traits.

In contrast, success in hunting and gathering requires continuous, creative adaptation to the ever-changing, unpredictable conditions of nature. For hunter-gatherers, each day's food supply comes from the cumulative efforts of diverse individuals and teams, each foraging in their own chosen way and using their own best judgment. The diversity of methods, coupled with the sharing of food among all members of the band, creates a hedge against the possibility that anyone will starve. Moreover, social success for the hunter-gatherer depends not upon obedience to anyone higher up, but upon the ability to assert one's thoughts and wishes effectively in the company of equals, where negotiation and compromise, not threat and submission, pave the way to agreement. Thus, the ideal hunter-gatherer is assertive, willful, creative, and willing to take risks; hunter-gatherers' permissive parenting served well to foster those traits.

More recently, research involving many types of societies has shown systematic relationships between a society's structure and its treatment of children. In one study, Carol and Melvin Ember analyzed massive amounts of data for approximately two hundred different societies, to determine which societal traits correlated most strongly with the use of corporal punishment to discipline children.[14] Not surprisingly, they found that the more violent a society was overall, the more likely it was that parents used corporal punishment. The beating of children correlated positively with frequencies of wife beating, harsh punishment of criminals, wars, and other indices of societal violence. But independently of that, it also correlated strongly with the degree of social stratification in the society. The greater the differentiation in power among people in a society, the more frequent the use of corporal punishment by parents. The researchers suggested, from this finding, that parents use corporal punishment ultimately to teach their children to respect the hierarchy of power. Some people are more powerful than others and must be obeyed, no questions asked.

Finally, I'd like to suggest an additional reason for the difference between hunter-gatherers and subsequent societies in child-rearing methods.[15] Agriculture brought to human beings more than a new way of procuring food. It introduced a new way of thinking about the relationship between humans and nature. Hunter-gatherers considered themselves to be part of the natural world; they lived with nature, not against it. They accepted nature's twists and turns as inevitable and adapted to them as best they could.[16] Agriculture, on the other hand, is a continuous exercise in controlling nature; it involves the taming and controlling of plants and animals, to make them servants to humans rather than equal partners in the natural world. With agriculture, I suggest, humans began to extend this idea of control over nature to other aspects of the natural world, including children.

Our own notions of child care and education are founded on agricultural metaphors. We speak of *raising* children, just as we speak of raising chickens or tomatoes. We speak of *training* children, just as we speak of training horses. Our manner of talking and thinking about parenting suggests that we own our children, much as we own our domesticated plants and livestock, and that we control how they grow and behave. Just as we train horses to do the tasks that we want them to do, we train children to do the tasks that we think will be necessary for their future success. We do that regardless of whether the horse or child wants such training or benefits from it as an individual. Training requires suppression of the trainee's will; it requires a concept of disciplining others that was foreign to hunter-gatherers.

Hunter-gatherers, of course, did not have agricultural metaphors. In their world all plants and animals were wild and free. Young plants and animals in nature grow on their own, guided by internal forces, making their own decisions. Each young organism depends, of course, on its environment, but its way of using that environment comes from within itself. The young tree needs and uses the soil, but the soil does not instruct the sapling as to how to use it. The young fox's environment includes its two parents, who between them provide milk, meat, comfort, and continuous examples of fox behavior; but it is the kit, not the parents, who determines when and how it will take the milk, meat, comfort, and examples. The parents to the kit, like the soil to the seedling, provide part of the substrate that the youngster uses in its own way for its own purposes. And that is the general approach that hunter-gatherers took toward child care and education. They provided part of the substrate, not the directing force, for their children's development.

The Further Effects of Feudalism and Industry

As agriculture spread across the useable land in Europe and Asia, landownership became tantamount to power and wealth. People without land became dependent on those who owned it. Landowners discovered that they could increase their wealth by getting other people to work for them. Systems of slavery, indentured servitude, and paid labor emerged as means to supply landowners with workers. Wars were fought to gain and control land and workers. This was the context in which children grew up.

By about the ninth or tenth century AD, feudalism was the primary form of social structure throughout Europe and much of Asia. In a prototypical feudal system (on which, though, there were many variations), a king owned all of the land in his kingdom but delegated portions of it to powerful nobles who, in turn, delegated sections of their land to less powerful nobles, and so on. At the bottom of this pyramid, making up the great majority of the population, were the serfs, who were provided with plots of land on which to grow their own food. In return, the serfs owed payments and services to their noble lords. Usually serfs were bound to their lords in a system of servitude that made it impossible for them to leave the land, even if other work was available, and their children were similarly bound. They were, for all practical purposes, slaves. Children of serfs, even the very young, worked from dawn to dusk in the fields. Others worked as servants in the great homes of nobles or in church monasteries, and some of the luckier ones worked for years as apprentices to tradesmen and developed skills that gave them some degree of independence in adulthood.[17]

The most valuable trait in medieval times, for most people, was obedience—obedience to the father within the family, to the lord within the manor, to the king within the kingdom, and to God in heaven, who was understood to be the "king of kings." In medieval society, the life purpose of those in the lower classes was to serve and obey those above them. It was in this way that education became synonymous with obedience training. Willfulness and the spirit of freedom had to be beaten out of people to make them good servants. Children were beaten not only by their parents, but by anyone who had power over them. For example, in one document dated as near the end of the fourteenth century, a French count advised that nobles' huntsmen should "choose a boy servant as young as seven or eight" and that "this boy should be beaten until he has a proper dread of failing to carry out his master's orders."[18]

In France, Spain, and England, feudal systems were replaced in the fifteenth century by absolute monarchies as kings gained power and nobles lost much of theirs. In an absolute monarchy, everyone serves the king directly, rather than indirectly through servitude to nobles. Farther east, however, feudalism survived much longer. Russia, for example, was feudal until the 1917 revolution. Ultimately the force that drove out large-scale feudalism nearly everywhere was industry coupled with capitalism.

Even in the Middle Ages, not everyone made a living by owning land or by working it. Some survived by filling the ever-increasing demand for material goods brought on by the agricultural way of life. They made farm equipment, household furnishings, and clothing, and they processed grain and other agricultural products purchased from farmers. To facilitate the exchange of goods and services, money economies, lending institutions, and capitalism emerged. Over time, with new inventions, new and more efficient means of producing goods and services were developed, but these means were affordable only to those who had acquired or could borrow a good deal of money. People with money formed businesses and hired those without it as employees. In England, factories capable of mass production began to multiply in the mid-eighteenth century. Capitalism and industry subsequently spread throughout the rest of Europe, leading to the rise of a new merchant class and, eventually, to the overthrow of monarchies. Business owners, who lacked positions of nobility but had economic power, demanded and received a voice in government.

Business owners, like landowners, needed laborers and could profit by extracting as much work from them as possible with as little compensation as possible. Everyone knows of the exploitation that followed and that still exists in some parts of the world. People, including young children, worked most of their waking hours, six or seven days a week, often in beastly conditions, just to survive. Child labor was moved from the fields, with its sunshine, fresh air, and occasional opportunities for play, into dark, crowded, dirty factories, or into coal mines. In England, overseers of the poor commonly farmed out paupers' children and orphans to factories, where they were treated as slaves. Thousands died each year of disease, starvation, and exhaustion. Industry also came to the United States, with similar consequences. By 1832, two-thirds of all employees in New England factories were children ages seven to seventeen, and the typical working day lasted from daybreak to 8 P.M., six days a week.[19]

It is with this history in mind that we must think about the origins of schools as we know them today.

The Early Religious Schools: Indoctrination and Obedience Training

Religious beliefs reflect political and economic realities and commonly serve the purposes of those in power. Hunter-gatherers' religions were nondogmatic and playful. Their deities, which generally represented the forces of nature, were relatively equal to one another, had little or no authority over humans, and were sources of amusement, inspiration, and understanding.[20] But as agriculture developed and societies became hierarchical, religions followed suit. Gods became more fearsome, demanding worship and obedience, and some gods came to be viewed as more powerful than others. This trend culminated in the development of monotheistic religions—Judaism, Christianity, and Islam—each founded on the idea of a steeply hierarchical cosmos headed by a single, all-powerful god who demanded continuous devotion and worship.

Catholicism and the Top-Down Control of Learning

The version of Christianity that held sway through the Middle Ages in Europe, of course, was Roman Catholicism. The Church, with its clear structure of authority—from God to pope, on down through cardinals, bishops, and priests, to parishioners at the bottom—mirrored the pyramid of feudalism. Just as the secular hierarchy transmitted material necessities downward, the Church transmitted knowledge and salvation downward. Those at the top were the arbiters of Truth. The task of those lower down was to learn, repeat, and follow.

Throughout the Middle Ages in Europe, the Roman Catholic Church held a monopoly on knowledge. The Church took on the task of preserving and interpreting not just the Bible but also the classical works of Greek and Roman scholars, and it prohibited new scientific or philosophical developments. Anyone who publicized a new idea risked burning at the stake. In the early seventeenth century, Galileo narrowly escaped torture and death by renouncing his blasphemous claim that the earth goes around the sun rather than vice versa. He was lucky to spend his remaining days under house arrest; others were less fortunate. Knowledge is power, and the Church suppressed new knowledge and dispensed even its own doctrines judiciously. To guard knowledge, the Church kept its dissemination in Latin. Anyone who had the means, desire, and official permission to enter one of the learned professions— that is, to become a theologian, lawyer, or physician—had to learn Latin and study in a Church-run university. The Church developed universities not for the purposes of free inquiry, but for the purposes of formulating and controlling doctrine.

One lesson that the Church did not withhold from the masses was the value of corporal punishment for children who disobeyed or sassed their parents. The hierarchical structure of medieval society and of the Church itself depended on unquestioned obedience, enforced by every means possible, including beatings, torture, death, and threats of hell. The doctrine of original sin justified human suffering, and it certainly justified the beating of children. Better to suffer the whip or the rod, or even be murdered, than suffer an eternity in hell. Here are three typical examples of the Bible's parenting advice: "Foolishness is bound up in the heart of a child, but the rod of correction shall drive it far from him" (Proverbs 22:15). "If a man has a stubborn and rebellious son who does not obey his father and mother and will not listen to them when they discipline him, his father and mother shall take hold of him and bring him to the elders at the gate of his town. . . . Then all the men of his town shall stone him to death" (Deuteronomy 21:18–21). "For God commanded, saying, Honour thy father and mother; and he that curseth father or mother shall be put to death" (Matthew 15:4).

The Rise of Protestantism and the Origin of Compulsory Education

Changes in economic conditions brought on religious changes. The rise of skilled crafts and businesses, beginning in the sixteenth century, produced capitalists who did not depend on the feudal hierarchy for their livelihoods. In their view, they had raised themselves up by their own bootstraps—that is, through their own God-given abilities and hard work. That view, spurred on by the writings of Martin Luther, John Calvin, and others, prompted the Protestant Reformation, which challenged the Roman Catholic hierarchy.

As Max Weber famously pointed out in *The Protestant Ethic and the Spirit of Capitalism,* the values espoused by Protestant sects closely matched those of capitalism.[21] One value was individuals' responsibility for their own success or failure. According to Protestant teachings, it is each person's duty to interpret God's word—that is, to read and understand the Bible—himself or herself and pray directly to God. This tended to put all people on an equal footing in their relationships to God. Another value was that of hard work. Early Protestant leaders taught that God's grace is reflected in people's devotion to and success at their earthly calling, their chosen line of work. To devout early Lutherans, Calvinists, and Puritans, regardless of how rich or poor they were, life was serious. The goal of work and earthly profit was not immediate enjoyment, but was to prove oneself to be in a state of grace with God, to be one of the select who would spend eternity in heaven, not hell.

That attitude fit well with the spirit of capitalism. Success as a capitalist required a person to work hard and then invest, not spend, the profits. Protestantism came to America in the form of Puritanism, and Americans, even more than Europeans, latched onto its spirit. The Protestant, capitalist ethic, at least in theory, replaced obedience to human masters with obedience to a set of stern principles concerning the route to future betterment, in this life and the next. In practice, beatings were still dispensed liberally, especially to children, but in theory the new goal was self-discipline, not discipline forced by others.

Protestants, far more than Catholics, promoted the idea of universal education. Martin Luther declared that salvation depended on each person's own reading and understanding of the scriptures. A corollary, not lost on Luther, was that each person must learn to read, as well as learn that the scriptures represent absolute truth. Luther and other leaders of the Reformation promoted universal education as Christian duty, to save souls from eternal damnation. By the end of the seventeenth century, Protestant-run schools could be found throughout much of Europe and in the American colonies.

In 1642, Massachusetts became the first American colony to mandate at least some degree of schooling—in schools run by Puritan clergy. The stated purpose was to turn children into good Puritans. By 1690, children in Massachusetts and adjacent colonies were learning to read from the New England Primer, known colloquially as "The Little Bible of New England."[22] It included a set of short rhymes to help children learn the alphabet, beginning with, "In **Adam's** Fall, We sinned all," and ending with, "**Z**accheus he, Did climb the tree, His Lord to see." The primer also included the Lord's Prayer, the Apostle's Creed, the Ten Commandments, and various lessons designed to instill in children a fear of God and a strong sense of duty to their elders. Schoolchildren also had to memorize and recite gruesome verses aimed at moral training, such as this little ditty created by the Puritan minister James Jameway:[23]

The Lord delights in them that speak
The words of Truth; but ev'ry Lyar
Must have his Potion in the Lake,
That burns with Brimstone, and with Fire.

Then let me always watch my Lips,
Lest I be struck to death and hell,
Since God a book of Reck'ning keeps
For ev'ry Lie that Children tell.

The primary method of instruction in the early Protestant schools was rote memorization. The goal was indoctrination, not inquisitiveness. The schools were also designed to enforce the Protestant work ethic. Learning was understood to be work, not play. In some schools children were permitted recesses for play, to let off steam, but play was not considered to be a vehicle of learning. In the classroom, play was the enemy of learning. The predominant attitude of Protestant school authorities toward play is reflected in John Wesley's rules for Wesleyan schools, which included the statement: "As we have no play days, so neither do we allow any time for play on any day; for he that plays as a child will play as a man."[24]

Repetition and memorization of imposed lessons are indeed tedious work for children, whose instincts urge them constantly to play and think freely, raise their own questions, and explore the world in their own ways. Children did not adapt well to forced schooling, and in many cases they rebelled. This was no surprise to the adults. By this point in history, the idea that children's own preferences had any value had been pretty well forgotten. Brute force, long used to keep children on task in fields and factories, was transported into the classroom to make children learn. Some of the underpaid, ill-prepared schoolmasters were quite sadistic. One master in Germany kept records of the punishments he meted out in fifty-one years of teaching, a partial list of which included: "911,527 blows with a rod, 124,010 blows with a cane, 20,989 taps with a ruler, 136,715 blows with the hand, 10,235 blows to the mouth, 7,905 boxes on the ear, and 1,118,800 blows on the head."[25] Clearly he was proud of all the educating he had done.

In his autobiography, John Bernard, a prominent eighteenth-century Massachusetts minister, described approvingly how he himself as a child had been beaten regularly by his schoolmaster.[26] He was beaten because of his irresistible drive to play; he was beaten when he failed to learn; he was even beaten when his classmates failed to learn. Because he was a bright boy, he was put in charge of helping the others learn, and when they failed to recite a lesson properly he was beaten for that. His only complaint was that one classmate deliberately flubbed his lessons in order to see him beaten. He solved that problem, finally, by giving the classmate "a good drubbing" when the school day was over and threatening more drubbings in the future. Those were the good old days.

The most concerted, large-scale effort toward the development of universal Protestant schooling occurred in Prussia, the largest of the German kingdoms, beginning in the late seventeenth century. The dominant Protestant sect in Prussia was Pietism, a reformed version of Lutheranism, and the leader of the Pietist schooling movement was August Hermann Francke, who established a system of schooling that would look familiar to us today. He developed a standardized curriculum (mostly of religious catechisms) and a method of training and certifying teachers to teach that curriculum. He arranged to have hourglasses installed in every classroom, so that everyone would follow a schedule dictated by time—a lesson that was part and parcel of the Protestant work ethic. He advocated "gentle" discipline methods when possible; the rod was to be used only to punish misbehavior, not mistakes in reciting lessons. Yet, he was clear in stating that the primary goal of his schools was to break, and then reform, children's will. He wrote, "The formation of the child's character involves the will as well as the understanding. . . . Above all, it is necessary to break the natural willfulness of the child. While the schoolmaster who seeks to make the child more learned is to be commended for cultivating the child's understanding, he has not done enough. He has forgotten his most important task, namely that of making the will obedient."[27]

Francke believed that the most effective way to break children's will was through constant monitoring and supervision in school. He wrote, "Youth do not know how to regulate their lives, and are naturally inclined toward idle and sinful behavior when left to their own devices. For this reason, it is a rule in this institution [the Pietist schools] that a pupil never be allowed out of the presence of a supervisor. The supervisor's presence will stifle the pupil's inclination to sinful behavior, and slowly weaken his willfulness."[28] The words used today may be a little different, but modern educators have expressed the same idea countless times. The belief that young people are incapable of making reasonable decisions is a cornerstone of our system of compulsory, closely monitored education.

Although Prussia was a Protestant kingdom, some Catholic schools were allowed to exist alongside the Pietist schools. King Frederick tolerated these largely because they stressed loyalty to rulers even more than did the Protestant schools. According to a 1768 manual for Prussian Catholic schoolmasters, one of the catechisms that pupils had to memorize was the following:[29]

Q: *Who is subject to the power of the ruler?*
A: *Everyone . . .*

Q: *Why must everyone submit to authority?*

A: *All power comes from God.*

Q: *From whence comes the power held by the ruler?*

A: *The power comes from God.*

Q: *Whom does God ordain?*

A: *Everyone who holds authority. Because all who exercise authority are ordained by God, subjects must be submissive, loyal, and obedient, even to a ruler not of our religion. This was taught by the Apostle Paul, who himself lived under the pagan Roman Emperors.*

Q: *What does it mean to resist authority?*

A: *To resist authority is to rebel against the divine order.*

Q: *What happens to those who do not submit to authority?*

A: *They will suffer eternal damnation.*

How Schools Came to Serve the State

By the beginning of the nineteenth century, churches throughout Europe had been forced out of political power, and states began to take over the task of educating the young.[30] The primary purpose of the new state-run schools was not literacy. By this time in history, the written word was everywhere, and literacy was high throughout Europe and North America. Children whose parents could read learned quite easily to read at home. By the early nineteenth century, roughly three-quarters of the population in the United States, including slaves, were literate, and percentages in most of Europe were comparable.[31] On both sides of the Atlantic, the percentage of literate people was far higher than was the percentage of jobs requiring literacy. The primary educational concern of leaders in government and industry was not to make people literate, but to gain control over *what* people read, what they thought, and how they behaved. Secular leaders in education promoted the idea that if the state controlled the schools, and if children were required by law to attend those schools, then the state could shape each new generation of citizens into ideal patriots and workers.

Just as the German kingdoms had been the leaders in developing Protestant schools, they became the leaders in developing state-run schools. During the eighteenth century, the German feudal system, in which each lord controlled the peasants who were tied to his land, was breaking down. The peasants were becoming increasingly difficult to control, uprisings were common, and talk of revolution filled the air. German educational leaders promoted compulsory state-run schooling primarily as a means to turn the peasants into loyal, well-behaved German citizens. For example, a 1757 article in a Prussian journal of economics predicted: "The inner contentment which the peasant will obtain from such schooling will not only dry the sweat of his brow, but cultivate in him the incentive to work for the good of society. . . . Disloyalty, laziness, idleness, disobedience, disorder, and drudgery would all disappear."[32]

In 1794, King Frederick William II of Prussia declared officially that children's education was henceforth a function of the state, not that of parents or churches. Schools were built in every community that didn't already have them, and compulsory attendance laws were so effectively enforced that by the late 1830s, roughly 80 percent of Prussian children were being educated in state-run elementary schools.[33] Other German states followed Prussia's lead. The principal theme of the German curriculum was nationalism. In the words of historian James Melton, "Perhaps no religion was ever more ardently espoused than that of the love of country in the Germany of William II. Children were made to feel that the German language was the most perfect of all languages, and German literature the most excellent of all literatures. . . . In geography the children were taught that Germany was bounded on the north, south, east, and west by enemies."[34]

Other countries followed suit. Schooling came to be seen as a state function that was essential for national security, not unlike the army. The state's power to forcibly conscript children into schools was understood as comparable to the state's power to conscript young men into the army. In France, Napoleon came to view schooling as a first step in military training.

England, which was the most fully industrialized country, was one of the last to adopt a system of universal compulsory education. A major force against it was the high prevalence of child labor. Industrialists wanted to keep poor children at work in factories, and parents were reluctant to give up the small but essential income that their children earned. Also, by the nineteenth century, England had a broad and rather successful network of church-run and private schools. Children who worked in factories studied religion and practiced literacy in Sunday schools. Nondenominational private schools sprang up, in wide variety, to complement or replace the apprenticeship system as a means of learning trades. The ruling classes in England had no interest in spreading literacy among the masses any further than it had already spread. If they could have put a stop to its spread, they would have. Already, by the beginning of the nineteenth century, the common people were reading and getting excited about such seditious works as Thomas Paine's "Rights of Man" and William Goodwin's "Enquiry Concerning Political Justice."

Finally, in 1870, the English Parliament passed the Education Act, which established a system of state-run elementary schools and mandated attendance for all children between the ages of five and thirteen. Among those who had pushed for this legislation were reformers who were genuinely concerned about children's welfare. They believed that getting children out of factories and into schools, for at least part of the day, would help to break the cycle of poverty and give poor children an opportunity for advancement. Allied with such reformers were members of the ruling classes who, like the German rulers, saw education as a means of controlling the masses. Among the most influential British proponents of compulsory public schooling was the prominent theologian and historian Rev. John Brown, who wrote, "'Tis necessary therefore, in order to form a good citizen to impress the infant with early habits, even to shackle the mind (if you please so to speak) with salutary prejudices, such as may create a conformity of thought and action with the established principles on which its native society is built."[35]

In the United States, Massachusetts—always a leader in American education—was the first state to mandate public schooling. In 1852, under the leadership of Horace Mann, who was secretary of the first state board of education in the United States, Massachusetts began to require every community to offer free public schooling and to compel all children between the ages of eight and fourteen to attend school for at least twelve weeks per year.[36] Mann was an early proponent of the Prussian school system. He saw compulsory schooling as a means of enlightening children in ways that served the interests of industry and the state.[37] One by one, other states followed, the last being Mississippi, which finally passed its compulsory schooling law in 1918.

The spirit behind compulsory education in the United States is laid out in the writings of Edward Ross, one of the founders of American sociology, who in the late nineteenth century published a series of articles that were later collected into the book *Social Control: A Survey of the Foundations of Order*. Ross advocated for compulsory public schooling as a means of maintaining social order. In his words, the job of the public school is "to collect little plastic lumps of human dough from private households and shape them on the social kneading-board."[38] Ross understood that children learned from their environment, especially from the people around them, and he wanted to ensure uniformity of that environment. He believed that children are highly suggestible and imitate adult models. He wrote, "Copy the child will, and the advantage of giving him his teacher instead of his father to imitate is that the former is a picked person, while the latter is not."[39] Yes, the teacher was a picked person—picked and certified by the state to teach the correct ideas and not the incorrect ones. Ross, like Frederick II in Prussia, saw compulsory public schooling as the secular replacement for religion in the task of maintaining social order. He wrote, "The technique of belief and religion has been understood for thousands of years, but the technique of education is the discovery of yesterday— or, shall I say, tomorrow?"[40] And he quoted approvingly Daniel Webster's idea that public schooling is "a wise and liberal system of police, by which property and peace are secured."[41]

The Ever-Increasing Power and Standardization of Schools

Once compulsory systems of state-run schools were established, they became increasingly standardized, both in content and in method. For the sake of efficiency, children were divided into separate classrooms by age and passed along, from grade to grade, like products on an assembly line. The task of each teacher was to add bits of officially approved knowledge to the product, in accordance with a preplanned schedule, and then to test that product before passing it on to the next station.

Female teachers generally replaced men in the classroom, largely because they could be hired more cheaply, but also because women would soften the image of schooling, reduce the use of corporal punishment, and make schooling more palatable to tender-minded parents.[42] At first, however, the female teachers were called assistants. They were assistants to the "principal teacher," who was almost always a male. We still have, especially in primary schools, mostly female teachers and male principals, and the principal is still charged with making sure that teachers follow the prescribed curriculum and that students obey the teacher. The school became, in some ways, a polygamous version of the hierarchical early twentieth-century family, with the man in a position of authority, the women working directly with children, and the children at the bottom. The task of the student, then as now, was to be punctual and obedient, to pay attention, to complete assignments on schedule, and to memorize and feed back to the teacher the lessons taught, without questioning either their content or the prescribed methods for learning them.

When compulsory public education was introduced into Massachusetts in the mid-nineteenth century, the required school year was only twelve weeks long, and only children from age eight to fourteen had to attend. Over time, in Massachusetts and everywhere, the school year was made longer and more years of schooling added on. As explained in Chapter 1, the first half of the twentieth century is considered to be the "golden age of children's free play," because most children no longer had to work long hours on farms or in factories and schooling was not as onerous as it later became. As the school day, school year, and years of schooling grew ever greater, as homework assignments grew, and as testing became ever more standardized and significant for the child's advancement from grade to grade, school gradually came to take over children's and family's lives—as described in Chapter 1.

Today most people think of childhood and schooling as indelibly entwined. We identify children by their grade in school. We automatically think of learning as work, which children must be forced to do in special workplaces, schools, modeled after factories. All this seems completely normal to us, because we see it everywhere. We rarely stop to think about how new and unnatural all this is in the larger context of human evolution and how it emerged from a bleak period in our history that was marked by child labor and beliefs in children's innate sinfulness. We have forgotten that children are designed by nature to learn through self-directed play and exploration, and so, more and more, we deprive them of freedom to learn, subjecting them instead to the tedious and painfully slow learning methods devised by those who run the schools.

4

SEVEN SINS OF OUR SYSTEM OF FORCED EDUCATION

CHILDREN GENERALLY DON'T LIKE SCHOOL. As if it needed confirming, a large-scale research study conducted a few years ago showed that children are less happy in school than in any other setting where they spend significant amounts of time each week.[1] When children do like school, it's usually because of the friends they meet there, not because of the lessons. Children's dislike of school is a national joke, not just in our nation but wherever children are forced by law to go to school. It's standard fare in the comic strips, where the first day of school each year is one of mourning for kids and joy for parents (who are apparently tired of having their kids around) and the last day is the reverse. And yet, if adults were treated as children are in school, nobody would find it funny.

Not long ago I read the book *Why Don't Students Like School?* by cognitive scientist Daniel T. Willingham. The book had received rave reviews from people involved in the school system, but I found that it fails to answer the question posed by its title. Willingham's thesis is that students don't like school (and also don't learn much there) because teachers don't have a full understanding of certain cognitive principles and therefore don't teach as well as they could. They don't present material in ways that appeal best to students' minds. Presumably, if teachers followed Willingham's advice and used the latest information cognitive science has to offer about how the mind works, students would love school. We've been seeing these kinds of books for decades—first from behaviorists, then from Piagetians, and most recently from cognitive and neural scientists who think that the latest fads and findings in their field of research will solve the school problem.

Willingham, like others who write such books, pretends not to see the big fat elephant sitting in the middle of the room, crushing the children. Children don't like school because to them school is—dare I say it—prison. Children don't like school because, like all human beings, they crave freedom, and in school they are not free.

The failure to acknowledge the elephant is not just Willingham's, but that of our entire culture. Everyone who has ever been to school knows that school is prison, but almost nobody beyond school age says it. It's not polite. We all tiptoe around this truth because admitting it would make us seem cruel and would point a finger at well-intentioned people doing what they believe to be essential. How could all these nice people be sending their children to prison or working for an institution that imprisons children? How could our democratic government, which is founded on principles of freedom and self-determination, make laws requiring children and adolescents to spend a good portion of their days in prison? I, like most people I know, went through the full set of years of public schooling. My mother taught in a public school for several years. My sister, two cousins, and many dear friends are or were public schoolteachers. How can I say that these good people—who love children and have poured themselves passionately into the task of trying to help them—are complicit in a system of imprisoning them?

A prison, according to the common, general definition, is any place of involuntary confinement and restriction of liberty. In school, as in adult prisons, the inmates are told exactly what they must do and are punished for failure to comply. Actually, students in school must spend more time doing exactly what they are told to do than is true of adults in penal institutions. Another difference, of course, is that we put adults in prison because they have committed a crime, while we put children in school because of their age.

Sometimes people use the word *prison* in a metaphorical sense to refer to any situation in which they must follow rules or do things that are unpleasant. In that spirit, some adults refer to their workplace as a prison, or even to their marriage as a prison. But that is not a literal use of the term, because those examples involve voluntary, not involuntary restraint. It is against the law in this and other democratic countries to force someone to work at a job where the person doesn't want to work, or to marry someone he or she doesn't want to marry. In contrast, it is against the law to *not* force a child to go to school if you are the parent and the child doesn't want to go. It is true that some parents have the wherewithal to find alternative schooling or provide homeschooling that is acceptable to both the child and the state, but that is not the norm in today's society. So, while jobs and marriages might in some sad cases *feel* like prisons, schools as we generally know them *are* prisons.

Given the historical origins of our schools, described in the last chapter, it should be no surprise that this is the case. To the Protestant reformers who started them, schools were meant to be correctional institutions, built on the assumption that children are natural sinners. To be saved from hell, children were required to go to schools where their sinful wills would be broken and then reshaped along lines consistent with Protestant teachings. Over time, the religious language was lost, but the idea remains: children are incompetent, untrustworthy, and in need of the coercive, corrective forces of schooling to shape them into the kinds of human beings that the elites of society think they should become.

Another term that I think deserves to be said aloud is *forced education*. Like the term *prison,* this term sounds harsh. But again, if we have *compulsory* education, we have *forced* education. The term *compulsory,* if it has any meaning at all, means that the person has no choice about it.

The question worth debating is this: Is forced education—and the consequent imprisonment of children—a good thing or a bad thing? Most people seem to believe that it is, all in all, a good thing and maybe even necessary. I disagree. In the remainder of this chapter I outline what I perceive to be *seven sins* of our system of forced education. Then, in the chapters that follow, I present abundant evidence that children learn beautifully, on their own motivation and in their own ways, if we give them the freedom and opportunities to do so, without coercion.

Sin 1: Denial of liberty without just cause and due process. This is the most blatant of the sins of forced education, and it provides the foundation for the others. A basic premise of our democratic system of values is that it is wrong to deny anyone liberty without just cause and due process. To incarcerate an adult, we must prove, in a court of law, that the person has committed a crime or is a serious threat to self or others. Yet we incarcerate children because of their age. According to our democratic system of values, it should be immoral to incarcerate children because of their age unless we have proven that children—all children within the specified age range—are a danger to themselves or others without such incarceration. No such proof exists, and as I will show, there is much evidence to the contrary.

Sin 2: Interference with the development of personal responsibility and self-direction. When Civil War hero David Glascow Farragut was nine years old, he was appointed midshipman in the US Navy. At age twelve, in the War of 1812, he temporarily led a navy team that included adults two to four times his age, when he was appointed commander of a ship captured from the British.[2] The great inventor Thomas Edison left school three months after starting it, at age eight, having been judged by his teacher to be unfit for it because of his "addled brain" (a condition that would probably be diagnosed today as ADHD). He then began systematically educating himself. By age twelve he was making an adult-size income from several businesses he had started, and two years after that he was publishing, on his own, a successful newspaper.[3]

Farragut and Edison were exceptional people, but the practice of children's assuming adult-like responsibilities was not exceptional in the early to mid-nineteenth century, before the era of state-enforced compulsory schooling. Today the typical twelve-year-old in a middle-class suburb is not trusted to babysit or even walk home from school unaccompanied by an adult. We have become a society that assumes that children are, merely because of their age, irresponsible and incompetent.

The belief that children and even teenagers are incapable of rational decision-making and self-direction is a self-fulfilling prophecy. By confining children to school and other adult-directed school-like settings, and by filling their time with forced busywork, which serves no productive purpose, we deprive them of the time and opportunities they need to practice self-direction and responsibility. And so, children themselves, as well as their parents and teachers, come to think that children are incompetent. Over time, as forced schooling has been extended to include people of ever-older ages, the belief in incompetence has been extended upward.

An implicit and sometimes explicit message of our forced schooling system is this: "If you do what you are told to do in school, everything will work out well for you." Children who buy into that message stop taking responsibility for their own education. They assume, falsely, that someone else has figured out what they need to do and know to become successful adults. If their life doesn't work out well, they take the role of a victim: "My school (or parents or society) failed me, and that's why my life is screwed up." This attitude of victimization, set up in childhood, may then persist for a lifetime. As schooling has become an ever more dominant force in young people's lives, the sense of individual helplessness has increased in our society, as I discussed in Chapter 1. Mark Twain was fond of saying, "I've never let school interfere with my education." Unfortunately, today, because of the great expansion of forced schooling since Twain's time, it's becoming harder and harder for anyone to live by that maxim.

Sin 3: Undermining of intrinsic motivation to learn (turning learning into work). Children come into the world burning to learn. They are naturally curious, naturally playful, and they explore and play in ways that teach them about the social and physical world to which they must adapt. They are little learning machines. Within their first four years or so they learn, without any instruction, unfathomable amounts of skills and information. They learn to walk, run, jump, and climb. They learn to understand and speak the language of the culture into which they are born, and with that they learn to assert their will, argue, amuse, annoy, befriend, and ask questions. They acquire an incredible amount of knowledge about the world around them. All this is driven by their inborn instincts and drives. Nature does not turn off this enormous desire and capacity to learn when children turn five or six. We turn it off with our system of schooling. The biggest, most enduring lesson of school is that learning is work, to be avoided when possible, not joyful play as children would otherwise believe.

The forced nature of schooling turns learning into work. Teachers even call it work: "You must do your work before you can play." But no matter what the teachers called it, learning in school would be work. Anything a person is forced to do, according to someone else's schedule, using procedures that someone dictates, is work. The very act of taking control of children's learning turns that learning from joy into work.

Albert Einstein, who loved to play with math but hated studying it in school, is one of many great thinkers who has pointed out the deleterious effects of forced instruction. In his autobiography he wrote:

It is nothing short of a miracle that the modern methods of instruction have not yet entirely strangled the holy curiosity of inquiry; for this delicate plant, aside from stimulation, stands mainly in need of freedom; without this it goes to wreck and ruin without fail. It is a very grave mistake to think that the enjoyment of seeing and searching can be promoted by means of coercion and a sense of duty.[4]

Elsewhere, concerning his formal education, Einstein wrote: "One had to cram all this stuff into one's mind, whether one liked it or not. This coercion had such a deterring effect that, after I had passed the final examination, I found the consideration of any scientific problems distasteful to me for an entire year." The genius of Einstein was that somehow he managed to survive schooling without losing forever his ability to explore and play with ideas.

When students are evaluated for their learning and are compared with other students, as they constantly are in school, learning becomes not only work but a source of anxiety. Students who are learning to read and are a little slower than the rest feel anxious about reading in front of others. Tests and fear of failure create anxiety in almost everyone who takes school seriously. I have found in my college teaching of statistics that a high percentage of students, even at my rather selective university, suffer from math anxiety, apparently because of the humiliation they experienced from math in school. A fundamental psychological principle (discussed in Chapter 7) is that anxiety inhibits learning. Learning occurs best in a playful state of mind, and anxiety inhibits playfulness.

Sin 4: Judging students in ways that foster shame, hubris, cynicism, and cheating. It is not easy to force people to do what they do not want to do. At first, the cane was the most common instrument of coercion in schools. Another early method was public shaming. Schoolmasters would ridicule misbehaving or poorly performing children in front of their classmates, sometimes verbally and sometimes by having them wear a dunce cap while seated on a special dunce's stool throughout the school day.

Today we rarely use the cane, though corporal punishment is still legal in twenty US states, and the dunce cap has vanished. But shaming has not. We rely now primarily on a system of incessant testing, grading, and ranking of children to motivate them to do their schoolwork. Children are made to feel ashamed (inferior) if they perform worse than their peers and proud (superior) if they perform better. Shame leads some to drop out, psychologically, from the educational endeavor or to struggle constantly with the sense of inferiority. Those made to feel excessive pride from the shallow accomplishments that earn them A's and honors may become arrogant, disdainful of the common lot who don't do so well on tests; disdainful, therefore, of democratic values and processes.

Our system of grading and ranking to motivate students seems almost perfectly designed to promote cynicism and cheating. Students are constantly told about the value of high grades. Advancement through the system and eventual freedom from it depend on them. Students understandably become convinced that high grades are the be-all and end-all of their schoolwork. By the time they are eleven or twelve years old, most are realistically cynical about the idea that school is fundamentally a place for learning. They realize that much of what they are required to do is senseless and that they will forget most of what they are tested on shortly after the test.

Students also come to realize that the rules about what is and isn't cheating in school are arbitrary and have little or nothing to do with learning. If you create a summary sheet of terms and facts and then consult that sheet while taking the test, you have cheated. However, if you create such a sheet and commit it to a form of short-term memory that lasts long enough for the test and then vanishes, you have not cheated. If you create a term paper by copying out large chunks of other people's writing and pasting them together, that is cheating, but if you do essentially the same thing and then paraphrase sufficiently, that is not cheating.

Students understand that the rules distinguishing cheating from not cheating in school are like the rules of a game. But it's a game they did not choose to play. They have little or no say in what they study, how they are tested, or the rules concerning what is or isn't cheating. Under these conditions, it's hard to respect the rules. It should be no surprise, therefore, to learn that cheating in schools is rampant. On anonymous questionnaires, approximately 95 percent of students admit to some degree of cheating, and roughly 70 percent admit to repeated acts of the most blatant forms of cheating, such as copying whole tests from other students or plagiarizing whole papers.[5]

The surveys also reveal an overall increase in the amount of cheating over recent years and a shift in who does most of it. In times past, the most frequent cheaters were the "poor students," who cheated out of desperation. Today, however, the highest incidences of reported cheating are among the "best students," the ones aiming for the top colleges and graduate schools, the ones who experience the greatest pressures to excel.[6] As one high school graduate put it in a call-in to a talk radio program, "I was in honors classes in high school because I wanted to get into the best schools, and all of us in those classes cheated; we needed the grades to get into the best schools."[7] Similarly, a young adult who had read one of my essays on school cheating wrote to me:

Although I am not proud of it, I was one of the many students cheating in high school and college. I never got caught. Even the valedictorian of my high school was a chronic cheater. I received above average scores, although I would have been an average student had I not relied on cheating. Being average was not an option at my house. I always felt that I was being pressured to be smarter, and unfortunately being "smart" was somehow better than being "honest." The result of the pressure is that students are rewarded for being dishonest, which is really very sad.

Teachers often say that if you cheat in school you are only cheating yourself, because you are shortchanging your own education. But that argument holds water only if what you would have learned by not cheating outweighs the value of whatever you did with the time saved by cheating. If by cheating in Subject X, you gain more time to really learn Subject Y, which you care about and which may or may not be a school subject, then you haven't really shortchanged your education. Students understand this argument well. In my experience talking with students, the argument against cheating that is most compelling to them is the argument that by cheating they are hurting students who didn't cheat. Most students don't want to hurt other students. They see the system as an enemy and hold few qualms about cheating to beat it, but they generally don't see other students as enemies, so they feel bad if they think they are hurting others. In fact, one of the main reasons cheaters are sometimes caught is that they share their cheating with other students, and somewhere in the sharing the word leaks out to school officials. The problems that arise from the students-versus-the-system attitude that coercive schooling promotes are serious and endless. The honest student, who reports the cheating, becomes a ratfink.

In other respects, cheating to get high grades seems to many students to be a win-win-win situation. They want to get high grades, their parents want them to get high grades, and their teachers want them to get high grades. Teachers generally don't look hard to see cheating and often ignore it when they do see it, because the higher grades, especially on standardized tests, make them look good, too. In fact, in this era of high-stakes testing and holding school personnel responsible, we hear of more and more cases where teachers and principals artificially raise students' scores as a way of protecting their jobs. And many parents, far from deploring their children's cheating, are ready to go to court to fight any school officials who dare make an accusation of cheating.

One of the tragedies of our system of schooling is that it teaches students that life is a series of hoops that one must get through, by one means or another, and that success lies in others' judgments rather than in real, self-satisfying accomplishments. Many people manage to get off that track, or partly off it, once they leave school and begin to experience more freedom. But too many others never get off it; they are perpetually like students, constantly more interested in impressing others than in real achievement. These are the ones who continue to cheat—in science, business, law, politics, or whatever career they pursue. For them, the habit of cheating that was cultivated in school remains for a lifetime.

Sin 5: Interference with the development of cooperation and promotion of bullying. We are by nature an intensely social species, designed for cooperation. Even in school children find ways to help one another. But regardless of the lectures that students might hear in school about the value of helping others, school works against such behavior. By design, it teaches selfishness. The forced competitiveness, the constant grading and ranking of students, contain the implicit lesson that each student's job is to look out for himself or herself and to do better than others. Indeed, too much help given by one student to another is cheating. Helping others may even hurt the helper, by raising the grading curve and lowering the helper's position on it. Some of those students who most strongly buy into school understand this well; they become ruthless achievers, more interested in beating others than in helping them.

Age segregation and lack of opportunities for free play add to the forces that work against the development of cooperation, compassion, and nurturance at school. Under normal conditions, children develop their abilities to cooperate and help one another in free, self-directed, social play, where they learn to resolve their differences and take into account one another's needs in order to keep the game going (see Chapter 8). Age-mixed play is especially valuable in this regard. Researchers have found that the presence of younger children naturally activates the nurturing instincts of older children (discussed in Chapter 9). Older children help younger ones when they play together, and in that way they learn to lead and nurture and develop a concept of themselves as mature and caring. But little of this can occur in school, where children are forced to associate only with others of their own age and where free, unsupervised play is rare or absent. It should come as no surprise that over the past few decades—as schooling has occupied ever-larger portions of children's lives and age-mixed play has declined—psychologists have documented a constantly rising prevalence of narcissism (defined as excessive self-concern and lack of concern for others) among young people.[8]

The age-segregated, competitive atmosphere of school, along with students' lack of any real voice in school governance, provides the ideal conditions for the generation of competitive coalitions, or cliques, which provide a foundation for bullying. Children who are not accepted into any of the prevailing cliques may be picked on mercilessly, and they have no way to escape.

Imagine what it is like to be bullied daily in school, as many kids are. Let's say you are fifteen years old, or thirteen, or eleven, and for some reason—a reason over which you have no control—you have been singled out by schoolmates as an object for scorn and humiliation. Every day at school, for you, is another day in hell. You are called "whore," "bitch," "slut," "fag," "pussy," "scum," or worse. People deliberately bump into you and knock your books out of your hands in the hallway. Nobody sits with you at lunch, or if they do, they are harassed until they stop. These are not the brutish-looking comic-strip bullies, whom nobody likes and who steal kids' lunch money. These bullies are among the popular kids—the athletes, cheerleaders, preppies. They are popular not only with the other kids but also with the teachers, school administrators, and adults in the larger community.

The law requires that you attend school, regardless of how you are treated. You are not among the minority whose parents have the means and will to send them to a private alternative school or to convince the school board that they can educate them adequately at home. You have no choice. What do you do? If you are like most of the hundreds of thousands of picked-on kids who suffer like this every school day, you somehow suck it up. You harden yourself and survive it. You may be the only person who will ever know the full extent of your suffering. You may think about killing yourself; you may even fantasize some violent revenge against the whole school; but if you are like most kids, such thoughts remain in the realm of fantasy. Every once in a while, however, in a particularly vulnerable person, the despair or rage or both erupt into violence, either against the self or against the whole school, and only then does school bullying become an issue to the larger community.

Here's how Helen Smith, in her book *The Scarred Heart*, tells one such story, that of the suicide of thirteen-year-old April Michelle Himes of Richland, Washington:

> Kids at school called her fat, threw things at her and pushed her around. They ridiculed her with rumors that she stuffed tissues in her bra. She attempted suicide and her parents admitted her to an inpatient mental hospital program and sought counseling but said it didn't help. After missing fifty-three out of the required one hundred and eighty days of school, she was told that she would have to return to school or appear before a truancy board which could then send her to a juvenile detention center. She decided the better alternative was to go into her bedroom and hang herself with a belt. . . . In times past, she could have just dropped out of school, but now kids like her are trapped by compulsory education.[9]

When events like this happen, school systems take bullying seriously, at least for a while. Their usual approach is to develop some sort of anti-bullying course or program and require all students to take it. A new required course—this is our culture's knee-jerk reaction to every problem we see among kids. Many such courses and programs have been tried over the past two or three decades, in other countries as well as in the United States, and many outcome studies have been conducted to see if they work. So far, no such program has proven itself to be effective over the long run.[10] None of the programs get at the root of the problem, and they can't without radically altering the basic structure of the school.

Bullying occurs in all institutions where people who have no political power and are ruled in top-down fashion are required by law or economic necessity to remain in that setting. It occurs regularly, for example, in adult as well as juvenile prisons. Those who are bullied can't escape, and they have no legislative or judicial power to confront the bullies. In their acclaimed book, *Will the Boat Sink the Water?*, Chen Guidi and Wu Chuntau describe the prevalence of bullying in rural China. The peasants are not allowed to move off the land and they are governed, top down, by petty bureaucrats. The peasants have no political power and no due process of law, and so the bullies, who can best intimidate others, rise to the top. Should we be surprised to discover that some of our schoolchildren respond to forced confinement and dictatorial governance in the same manner as adult prisoners and Chinese peasants?

By segregating children by age, by caging them in so they can't avoid those who harass them, by indoctrinating them in a setting where competition and winning—being better than others—are the highest values, and by denying them any meaningful voice in school governance, we establish the breeding grounds for bullying.

Sin 6: Inhibition of critical thinking. Presumably one of the great general goals of education is the cultivation of critical thinking. But despite all the lip service that educators devote to it, most students learn to avoid thinking critically about their schoolwork. They learn that their job in school is to get high marks on tests and that critical thinking interferes. To get a good grade, you need to figure out what the teacher wants you to say and then say it. I've heard that sentiment expressed countless times by college students as well as by high school students, in discussions held outside the classroom. I've devoted a lot of effort toward promoting critical thinking at the college level.[11] But truth be told, the grading system, which is the chief motivator throughout our system of education, is a powerful force against honest debate and critical thought in the classroom. In a system in which we teachers do the grading, few students are going to criticize or even question the ideas we offer, and if we try to induce criticism by grading for it, we generate false criticism.

To think critically, people must feel motivated and free to voice their own ideas and raise their own questions. But in school students learn that their own ideas and questions don't count. What counts are their abilities to provide the "correct" answers to questions that they did not ask and that do not interest them. And "correct" means the answers that the teachers or the test producers are looking for, not necessarily answers that the student really understands or cares about, or really believes are correct, or finds useful in daily life.

A high school student I was trying to help with math homework summed it up nicely to me. After a few minutes of pretending politely to listen to my explanation of *why* a certain way of solving certain equations worked and another did not, she exclaimed, "I appreciate what you are trying to do, but I don't need or want to know why the method works! All I need to know is how to follow the steps that the teacher wants and get the answers that she wants." This was someone widely recognized to be a "good" student; she could have been speaking for the great majority of such students.

Students recognize that it would be impossible to delve deeply into their school subjects, even if they wanted to. Time does not permit it. They must follow the schedule set by the school. Moreover, many students have become convinced that they must also engage in a certain number of formal extracurricular activities, to prove that they are the "well-rounded" individuals top colleges are seeking. Students who allowed themselves to pursue a love of some subject would risk failing all the others. To succeed, students must acquire the limited information and shallow understanding needed to perform well on the tests.

Another great inhibitor of critical thinking in school is anxiety. The continuous evaluation of students that occurs in school reduces critical thinking not only because it leads students to look for what the teacher wants, but also because it promotes anxiety. Critical thinking is founded in creativity, and creativity always requires a degree of playfulness (see Chapter 7). The critical thinker plays with ideas—tries them out, turns them upside down to see what happens, explores their consequences. Anxiety prevents such play and forces thought along well-worn channels. Anxiety facilitates the ability to feed back what one knows by rote, but it inhibits the generation of new ideas or insights.

Sin 7: Reduction in diversity of skills and knowledge.   By forcing all schoolchildren through the same standard curriculum, we reduce their opportunities to follow alternative pathways. The school curriculum represents a tiny subset of the skills and knowledge that are important to our society. In this day and age, nobody can learn more than a sliver of all there is to know. Why force everyone to learn the same sliver? In the next chapter I'll present evidence that when children are free to follow their interests, they take diverse and unpredicted paths. They develop passionate interests, work diligently to become experts in the realms that fascinate them, and then find ways to use their skills, knowledge, and passions to make a living. Students forced through the standard curriculum have much less time to pursue their own interests, and many learn altogether too well the lesson that their own interests don't count. Some get over that and explore paths outside of the school curriculum, but too many do not.

In the real world, outside of school, diversity in personality as well as in knowledge is valued. Part of the task of growing up is to find niches that best fit one's personality. In the modern school classroom, however, there is only one niche, and those whose personalities don't fit are seen as failures, or as suffering from a "mental disorder." Instead of adjusting to the diversity of personalities, schools try to mold personalities to fit the school, often with drugs. The most obvious current example of this concerns the high rate of diagnosis of ADHD (attention-deficit/hyperactivity disorder) among schoolchildren today.

Some children are naturally more active and impulsive than others, and this gets them into trouble in school. It is even harder for them than for the typical child to sit still for hours every day, to attend to assignments that don't interest them, and to tolerate tedium. In today's world of high-pressure schooling, those kids get labeled as having a mental disorder, ADHD. According to the most authoritative data at the time of this writing, roughly 12 percent of school-age boys and

4 percent of school-age girls in the United States have been diagnosed with ADHD.[12] The great majority of such diagnoses are initiated by complaints from schoolteachers. Think of it! Twelve percent of boys— one out of every eight—have been labeled as *mentally disordered* because of inability or unwillingness to attend for long periods to schoolwork that they find boring. That by itself is a sin. Today we even hear, increasingly, of three- and four-year-olds being diagnosed with ADHD and drugged because they can't or won't sit still at *preschool*!

When I was in elementary school, decades ago, the adults seemed to recognize that it is not natural for children to spend long hours sitting and studying. We had a half-hour morning recess, an hour of outdoor play at lunch, and another half-hour afternoon recess, and we almost never had homework. Our six-hour school day consisted of two hours of outdoor play and four hours in the classroom. I'm not saying that school back then was great; it just wasn't as bad as it is now. Elementary schools today no longer provide such breaks. Instead the kids who can't adapt to school's tedium are diagnosed with ADHD and are put on powerful psychoactive drugs, which have the immediate effect of reducing their spontaneity so they can attend to the teacher and complete the senseless busywork. Nobody knows the long-term effects of these drugs on the human brain, but research with animals suggests that one effect may be to *interfere* with the normal development of the brain connections that lead children generally to become more controlled, less impulsive, with age and maturity.[13] Perhaps that helps to explain why today we see more and more cases of ADHD extending into adulthood. As with lots of psychoactive drugs, the drugs used to treat ADHD may be creating long-term dependency.

Not long ago, I solicited reports from parents who had withdrawn a child from public school and begun homeschooling sometime after the child was diagnosed with ADHD. In the great majority of cases, according to the reports, the children were taken off the drugs and had no particular problems learning under the conditions of homeschooling.[14] When they could pursue their own interests rather than paths laid out for them by others, and when they could play to their hearts' content, most had no trouble learning and no need for psychoactive drugs.

MY LIST OF SINS HERE IS NOT NOVEL. Many teachers I have spoken with are aware of these harmful effects of forced education, and many work hard to try to counteract them. Some try to instill as much of a sense of freedom and play as the system permits; many do what they can to mute the shame of failure and reduce anxiety; most try to allow and promote cooperation and compassion among the students, despite the barriers against it; many do what they can to allow and promote critical thinking. But the system works strongly against them, especially today as we move the system ever more toward its logical conclusions. It may even be fair to say that teachers in our school system are no freer to teach as they wish than are students to learn as they wish. One teacher, in response to an early sketch of this chapter, wrote, "I don't choose what I teach; the state does. Teachers know wonderful things about how children learn, but we're not allowed to do anything about it. . . . My ability to keep my job is based on how many of my students pass the [state-mandated] test." But teachers, unlike students, are free to quit.

I must also add that human beings, especially young ones, are remarkably adaptive and resourceful. Many students find ways to overcome the negative feelings that forced schooling engenders and to focus on the positive. They fight the sins. They find ways to cooperate, to play, to help one another overcome feelings of shame, to put undue pride in its place, to combat bullying, to think critically, and to spend some time on their true interests despite the forces working against them in school. But to do all this while also satisfying the demands of the forced education takes great effort, and many do not succeed. At minimum, the time students must spend on wasteful busywork and following orders in school detracts greatly from the time they can use to educate themselves.

I have described here *seven sins* of forced education, but I have resisted the temptation to call them *the* seven sins. You may want to add others. One reader suggested that I should add *interference with family life* as an eighth sin. Schooling eats into the time that families can spend together, on their own activities. It also interferes with family harmony, as parents must be enforcers of homework, cope with the negative effects that schooling has on children's moods and home behavior, and in some cases do battle with their kids every day to get them to go to school.

Reducing the amount of time that children must spend at school, reducing homework, and increasing recesses—to levels comparable to the norm of decades ago—would help, but it would not solve the problem. To rid ourselves of the sins described in this chapter we would need to ditch the line of thinking and behaving that arose out of the dark period of human history when we assumed that children were natural sinners in need of reform and that the primary goal of education was obedience to lords and masters. We would need to throw out the whole system and think afresh about how to help children learn, in their own self-directed ways, rather than about how to force them to learn what others have decided they should learn. This would be a huge and wonderful leap backward as well as forward. Hunter-gatherers had it right, and their understanding that children need freedom to educate themselves is as valid for children in our social world today as it was in theirs.

5

LESSONS FROM SUDBURY VALLEY: MOTHER NATURE CAN PREVAIL IN MODERN TIMES

IN THE EARLY TO MID-1960s, Daniel Greenberg was a young professor, first in physics and then in history, at Columbia University and a rising star in the newly developing field of history of science. Everyone who knew him predicted a long, stellar academic career. Greenberg was also a popular teacher, and it was teaching that got him thinking about something that seemed even more important than the new translation of Aristotle he had been working on. Undergraduates claimed they loved his courses, but he couldn't help but observe the passive approach they took to their studies. Here, even in this Ivy League school, students taking physics or history seemed motivated to get the highest grades they could while learning the least possible amount of the subject matter. Why, he wondered, are they taking courses in these subjects when they don't really want to learn them? Then he asked: What is wrong with our educational system that prevents students from developing passionate interests and then pursuing those interests in their education?

Most bright young professors, in my experience, go through a phase of fretting about the educational system. Then at some point, they brush it off and move on. They go on teaching, year after year, assuming that their job is to push and prod unmotivated students to go through the motions of learning and to get good grades on tests. But Greenberg is not the kind of person who easily brushes things off. He began to see the university as complicit in a system of education that he could no longer tolerate. In fact, he realized, it was universities, through their education departments, that promoted the K–12 schooling policies that he deplored. Then Greenberg took a step that shocked everyone. He resigned from his professorship and, with his wife, Hanna, moved off into what was to them the "wilderness" of the Sudbury River region of eastern Massachusetts, to ponder the nature of education and to write about it.

Among Greenberg's early writings of that era was the treatise *Outline of a New Philosophy,* in which he challenged the theory that knowledge consists of certain fixed truths.[1] Knowledge is fluid, he argued. The truths of today are the myths or half-truths of tomorrow. Two ideas that logically contradict each other can both be true, from different vantage points, for different purposes. What we call knowledge might better be called models, or explanatory concepts, which help people to make sense of the world around them. From this perspective, knowledge is to be judged not so much by its truth or falseness as by its usefulness. A good idea is one that helps a person make sense of some aspect of his or her social or physical world and thereby helps that person to navigate that world.

This view of knowledge negates the value of a fixed educational curriculum. What is most desirable is that people have the freedom to develop their own models, their own concepts to explain what they need or wish to explain, using whatever resources they find useful—including, but not limited to, others' teachings and writings. People naturally want to make sense of their world. That, to Greenberg, is the essence of human curiosity. As they strive to answer questions that truly interest them, people are automatically motivated to use any resources that help them to address those questions. But the questions that interest one person do not necessarily interest another, and the resources that are helpful to one are not necessarily helpful to another.

Greenberg also thought deeply about the principles of American democracy and their relevance to education. In the book *The Crisis in American Education,* he and a group of other reformers, with whom he went on to found a new school, argued, "The educational system in our country today is the most un-American institution we have in our midst."[2] They pointed out that our democracy rests on three root ideas: (1) human beings have certain fundamental rights; (2) the people affected by a decision should have a voice in making that decision; and (3) all people should have equal opportunities to succeed in life. These ideas get lip service in schools but are not practiced there. The rights of free speech, free assembly, freedom to choose one's own path to happiness, and fair trial when accused of a misdeed are nonexistent for students. Students generally have no voice in the formation of school rules and little voice in decisions about how they will spend their time each day. Equality of opportunity is subverted by a system that passes and fails students for their progress along the school's preplanned path and does not support those whose proclivities would lead them in different directions. A major purpose of schooling in a democracy, argued Greenberg, should be to help people prepare for the opportunities and responsibilities of democratic citizenship; and you don't do that effectively by depriving students of those opportunities and responsibilities as they are growing up.

In the same book, Greenberg and his colleagues argued that a democratic school should be "a free market place of ideas, a free enterprise system of talents."[3] Students should be free to explore any ideas that engage their interests and should be allowed to come to their own conclusions, in an environment where they can hear all sides of any question. In a democracy, a school should be a setting for exploration and discovery, not indoctrination.

A Truly Democratic School

In 1968 Greenberg and his wife, Hanna, along with a group of other parents of school-age children, founded such a school. They called it the Sudbury Valley School. The school has been operating ever since, and at this writing, both Greenbergs are still staff members there. They have been reelected to the staff, by the School Meeting, every year for forty-four years.

For more than four decades, Sudbury Valley has been perhaps the best-kept secret in American education. Most education students have never heard of it. Professors of education ignore it, not out of malice but because they cannot absorb it into their framework of educational thought. But the secret is getting out, spread largely by the schools' graduates and others who have experienced the school directly. Today roughly three dozen schools throughout the world are modeled explicitly after Sudbury Valley. I predict that fifty years from now, if not sooner, the Sudbury Valley model will be featured in every standard textbook of education and will be adopted, with variation, by many if not all public school systems. In fifty years, I predict, educators will see today's approach to schooling as a barbaric relic of the past.

To visualize the Sudbury Valley School, you have to set aside all of your notions of what traditional schools look like, including your notions of what progressive versions of traditional schools look like. Sudbury Valley is not a Montessori school or a Dewey school or a Piagetian constructivist school. Schools of those sorts may use methods more in line with children's natural ways of learning than do typical traditional schools, but teachers still run the show. Teachers in those schools still strive to get students to learn a preplanned curriculum according to a preplanned schedule, and they evaluate the students along the way. Sudbury Valley is something entirely different. To understand the school you have to begin with the thought: *Adults do not control children's education; children educate themselves.*

Sudbury Valley is a private day school located in a semi-rural portion of Framingham, Massachusetts. It accepts students, age four on through high school, without regard to test scores or other indices of ability. The only admissions criteria are an interview and a visiting week designed to ensure that potential students and their parents understand the school before they enroll. In recent years the population of the school has consisted of between 130 and 180 students and nine to eleven adult staff members. The school charges a low tuition and operates on a per-pupil budget that is about half that of the surrounding public schools and far less than that of other private schools. This is by no means an elite school. If all public schools in the United States followed the Sudbury model, hundreds of billions of dollars in taxpayer money would be saved each year.

The school is, first and foremost, a democratic community. The primary administrative body is the School Meeting, which includes all students and staff members and operates on a one-person-one-vote basis, regardless of the person's age. This body, which meets once a week, legislates all rules of behavior, hires and fires staff, makes all major decisions about budgetary expenditures, and in general has full responsibility for running the school. As in most democracies, participation in governance is not required. Most staff and a good number of students attend most or all of the meetings, while others, especially the youngest students, participate only when the agenda is directly relevant to them. For example, a proposal to close the playroom because of messiness will draw a crowd of four- to seven-year-olds who otherwise rarely attend. The great majority, however, takes part in the annual staff elections, which occur each spring and provide the basis for hiring staff members for the following year.

The school's rules are enforced by the Judicial Committee, which changes regularly in membership but always includes one staff member, two elected student clerks who chair the meetings, and five other students selected in such a way that they represent the entire age span of students at the school. When a student or staff member is charged by another school member with violating a rule, the accuser and accused must appear before the Judicial Committee, which hears testimony, gathers other evidence if needed, determines innocence or guilt, and in the latter case, decides on an appropriate sentence. Cases range from such minor issues as being noisy in a designated "quiet room" (for which the punishment might be banishment from that room for some period of time) to rare cases of theft, vandalism, or illegal drug use (for which the punishment might be suspension or, very rarely, after repeated suspensions, expulsion from the school). Contested cases and all of the most serious cases are appealed to the whole School Meeting for review.

Staff members, even those founding members who are still on the staff, are all on one-year contracts and must be rehired each year by the School Meeting if they are to remain. As the students outnumber the staff by a ratio of roughly fifteen to one, the staff members who survive this process and are reelected year after year are those who are admired by the students. They are people who are kind, ethical, and competent, and who contribute significantly and positively to the school's environment. They are adults whom the students may wish in some ways to emulate.

Stated most simply, the staff's role is to be the adult members of the school community. They are there to ensure students' safety; comfort those who need comforting; perform many of the chores needed to keep the school running efficiently and legally (always at the behest of the School Meeting); protect the school from outside infringements; and serve as resources for those students who wish to take advantage of their skills, knowledge, or thoughts. For example, one staff member I know well has primary responsibility for keeping the computers up to date and running smoothly, but he is also much engaged by students who share his love of role-playing games, politics, theology, literature, modern and ancient history, and psychology. Like other staff members, he is charged with executing many of the decisions made by the School Meeting. The staff members do not call themselves "teachers," because they recognize that students learn more from one another, and from their own play and exploration, than they do from the adult school members. The staff members are subject to the same school rules as are students, and when they are accused of violating a rule, they are tried in the same way. Nobody is above the law.

Students are free all day to move about the school buildings (a large Victorian farmhouse and renovated barn) and ten-acre campus as they please and to associate with whom they please. They are not assigned to spaces or to groups. There are no "first graders," "middle schoolers," or "high school students." Books line the walls of many of the school's rooms, computers are available for everyone's use, and equipment and staff expertise are available to aid education in a wide variety of subjects and skills, but students are always free to use or not use those resources as they choose. Students age eight and above are free to venture off campus at any time of day—though, if they are under thirteen, they must go with another student and sign out so that people at the school know their destination and expected time of return. A common destination is the large, forested state park adjacent to the school's campus. Classes in specific subjects are offered when students request them, but no one is required or particularly encouraged to join a class and many students never join one. Classes have no formal status and last only as long as student interest lasts.

The basic premise of the school's educational philosophy is that each person is responsible for his or her own education. The school establishes no curriculum, gives no tests, and does not rank or in other ways evaluate students. There are, however, two exceptions to the policy of non-evaluation: (1) students who wish to use expensive or potentially dangerous equipment—such as computers, kitchen appliances, or woodworking tools—must first become "certified" for that equipment by proving that they can use it appropriately; and (2) students who desire a diploma from the school must prepare and defend a thesis explaining why they are ready to graduate and how they have prepared themselves for responsible adult life outside of the school. Theses are evaluated by outside reviewers who are knowledgeable about the school's philosophy. They are deliberately not evaluated by staff members at the school because of concern that that would jeopardize the nonjudgmental, nonadversarial, supportive nature of the relationship between staff and students.

All in all, the school operates in a manner that is almost the opposite of conventional schooling. Visitors, arriving at any given time of the school day and knowing only that Sudbury Valley is a school, would assume that they must have arrived at recess time. They would observe students playing, talking, hanging out, and enjoying a wide variety of self-directed activities. Outside, groups might be seen eating lunch on the grass, climbing trees, fishing in the millpond, playing four square or basketball, fencing with padded swords, riding bicycles and unicycles, or swinging and sliding on the playground equipment. Inside, students might be found cooking, playing cards, playing video games, programming a computer, strumming guitars and making up songs, roughhousing (within the limits of the rules), discussing a movie or the latest teen vampire novel, gossiping, arguing politics, watching a music video, building with Legos, reading a book to themselves or aloud to younger children, painting in the art room, or selling cookies to raise money for a school activity. The visitors would find little that looks like academic schoolwork—perhaps a handful of students and a staff member engaged in a history seminar, a couple of teenagers solving math problems, and a small child intently and meticulously writing out the alphabet on a chalkboard, apparently for her own amusement, asking a nearby older student for help when she was stuck.

The school fulfills, in reality, all aspects of the vision set out in the early writings of Daniel Greenberg and the other school founders. It is a fully democratic community, where students continuously enjoy the freedoms and practice the responsibilities that accompany democratic citizenship. It is a place where students take full charge of their own educations, where all ideas that interest anyone are freely aired, and where all endeavors are equally valued, as long as they do not hurt others or disrupt the school. But does it work? Do students learn there what they need to know for success in our culture?

The School as an Educational Institution

As I explained in the prologue, my interest in Sudbury Valley began when my son became a student there, at age ten, many years ago. I could see right off that the school made him happy, which made me happy. In his view, Sudbury Valley was everything that a school should be. But I had some concerns. The school is radically different from the norm, and anything not normal—anything *ab*normal—is frightening to those of us who have spent our lives doing, more or less, what others expected of us. By attending such a school, might he be narrowing his future options? Could he go to college? Might certain potential career paths be cut off? I received reassurances from staff members and from parents of former students, in the form of anecdotes about graduates who had gone on and done well in various walks of life, but as a scientist and as a conscientious parent I was not fully satisfied. At the same time I also began to develop an academic interest in the school. I was curious to learn all I could about it and how it worked. Up until then all of my research had been conducted in my university laboratory, with rats and mice as subjects, aimed at learning about hormonal and brain mechanisms underlying certain basic mammalian drives and emotions. But now I was becoming interested in human children's play, exploration, and natural means of learning.

To address my concern as a parent, and as a first step toward satisfying my academic curiosity, I decided to conduct a systematic survey of the school's graduates. I discovered that David Chanoff—an author of biographies and, at that time, a part-time staff member at Sudbury Valley—was also interested in conducting such a survey, so we decided to collaborate. We conducted the study through the auspices of the university where I worked.

Our goal was to survey all of the students who had graduated from the school at least one year earlier. As "graduates" we included students who had left with a high school diploma and those who had left at age sixteen or older without a diploma but with no plans for further secondary schooling. At the time of our study, the school was much smaller than it is now and had been in existence for only fifteen years. The school's files showed that eighty-two former students met our criteria (four of whom had left without a diploma). We were able to locate seventy-six of these eighty-two, and sixty-nine of them agreed to participate and actually did participate—a response rate of 91 percent of the graduates who could be located, or 84 percent of the total graduates. Most of them responded by filling out an extensive written questionnaire that we mailed to them, but some responded to the same questions in a telephone interview, and we interviewed a few personally. We asked the graduates to recall and describe the activities they had engaged in at school. We asked detailed questions about their further education and/or employment after leaving Sudbury Valley. And we asked them to describe how their attendance at such an unusual school might have handicapped or benefited them in various aspects of their life after Sudbury Valley. We also asked questions about their family backgrounds and their original reasons for attending Sudbury Valley.

The results of the study, which we published in the *American Journal of Education,*[4] convinced me that the school functions very well as an educational institution. Those graduates who had pursued higher education (about 75 percent of the total) reported no particular difficulty getting into the schools of their choice or doing well there once admitted. Some, including a few who had never previously taken a formal course, had gone on to highly prestigious colleges and universities and performed well. As a group, regardless of whether they had pursued higher education, the graduates were remarkably successful in finding employment that interested them and earned them a living. They had gone on, successfully, to a wide range of occupations, including business, arts, science, medicine, other service professions, and skilled trades.

In response to our questions about how attendance at such an unusual school might have handicapped them, the majority (71 percent) said they experienced no handicap at all. Those who did report handicaps said they were easily overcome. For example, some who had gone on to college said that at first they felt ignorant of some of the standard school subjects that others had studied, but that they had no difficulty catching up where the gap was real. A finding that surprised me, at the time, was that none of the graduates complained about difficulty adjusting to the formal structure of college or employment. When we followed this up in interviews, they typically told us that their decisions to continue their schooling or to work at particular jobs were their own, that they enjoyed what they were doing, and that they fully recognized and accepted the fact that these pursuits involve certain regimens that must be followed. People who had rebelled against required schoolwork when they had no choice in the matter, before going to Sudbury Valley, were not rebelling against the requirements of college and jobs because these had been their own choices. They also pointed out that there was much more minute-to-minute and day-to-day freedom in their college and work experiences than had been true in the standard schools they had attended.

The great majority (82 percent) of respondents said that their attendance at Sudbury Valley had benefited them for their further education and careers. Most of the benefits they described could be distilled into four categories. One category had to do with being *responsible and self-directed*. Graduates explained that at Sudbury Valley they had always had to make their own decisions about how to spend their time, that there was nobody to blame but themselves for mistakes they made, and that they had had to work through the school's democratic procedures for any changes they had wanted in the school. The resultant sense of personal responsibility remained with them, they said, and served them well in higher education and employment.

A second category of benefits, closely related to the first and offered equally often, had to do with their *high motivation* for further learning and work in their chosen careers. Their experience in a setting where learning had always been fun led them to want to continue learning. They wrote of being curious and having strong desires to learn more about certain activities or ideas that greatly interested them. Moreover, most of the graduates reported that they had gone on to endeavors that they enjoyed and had chosen, and as a result their motivation was high. One graduate, who had been a student at Sudbury Valley since age nine and was currently an honors student in college, put it this way:

> A lot of the people there [in college] have had more experience in some of the substantive areas. But the attitudinal difference seems to allow me to catch up quickly. The substantive things are trivial to acquire. . . . My attitude is that I'm going to college for fun and I fully intend to enjoy myself by taking advantage of whatever it has to offer. The attitude of many people is that they're going because they were kind of corralled. It never occurred to them that there was something else they could do.

A third category of benefits had to do with the particular *skills and knowledge* they had acquired. Through their play and self-motivated exploration at Sudbury Valley, many of the graduates had acquired unusual skills and deep understanding in the realms that interested them most and had gone on to careers or higher education in those areas. I will say more about this shortly.

The fourth category of often-mentioned benefits had to do with *lack of fear of authority figures,* which the graduates attributed to the respectful relationships that they had had with adults at Sudbury Valley and to their experiences articulating their views at sessions of the School Meeting and Judicial Committee. The graduates reported that they had good relationships with professors and employers, communicated easily with them, and had no difficulty asking them for help or advice when needed. For example, one graduate, who had earned a bachelor's degree in economics from a prestigious private university, told us, "I would hang out in the economics department, just as I would hang out in the office at Sudbury Valley, just hang out and talk with professors. I always felt I had as much right to be there as anyone else. Most of the students felt a tremendous gap between themselves and professors— they weren't used to relating to the 'enemy' in that way. I didn't have

that kind of feeling." This person then described a club she had organized to bring students and faculty together.

In response to a final question in our survey, none of the graduates
said that their life would be better if they had attended a traditional
school rather than Sudbury Valley. All of them, except two who omitted
the question, indicated that they were "glad" (eleven selected this) or
"very glad" (fifty-six selected this) that they had attended Sudbury Valley
rather than a more traditional school. As reasons, many referred to the
types of benefits already mentioned, having to do with their preparation
for life after graduation. In addition, many said they were glad they had
attended the school, because it had allowed them to enjoy their childhood, to be free, and to feel respected and valued as individuals. Some
wrote specifically about the importance to them of the democratic atmosphere and procedures at the school. For example, one graduate
wrote, "The articulation of democratic philosophy, particularly the de-
bates on responsibility of individuals, impressed me deeply. I continue
to try very hard to know what my responsibilities are and to carry them
out. And that, of course, has been helpful in every area of my life."

Since the time of our original study, the school itself has conducted
and published, as books, two further systematic surveys of former students.[5] By the time of these later studies, the school had many more
graduates than it did when Chanoff and I conducted our survey, and
the average graduate had more years of life experience after Sudbury
Valley; yet the general conclusions are similar to ours. The graduates
have continued to do well in higher education and in their careers, and
the great majority of them attribute much of their success to the skills,
attitudes, and values they acquired during their years at the school.

How Can the Success of
the Graduates Be Explained?

Sudbury Valley runs strongly against the grain of our culture's thinking
about education. Most people believe that children need to sit through

lessons and work hard at assigned schoolwork in order to succeed in life. In fact, to suggest otherwise borders on blasphemy. Even if some children complain or rebel, even if some must be given strong drugs so they will concentrate on their assigned schoolwork, such work, most believe, is necessary.

Most people who hear of the success of Sudbury Valley graduates quite naturally look for ways to explain it without upsetting their prior beliefs. One approach is to suggest that somewhere, behind the scenes, adults are giving lessons. Perhaps these children are being schooled at home by their parents, or perhaps the school's staff are extraordinarily clever educators who manipulate children into wanting to do the things they must to learn.

I can assure you that neither of these is the case. A few parents enroll their children at Sudbury Valley with the idea that they will school them at home, but they quickly give up that idea. The attempt to enforce a curriculum at home is so much in conflict with the school's philosophy that parents either stop the homeschooling or remove their children from Sudbury Valley. The staff members at the school are highly capable people, and they no doubt influence students' learning through the examples they set and through conversations with students; but they have no interest in manipulating students into learning particular lessons. They believe strongly that children learn best on their own initiative, through their own self-chosen and self-directed means, and that the best way to help children learn is to leave them alone except when a child asks for help or advice. And even then, they believe, the help or advice should be limited to what has been requested, not more.

Another approach some take to rationalizing the school's success is to suggest that the students who attend are a special group to begin with, destined to do well no matter what sort of education they have. Although the school has no entrance requirements, only a self-selected few choose to enroll (or have parents who permit them to enroll). But consider, who are the students who do enroll? What are their "special" characteristics? They are not, as a group, people for whom most traditional educators would make glowing predictions of success, though some are in that category. In our survey of graduates, somewhat more than half of the respondents said they had experienced serious problems in public school before enrolling at Sudbury Valley. These included persistent rebellion, repeated failure of classes, and in some cases, diagnosed learning disabilities. The others either started their schooling at Sudbury Valley, simply because their parents believed in it, or came to the school later because they found it attractive despite the fact that they had been faring well or at least not badly in public school.

My own observations convince me that there is no particular personality type that fails to do well there. Some students are adventuresome; others are cautious. Some are highly independent; others are very much group oriented. Some are well behaved; others get into trouble repeatedly with the school's judicial system. Some are academically inclined; others are not. Some prefer a highly structured environment, which they create for themselves at the school; others prefer relative chaos. In a setting where students can make their own choices, students structure their own time in ways that meet their unique needs and wishes. No one is forced into a mold; rather, students mold their environment to fit themselves, and they change that mold as they grow and change.

To me, the idea that Sudbury Valley works only for certain special students makes no sense at all. The only students who do not succeed at the school, by my observations and according to reports of staff, are those very few whose behavior is so continuously and greatly disruptive that they are expelled, through due process involving the Judicial Committee and School Meeting, or who have a severe mental disorder that makes them unable to learn through social interaction and play. Children diagnosed with ADHD do well at the school, but a child with severe autism—which includes a lack or absence of the normal drive to play and to engage socially with other people—would generally not do well there. To me, it seems clear that the school works well for all normal children because it provides the conditions that optimize children's natural instincts to take charge of their own lives, to develop social bonds with those around them, and to learn what they need to know to function well in the culture within which they are developing. It works because it is the functional equivalent, for our time and place, of a hunter-gatherer band.

How Sudbury Valley Is Like a Hunter-Gatherer Band[6]

The founders of the Sudbury Valley School did not set out to model a hunter-gatherer band. Their aim was to create a school that is consistent with the tenets of American democracy. However, to my eyes, the school contains precisely those elements of a hunter-gather band that are most essential for children's self-educative instincts to operate well. Perhaps this is no coincidence. As many anthropologists have pointed out, hunter-gather societies were the original democracies.[7] Here I offer a list of what seem to me to be the conditions that optimize children's abilities to educate themselves effectively—conditions that exist both in hunter-gatherer bands and at the Sudbury Valley School.

Time and Space to Play and Explore

Self-education through play and exploration requires enormous amounts of unscheduled time—time to do whatever one wants to do, without pressure, judgment, or intrusion from authority figures. That time is needed to make friends, play with ideas and materials, experience and overcome boredom, learn from one's own mistakes, and develop passions. In hunter-gatherer bands adults placed few or no demands on children and adolescents, partly because they recognized that young people needed to explore and play on their own to become competent adults. The same is true at Sudbury Valley.

Self-education also requires space—space to roam, to get away, to explore. That space should, ideally, encompass the range of terrains relevant to the culture in which one is developing. Hunter-gatherer adults trusted their children to use good judgment in deciding how far they should venture away from others into possibly dangerous areas. At Sud-

bury Valley, children are likewise trusted, within the limits set by pru-
dence in our modern, litigious society. They can explore the surrounding
woods, fields, and nearby stream, go to local stores and museums, or
go wherever they wish to pursue their interests as long as they let others
know where they are going and take adequate safety precautions.

Free Age Mixing Among Children and Adolescents

As I noted in Chapter 2, hunter-gatherer children necessarily played
in age-mixed groups, as there were not enough children of any given
age for age-segregated play. At Sudbury Valley there are enough children
that students could play exclusively with others close in age, but they
don't. Research studies have shown that students at the school regularly,
of their own volition, play across large age ranges.[8] As I'll explain in
Chapter 9, age-mixed play allows the younger children to learn skills
and sophisticated ways of thinking from older ones, and it allows the
older ones to learn how to nurture, lead, and, in general, be the mature
person in a relationship.

Access to Knowledgeable and Caring Adults

In hunter-gatherer bands, the adult world was not segregated from the
children's world. Children saw what adults did and incorporated that
into their play. They also heard the adults' stories, discussions, and de-
bates, and they learned from what they heard. When they needed adult
help, or had questions that could not be answered by other children, they
could go to any of the adults in the band. All of the adults cared for
them. Many of the adults, in fact, were literally their aunts and uncles.

At Sudbury Valley, too, adults and children mingle freely, though
the ratio of adults to children is much smaller there than in a hunter-
gatherer band. There is no place in the school where staff members
can go where students are not welcome. Students can listen into any
adult discussions and observe whatever the adults are doing, and they
can join in if they wish. Students who need help of any kind can go to

any of the staff members. A child who needs a lap to sit on, or a shoulder to cry on, or personal advice, or the answer to some technical question that he hasn't been able to find on his own, or (occasionally) more prolonged help in the form of a tutorial or course, knows which adult will best satisfy that need. The adults act much like aunts and uncles. They know all of the students and take pride in watching them develop over the years. Since the staff members must be reelected each year by a vote that includes all of the students in the school, they are necessarily people who like kids, are liked by kids, and serve kids' needs effectively.

Access to Equipment and Freedom to Play with It

To learn to use the tools of a culture, one must have access to those tools. Hunter-gatherer children played with knives, digging sticks, bows and arrows, snares, musical instruments, dugout canoes, and the like. At Sudbury Valley, children have access to a wide range of the equipment that is of most general use to people in our culture, including computers, cooking equipment, woodworking equipment, art materials, musical instruments, sporting equipment of various types, and walls filled with books; and they have access to other equipment through the school's open-campus policy.

Free Exchange of Ideas

Intellectual development occurs best in a setting where people can share ideas freely, without censorship or fear of being ostracized. According to anthropologists' reports, hunter-gatherers were nondogmatic in their beliefs, even in religious beliefs.[9] People could say what they thought, and ideas that had any consequence to the group were debated endlessly. The same is true at Sudbury Valley. The school has deliberately refrained from aligning itself with any particular political or religious ideology. All ideas are on the table. In this kind of environment an idea is something to think about and debate, not something to memorize and feed back on a test. Children who may not hear much discussion of politics, religion, or philosophical ideas at home hear it at school, and they hear every side of every issue.

Freedom from Bullying

To feel free to explore and play, a person must feel safe, free from harassment and bullying. Such an environment prevailed to a remarkable extent in hunter-gatherer bands, as it does at Sudbury Valley. According to anthropologists, the close-knit personal relationships, the age mixing, and the noncompetitive, egalitarian ethos of hunter-gatherer cultures worked effectively to prevent bullying.[10] If one child appeared to be picking on another, older children would step in quickly and stop it. The same occurs at Sudbury Valley and, in addition, research at the school suggests that the simple presence of young children has a pacifying effect on older children (discussed in Chapter 8). Moreover, at Sudbury Valley the democratically created rules and judicial system prevent serious bullying. A student who feels harassed in any way can "bring up" the offender, to appear before the Judicial Committee, which comprises school members of all ages. Because students make the rules and have responsibility for enforcing them, they have far more respect for the rules than do students in a standard school.

Immersion in a Democratic Community

Hunter-gatherer bands and the Sudbury Valley School are, in effect, democracies. As I noted earlier, hunter-gatherer bands did not have chiefs who made decisions for the group. Instead, group decisions were made through long discussions until all who cared came to an agreement. Sudbury Valley is administered through a formal democratic process, involving discussions and votes of the School Meeting. Immersion in the democratic process endows each person with a sense of responsibility that helps to motivate education. If my voice counts, if I have a real say in what the group does and how it operates, then I'd better think things through carefully and speak wisely. My education is not just for myself, but also for my community.

Continuity Between Students' Activities at the School and Subsequent Careers

I'll discuss much more in the next four chapters about how children educate themselves at Sudbury Valley and in other settings where they are allowed to play and explore freely. First, however, I want to illustrate a general theme that has emerged from interviews with the school's graduates: that of continuity between activities at the school and subsequent employment. Through play and exploration, students discover activities they enjoy, become good at those activities, and quite often go on—still in the spirit of play—to make a living at those or similar activities. What follow are some examples of graduates for whom that connection is most direct. Except where otherwise noted, all of the direct quotations here are from the book *Kingdom of Childhood*, in which thirty-one former Sudbury Valley students describe, in their own words, their experiences at the school.[11]

- Carl, who was twenty-two years old when he participated in Chanoff's and my initial study of graduates, was already the founder and president of a computer software development company, doing more than a million dollars in business a year. He had come to Sudbury Valley after seventh grade, with a poor record at public school, and had developed there a fascination with computers and computer programming, at a time when the home-computer industry was germinating. His interest in bringing computers into the school led him to become head of the school's supply corporation, which taught him a great deal about business. By the time he graduated, he not only was an expert software developer, but also had an excellent understanding of how businesses operate and how to interact with people in the business world. In our interview with him, he noted, ironically, that one of his clients was the same public school district that a few years earlier had given him failing marks. The difference between a young person laboring (or resisting) under another's forced instruction and the same young person pursuing his or her own true interests is one of night and day.

- Carol, who went on to become captain of a cruise ship, developed a love of boats during her time at Sudbury Valley. She played with small boats on the millpond located on the school's campus. As a teenager, she took advantage of the school's open-campus policy to spend as much time as possible at a nearby seacoast area, where she studied navigation and sailing.

- Fred, who had done all of his primary and secondary education at Sudbury Valley, became a professor of mathematics at a major university. In an interview, conducted not long after he graduated from Sudbury Valley, he explained that as a young child he was obsessed with science fiction, which led to an equally strong passion for physics and math, subjects he studied largely on his own during his later years at the school. In commenting on the connection between science fiction and math, he said, "Science fiction tends to deal with things that are on the borderline of real possibilities. Good science fiction attempts to do one of two things. Either it attempts to contradict no known facts, or to change one assumption and work with that, which is kind of similar to many mathematical concepts."[12]

- Fran became a master patternmaker and head of a facility in the high-fashion clothing industry. She was fascinated with fabrics and sewing as a child. First she made doll clothes and then, as a teenager, she began making clothes for herself and her friends. In an interview, she said, "When Alexis and I figured out how differently shaped a woman's sleeve is from a man's sleeve, [that] was the real beginning of my learning how to make patterns. . . . I sewed for other people. I made shirts for my boyfriend. I made leather vests for people. I did embroidery for money. I only wore jeans, but I had embroidered them beautifully. Then I started preparing a wardrobe to wear for work when I got a job." The school helped her arrange an apprenticeship with a clothing designer in Boston, and her career took off from there.

- Who would ever expect a child to develop the goal of becoming a mortician? It happened with Henry, apparently because of the comforting role a mortician had played concerning a death in his family. At Sudbury Valley he pursued this interest by, among other things, dissecting dead animals. In an interview he had this to say about his experiences after coming to Sudbury Valley in his early teens: "As soon as I found people with the same interests, like science and biology, we did dissections and went marauding for dead animals. One of my fondest memories is driving around with Melanie and finding dead animals on the road. We would pick them up with garbage bags and people would look at us like we were very sick. . . . We took the flesh off and kept the skulls to look at and to compare. . . . I doubt that there'd be any other school that would let me boil down skeletons. . . . 'Real' schools don't let you dissect raccoons on the kitchen table." Now Henry is a successful mortician and estate planner.

- Helen became a physician. She came to the school as a teenager, despite her parents' resistance, and paid much of her own tuition by working early mornings at a restaurant. In an interview, she said, "Where the school and I and going to medical school all cross is at the point of being idealistic, I guess. I always looked for what was wrong with things and how to fix them and how they could be right. When I was thirteen years old I was reading *Siddharta.* I was interested in Eastern religions. I did yoga and I meditated then too. I knew something was wrong and I wanted to fix it, and it's been almost like everything I've done has somehow been on that path. . . . I always read a lot. I remember Carla gave me *Spiritual Midwifery* when I was going to the school. . . . Almost every book anybody gave me had to do with something health-related. It was an early interest. . . . Learning about raising children was also really important to me. Learning things that are totally different from anything I'd ever thought about: that people would breast feed their babies for a long time, or would sleep with kids in their own bed until they were a little older, and things like that. They had never occurred to me, but when I saw it or heard about it, it was exciting to me. So in terms of forming a world view or just seeing the world as a bigger place than I knew it to be, the staff was really important to me. I have to qualify that: the staff and students."

- Tom became a master machinist and inventor of high-tech industrial machines. I'll relay his story—the final one of the chapter—a bit more fully than the others, entirely in his words, taken from an extensive interview in *Kingdom of Childhood.* The story sums up a lot of what the school is about.

"My parents were supportive of me during the troubles I had in public school. I was in sixth grade, and I was doing anything I could to rebel against the system. That's not a good way to learn. . . . I noticed as soon as I got to Sudbury Valley that I no longer had anything to rebel against, so there was no reason to do all those things that I was starting to do, like starting to smoke. If nobody's telling you to do things that you want to rebel against, there's no more point in rebelling. So we just played. . . .

"*Plasticene [a type of modeling clay that does not harden] was probably one of the most intense things I've ever done. There were days when [my friends and I] would show up, go to the art room, work steadily at it until lunch time, eat lunch at the table, and keep on going until we had to leave that night; and we'd never, never leave the room. . . . Sometimes we'd be building a gold mining community. Sometimes it would be a bunch of towns with hotels and saloons. It usually involved a lot of buildings, a lot of vehicles, a lot of people, and we'd make all this stuff. Then we would enact various scenes with it. . . . But for the most part we were building. We'd be building tanks and airplanes, just one after another. I did exactly what I'm doing now, except I'm doing it now in real life. Same thing. And very intensely. Day in and day out. Except that when you're a kid you don't really have as many of the same complications you have when you're an adult.*

"*With the plasticine I was making businesses. I made a lot of factories. I had a cannery at one time. I could picture it—I had seen films and gone through books that would show you pictures of bottling plants and things. It had to be realistic. . . . We had only so much clay and the fun was in the creating. Afterwards, the only thing you could do with it was to smash it and start over again. It was a constant build and smash. . . .*

"*Then we [my friends and I] had projects. We'd try to make go-carts out of old wheels and things. We used to go down into the basement and fix up old stuff people had donated—bicycles and things like that. . . . Then there were trips to the Sudbury town dump, getting staff members or other students to take us. There were certain items we always looked for: anything that had anything to do with a bicycle or tricycle. We'd take these parts back and build new ones. It was like a little business. We'd fix them up, and sometimes we'd paint them. We put price tags on them—50 cents, 75 cents—and we would sell them.*

"*Nobody at the school knew much about what I wanted to know, but they all could teach me how to find information. So, if I needed to find something, they might show me how to use the library catalog, or how to talk to somebody [outside the school] who did know. I think the school taught me how to learn better than if I was just at home. . . .*

"*If I had an alcoholic beverage at the school, it was because I had made a still. . . . There's a big difference between a kid who smuggles a fifth of whiskey into his lunch box and a kid who, over a period of three or four months, makes a still, grinds his own grain, makes some whiskey; and the fact is I never even drank the whiskey I made. What fascinated me was how to make the stuff. So I made whiskey at school, and I possessed it at the school, because I had made it there, and I was allowed to, because I had gone through all those steps. If I had just said I want to have whiskey at school, everybody would have said, 'Forget it, that's against the law. Kids can't have whiskey at school.' . . .*

"*Then there is the story of the squirt. It was April Fool's Day. The school had an old annunciator control panel in the kitchen. . . . Some of the wires were still there, and some of them went down into the basement. I connected a windshield washer pump to a battery that was downstairs and hooked it to a little squirt nozzle that I stuck between the two stoves, aimed at a certain spot. I would wait until somebody would sit in the seat that the thing was aimed at, and I would push one of those little buttons that was already there, and they would get squirted. . . .*

"*I am the same person now that I was then. . . . Did the school make me the way I am now? It's something I wondered often. I don't know if it did, but I wouldn't be surprised if it did. It certainly helped. It took away those stomachaches [that I had experienced in public school], and it kept me from wasting my time doing silly things of protest.*"

6

THE HUMAN
EDUCATIVE
INSTINCTS

ON JANUARY 29, 1999, Sugata Mitra, then science director of an educational technology firm in India, initiated a fascinating experiment on children's capacity for self-education. He turned on a computer he had installed on an outside wall of the building where he worked, facing one of the poorest slums in New Delhi—it was a community where most children were unschooled and illiterate, and had never previously seen a computer. Mitra turned the computer on, left it on, and told the children who crowded around that they could play with it. He then used a permanently installed video camera to monitor activity around the computer.

Children, mostly between the ages of seven and thirteen, immediately began to explore this odd installment, which looked to them like some kind of television set. They touched some of the parts and, by accident, discovered that they could move a pointer on the screen by moving their finger across the touch pad. This led to more exciting discoveries. The pointer turned into a hand when it was moved to certain parts of the screen. By pushing (clicking) on the touch pad when the pointer was a hand, they could get the screen to change. They eagerly sought out their friends to tell them about this fascinating machine. Each new discovery, made by one child or a group, was shared with others. Within days, without any instruction from adults, dozens of children were using the computer to play music and games, to draw with Microsoft Paint, and to do many of the other things that children everywhere do when they have access to a computer.

Subsequently, Mitra and his colleagues repeated the experiment in other places in India, rural as well as urban, always with the same general results. Wherever a computer was made publicly available, children quickly gathered, explored the apparatus, began playing with it, and with no help except what they provided to one another, discovered exciting ways to use it.[1] The children made up names to refer to the computer, its parts, the various icons that appeared on the screen, and the activities that could be performed with it. For example, one group referred (in their native Hindi language) to the pointer as a "needle" and to folders as "cupboards."

Where the computers had Internet connections, children learned how to search the Web. The computer gave them access to the whole world's knowledge. Children who could not read began to learn to do so through their interactions with the computer, and those who could read sometimes found and downloaded articles that interested them, in the language in which they were literate (typically Hindi or Marathi). Children who were at an early stage of learning English learned many words through interacting with the computer and talking with others about it. In one remote Indian village, children who previously knew nothing about microorganisms learned about bacteria and viruses through their interactions with the computer and began to use this new knowledge appropriately in their everyday conversations.[2]

Mitra estimates that for every computer he and his colleagues set up, three hundred children became computer literate within three months of the computer's becoming available. That's 30,000 computer-literate children for one hundred computers in three months. By *computer literate,* Mitra means they could do most or all of the following tasks: "use all Windows operational functions (such as click, drag, open, close, resize, minimize, menus, navigation, etc.); draw and paint with the computer; load and save files; play games; run educational and other programs; browse and surf the Internet if a connection is available; set up email accounts; send and receive email; chat on the Internet; do simple troubleshooting, for example, if the speakers are not working; download and play streaming media; download games."[3] Mitra and his colleagues refer to their demonstrations as examples of *minimally invasive* education, a descriptor borrowed from surgery. It is education with minimal intrusion into children's lives.

Mitra's experiments illustrate how three core aspects of our human nature—curiosity, playfulness, and sociability—can combine beautifully to serve the purpose of education. *Curiosity* drew the children to the computer and motivated them to explore it; *playfulness* motivated them to practice many computer skills; and *sociability* allowed each child's learning to spread like wildfire to dozens of other children. In previous chapters I have referred to the human "educative instincts," provided hints about their nature, and presented evidence that they can provide the foundation for education in our present-day culture as they did in hunter-gatherer cultures. Here we shall look in more detail at the powerful human drives for self-education.

The Educable Animal

From an evolutionary perspective it is reasonable to say that we humans are, first and foremost, the *educable* animal. We are educable to a degree that goes way, way beyond that of any other species. Education, as I defined it in Chapter 2, is cultural transmission. It is the set of processes by which each new generation of humans acquires and builds upon the skills, knowledge, rituals, beliefs, and values of the previous generation. Education, thus defined, has to do with a special category of learning. All animals learn, but only humans learn to a significant degree from others of their species and thereby create, transmit, and build upon culture, from one generation to the next.

At least two million years ago, our human genetic line began moving along an evolutionary track that made us ever more reliant on cultural transmission. Over time we developed means of hunting, gathering, processing foods, protecting ourselves from predators, birthing, caring for infants, and combating diseases that depended on detailed knowledge and well-honed skills. Such knowledge and skills went way beyond what any individual or any group of individuals living together could discover on their own. Our survival came to depend on the accumulated achievements of prior generations, each building on the accomplishments of their ancestors. We also became increasingly dependent on our ability to cooperate and share with others of our kind, within and across bands, which required the transmission of social mores, rules, rituals, stories, and shared cultural beliefs and values. In short, we came to depend on education.

Today when most people think of *education* they think of schooling. In other words, they think of education as something done *to* children *by* adults. But education long predates schooling, and even today most education occurs outside of school. To say that we are the educable animal is to say that we have, built into us, instinctive drives to acquire and build upon the culture into which we are born. Today, in the minds of most people, the onus for education lies with adults, who have the responsibility to make children acquire certain aspects of the culture, whether or not the children want to acquire them. But throughout human history the real onus for education has always laid with children themselves, and it still does today. Just as children come into the world with instinctive drives to eat and drink what they must to survive, they come into the world with instinctive drives to educate themselves—to learn what they must to become effective members of the culture around them and thereby to survive. Those instinctive drives, broadly construed, are *curiosity, playfulness,* and *sociability.*

Natural selection works largely by building upon and modifying structures and instincts that are already present. All mammals are to some degree curious, playful, and sociable. But in our species these traits have been greatly expanded and shaped in ways that suit our unique educative needs.

Curiosity: The Drive to Explore and Understand

Whenever Mitra and his colleagues set up an outdoor computer in an area in which it was a novelty, children crowded around it because they were curious. They wanted to know what this strange thing was and how it worked. They especially wanted to know what they could *do* with it.

Aristotle, writing in the fourth century BC, began his great treatise on the origin of scientific thought with the words, "Human beings are naturally curious about things."[4] Nothing could be more obvious. Within hours of their births, infants begin to look longer at novel objects than at those they have already seen. On their deathbeds, people sometimes make heroic efforts to remain alive a little longer, sometimes in great pain, because they are curious to see what will happen next. During all of our waking time between birth and death, our senses are alert to changes in the world around us—our curiosity is continuously provoked. To confine a person to an unchanging environment (to the degree that that is possible), in which there is nothing new to explore, nothing new to learn, is everywhere considered cruel punishment, even if all other drives are satisfied. In a healthy human being, the thirst for knowledge is never quenched.

OF COURSE HUMANS ARE NOT the only species that is motivated to explore. All organisms probe their environment to find what they need for survival. For some animals, exploration involves simply random or quasi-random movement. An amoeba moves randomly until it makes contact with chemical molecules indicating that food is nearby, and then it keeps moving in the same direction until it engulfs the food. Foraging ants move out in random directions from their colony's nest, leaving faint chemical trails as they do.[5] If one ant finds a source of food, it returns to the nest and leaves a stronger trail, which others in the colony can follow. Mammals explore in more directed ways than do protozoa or insects—ways that seem well designed for the acquisition of multiple kinds of information about their environment. Through exploration, they gain information about the general layout of their corner of the world, about food sources, predators, escape routes, potential hiding places, safe places to sleep or to raise young, and about the presence or absence of other members of their species, whether foes, friends, or potential reproductive partners.[6]

The most systematic studies of exploration have been conducted with laboratory rats. When placed in a novel environment—typically a large open-topped box or maze with various objects, pathways, and barriers—the rat's strongest initial drive is fear. The animal cowers motionless in a corner. Gradually, however, the fear diminishes and the exploratory drive begins to manifest itself and the rat starts to make brief excursions. On each excursion it may rear up several times on its hind legs and look around and sniff before scurrying back to the corner. Over time, the rat becomes bolder and begins to explore larger areas, sniffing everywhere and feeling objects with its whiskers and forepaws. Even after it has thoroughly explored the apparatus, the rat continues to patrol periodically, checking to see if anything has changed. If a new object appears in an otherwise familiar environment, the rat approaches it, at first cautiously, and explores it until it, too, becomes familiar. Many experiments have shown that rats acquire useful information through such exploration.[7] In one set of experiments, for example, rats that had an opportunity to explore a complex arena that contained one or more hiding places ran much more quickly to a hiding place when they were deliberately frightened in a later test than did rats that had not previously explored the arena.[8]

MOST RESEARCH ON HUMAN CURIOSITY and exploration has been conducted with infants, toddlers, and preschool children. In hundreds of experiments, babies have been found to gaze much longer at scenes they have never seen before than at ones they have previously seen. In fact, this preference for novelty is so reliable that researchers use it to assess babies' abilities to perceive and remember. Babies who look significantly longer at a new pattern or object than at one they have already seen must perceive the difference between the two and must, at some level, remember having seen the old one before.[9] Babies also look much longer at events that seem to defy the laws of physics than at those that abide by them.[10] For example, given a choice between watching objects fall *down* or *up* when shoved off the end of a shelf, babies as young as three months old look much more at the latter than at the former. In their attempts to understand the world around them, babies seem to be attracted to all events that run counter to their expectations.

By about six months old, babies begin to explore with their hands as well as with their eyes. They grab any novel object within reach and hold it in front of their eyes, turn it from side to side, pass it from hand to hand, rub it, squeeze it, pull on it, drop it, pick it up again, and in general act as if they are deliberately testing the object's properties.[11] Such actions decline sharply as the infant becomes familiar with a given object, but return in full force when a new, different object is substituted for the old one. Through such actions, babies quickly learn about the properties of the objects around them and how to use those properties. They learn how to make objects squeak, come apart, twist into new shapes, bounce, or shatter, depending on the object's nature. During the exploration process, the baby's face is serious and intense, like that of a scholar poring over a book or a scientist working feverishly with test tubes; with each discovery comes a eureka moment of delight. If you want to see the raw emotions of curiosity and discovery writ large on the face of a scientist who doesn't hide emotions, watch any normal nine-month-old baby exploring a new object.

As children grow older, their curiosity does not diminish but motivates increasingly sophisticated forms of exploration. Research psychologist Laura Schulz and her colleagues have performed many experiments with children showing how they go about solving mysteries in the world around them. In one experiment, the researchers presented four-year-olds with a box that had two levers sticking out of it.[12] Pressing one lever caused a toy duck to pop up through a slit on top of the box, and pressing the other caused a puppet made of drinking straws to pop up. The box was demonstrated to different children in two different ways. In one demonstration condition, the experimenter pressed each lever separately, so the child could see the effect that each lever produced when pressed. In the other condition, the experimenter always pressed the two levers simultaneously, so the child could not know which lever controlled which object. Then each child was allowed to play with the two-lever box or with a different toy. The result was that children who had seen only the two levers operated simultaneously chose to play much more with the demonstrated box than with the new toy, while the opposite was true for the other children.

The logical interpretation is this result: The children who were shown what each lever did were no longer much interested in the box because they had little to learn from it. In contrast, those who had only seen the two levers pressed simultaneously wanted to explore the box so they could try each lever separately and discover whether it moved the duck, the puppet, or both. The children were motivated by curiosity to discover how the box worked; they were not much interested in producing already known effects. The experiment also showed that four-year-olds are capable of rather sophisticated cause-effect reasoning. They realized that to know fully how the box worked, they had to see what each lever did separately, not just what the two levers did when operated together.

In another set of experiments, Schulz and her colleagues showed that teaching can interfere with exploration.[13] Four- and five-year-olds were allowed to explore a toy that could produce four different effects when acted upon in different ways. It squeaked when one tube was pulled out from inside another; it lit up when a small button hidden inside the end of a tube was pressed; it produced musical notes when certain parts of a small yellow pad were pressed; and it produced a reverse image of the child's face when the child looked into one of the tubes. In the *teaching* condition, the experimenter deliberately showed and explained to the child how to produce one of the effects, the squeak. In the *experimenter play* condition, the experimenter squeaked the toy in front of the child, but did so as if for her own enjoyment rather than in a teaching mode. In the *control* condition, the experimenter did nothing with the toy before giving it to the child. The result was that the children in the control condition and in the experimenter play condition subsequently spent much more time exploring the toy, and discovered how to produce more of its effects than did children in the teaching condition. Apparently children in the teaching condition tended to conclude that the only thing the toy could do was squeak, because that was all the experimenter showed them. Those in the nonteaching conditions had no reason to believe the experimenter had shown them all there was to know about the toy, so they explored it more fully to discover its possibilities.

There is reason to believe that this kind of inhibitory effect of teaching on curiosity occurs in schools all the time. A teacher shows students one way to solve an arithmetic problem, for example, and the students conclude that it must be the only way. They don't explore alternative ways to solve the problem (even if they are allowed to, which they often are not), and they therefore fail to learn all the dimensions of the problem or the full power of arithmetic operations. Ultimately they are deprived of the joy of discovery in the realm of numbers and learn not to go beyond what was taught.

Playfulness: The Drive to Practice and Create

Playfulness (the drive to play) serves educative purposes complementary to those of curiosity. While curiosity motivates children to seek new knowledge and understanding, playfulness motivates them to practice new skills and use those skills creatively. In Mitra's experiments, curiosity led the children to approach the computer and manipulate it to discover its properties; then playfulness led them to become adept at using those properties for their own, creative purposes. For example, after exploring the computer's Paint program, children played extensively with it, using it to paint pictures that were their own creations, not inherent properties of the computer. Similarly, after exploring the Word program, many used it to write notes of their own creation, just for fun. In the process, they became skilled in computer painting and computer writing.

In a classic series of research studies, British developmental psychologists Miranda Hughes and Corrine Hutt documented the behavioral differences between exploration and play in two-year-olds.[14] When first presented with a complex new toy, the typical child explored it intensely, exhibiting a serious face and eyes riveted on the toy. As the child manipulated the toy to discover its properties, the focused concentration continued, punctuated by momentary expressions of surprise, sometimes mixed with joy, as new discoveries were made. Only after exploring the toy for some time did the child begin to *play* with it, by repetitively acting on it to produce known effects or by incorporating it into a fantasy game. The shift from exploration to play was marked by a shift from a focused, serious facial expression to a more relaxed, smiling one. It was also marked by a change in heart rate. The heart rate during exploration was slow and steady, indicative of intense concentration; during play it became more variable, indicative of a more relaxed attitude. During exploration, the child screened out the researcher and other potential distractions; during play the child became more willing to interact with the researcher and to incorporate other events and objects into the play.

Play is not as widespread among animals as is exploration, but it does appear to occur in all species of mammals and in some species of birds. From a biological, evolutionary perspective, play is nature's way of ensuring that young mammals, including young humans, will practice and become good at the skills they need to develop to survive and thrive in their environments. This practice theory of play was first proposed and developed more than a century ago by the German philosopher and naturalist Karl Groos, who presented evidence for it in two books: *The Play of Animals* (1898) and *The Play of Man* (1901).

GROOS WAS AHEAD OF HIS TIME, in his thinking about evolution and about play. He understood the writings of Charles Darwin and had a sophisticated, modern understanding of instincts. He recognized that animals, especially mammals, must to varying degrees *learn* to use their instincts. Young mammals come into the world with biological drives and tendencies (instincts) to behave in certain ways, but to be effective such behaviors must be practiced and refined. Play in animals, according to Groos, is essentially an instinct to practice other instincts. He wrote, "Animals cannot be said to play because they are young and frolicsome, but rather they have a period of youth in order to play; for only by doing so can they supplement the insufficient hereditary endowment with individual experience, in view of the coming tasks of life."[15] Consistent with his theory, Groos divided animal play into categories related to the types of skills the play promotes, including movement play (running, leaping, climbing, swinging in trees, and so on), hunting play, fighting play, and nursing play (playful care of infants).

Groos's explanation of play's biological purpose allows us to make sense of the patterns of play seen throughout the animal world. For starters, it explains why young animals play more than older ones; they play more because they have more to learn. It also explains why mammals play more than do other classes of animals. Insects, reptiles, amphibians, and fishes come into the world with rather fixed instincts; they don't need to learn much to survive, given their ways of life, and there is little if any evidence in them of play. Mammals, on the other hand, have more flexible instincts, which must be supplemented and shaped through learning and practice provided by play.

Groos's theory also explains the differences in playfulness found among different orders and species of animals. Those animals whose way of life depends least on rigid instincts and most on learning are the most playful. Among mammals, primates (monkeys and apes) have the most to learn, and they are the most playful of all animal orders. Among primates, human beings, chimpanzees, and bonobos (a species of ape closely related to chimpanzees and to humans) have the most to learn, and they are the most playful species. Also among mammals, carnivores (including the dog-like and cat-like species) are generally more playful than herbivores, most likely because success in hunting requires more learning than does success in grazing. Aside from mammals, the only other animal class in which play has been regularly observed is that of birds. The most playful birds are the corvids (crows, magpies, and ravens), raptors (hawks and their relatives), and parrots. These are all long-lived birds, with larger brain-to-body-weight ratios than other birds, which exhibit much flexibility and cleverness in their social lives and ways of obtaining food.[16]

The idea that play's purpose is to promote skill learning also helps us to understand why different species of animals play in different ways. To a considerable degree, you can predict what an animal will play at by knowing what skills it must develop to survive and reproduce. Lion cubs and the young of other predators play at stalking and chasing; zebra colts, young gazelles, and other animals that are preyed upon play at fleeing and dodging; young monkeys play at swinging from branch to branch in trees. Among species in which males fight one another for access to females, young males engage in more play fighting than do young females. And at least among some species of primates, young females, but not young males, engage in much playful care of infants.

In *The Play of Man,* Groos extended his insights about animal play to humans.[17] He pointed out that human beings, having much more to learn than do other animals, play much more than do other animals. Indeed, young humans everywhere, when left to their own devices, play at the kinds of skills that people must develop to thrive as adults. He also pointed out that human beings, much more so than the young of any other species, must learn *different* skills depending on the unique culture in which they develop. Therefore, he argued, natural selection led to a strong drive, in human children, to observe the activities of their elders and incorporate those activities into their play. Children in every culture play at the general categories of activities that are essential to people everywhere, and they also play at the specific variations of those activities that are unique to their native culture.

HERE, TO EXPAND UPON Groos's theory, is my own list of universal types of children's play and the relation of each type to basic human survival skills.

- *Physical play.* Like all mammals, we must develop strong bodies and learn to move in coordinated ways, and so we engage in physical play, including running, leaping, chasing, and rough-and-tumble games that resemble the play of other mammals. Children on their own initiative don't lift weights or run laps to keep in shape. Nothing would be more dull and wearisome. Instead, they chase one another around, and wrestle or play at sword fighting to happy exhaustion, many times per day if given the opportunity. While some forms of physical play, such as chasing one another around, occur in all cultures, others, such as playful sword fighting or bicycle riding, are unique to cultures in which the appropriate artifacts and models are present.
- *Language play.* We are the linguistic animal, and so we engage in language play to learn to talk. Nobody has to teach language to young children. They learn it on their own, through play. At about two months of age, infants begin to make repeated, drawn-out vowel-like cooing sounds—*ooh-ooh-ooh, eeh-ahhh-eeh-ahhh.* At about four or five months, the cooing gradually changes to babbling, as the baby begins to put consonants and vowels together—*ba-ba-boo-ba-ga-da-da-da-badada.* Such language-like sound production occurs only when the baby is happy; it has structure; it is self-motivated; it is not done to get something—it is done purely for its own sake. All that makes it play. With time, the babbled sounds come increasingly to resemble the sounds of the child's native language, and by about one year of age the

child's first words appear and may be repeated over and over in a playful manner. After that, the child's linguistic play becomes ever more complex and takes forms that are ever more shaped by the specific linguistic culture in which the child is developing. Children play with phrases, puns, rhymes, alliterations, and alternative grammatical constructions—all of which help to consolidate their growing understanding of all aspects of their native language. Listen closely to any young child playing with language, either alone or in pseudo dialogues with others, and you will find many instances of practice at linguistic constructions that are joyful challenges to the child. When language play is carried into adulthood, we call it poetry.

- *Exploratory play.* We are *Homo sapiens,* the wise animal, who make sense of the world, and so we have exploratory play, which combines exploration and play to promote understanding. I distinguished earlier between exploration and play, but I hasten now to add that in our species the two often blend. Much if not most of children's play is exploration as well as play. As children develop skills in play, they continue to be open to new discoveries made during play. In Mitra's experiments, the children who had reached the stage of playing with one or another of the computer's programs were still making new discoveries about the program's capacities. As I will describe in Chapter 7, whenever children or adults bring imagination and creativity into their efforts toward discovery, they are combining play and exploration. In adults, we call that science.

- *Constructive play.* We are the animal that survives by building things—including shelters, tools, devices to help us communicate, and devices to help us move from place to place—and so we have constructive play, which teaches us to build. In constructive play a child strives to produce some object that he or she has in mind. A child making a sand castle, or creating a spaceship from blocks, or drawing a giraffe, is engaged in constructive play. In many cases the objects built in constructive play are miniature or pretend versions of "real" objects that adults in the culture build and use. Hunter-gatherer children make small versions of huts, bows and arrows, blow-guns, nets, knives, slingshots, musical instruments, digging sticks, rafts, rope ladders, mortars and pestles, and baskets. Through such play they become good at building, and by adulthood they are making well-crafted, useful versions of the real things. Constructive play can be with words and sounds as well as with substances, and people everywhere, adults and children alike, produce stories, poems, and melodies in their play. Among the countless kinds of constructions playfully made by children in our culture today are computer programs, written stories, and secret codes with invented symbol systems. Constructive play can be intellectual as well as manual.

- *Fantasy play.* We are the imaginative animal, able to think of things that do not exist or are not present, and so we have fantasy play, or pretend play, which builds our capacity for imagination and provides a foundation for the development of logical thought. In this type of play children establish certain propositions about the nature of their pretend world and then play out those propositions logically. In doing so they develop and exercise the imaginative capacities that allow people to consider things that are not immediately present, which is what we all do when we plan for the future and what scientists do when they develop theories to explain or predict events in the real world. I will say more about this in Chapter 7.

- *Social play.* We are an intensely social species, who must cooperate with others to survive, and so we have many forms of social play, which teach us to cooperate and to restrain our impulses in ways that make us socially acceptable. When children play imaginative games together, they do more than exercise their imagination. They enact roles, and in doing so they exercise their capacities to behave in accordance with shared conceptions of what is or is not appropriate. They also practice the art of negotiation. As they decide who will play what roles, who may use which props, and just what scenes they will enact and how, the players must all come to agreement. Getting along and making agreements with others are surely among the most valuable of human survival skills, and children continuously practice those skills in social play. I will say much more about social play in Chapter 8.

The types of play italicized in the above list are not mutually exclusive categories. They are functional types, meaning that they refer to the different functions that play can serve. Any given instance of play may serve more than one function. A lively outdoor group game may be physical play, language play, exploratory play, constructive play, fantasy play, and social play all at once. Play, in all its varieties taken together, works to build us into fully functioning, effective human beings.

Children everywhere, when allowed freedom and access to other children, play in all of these general ways. However, the specific details vary from culture to culture. Consistent with Groos's theory, children play especially at the kinds of activities most valued by their culture. Children in hunting and gathering cultures play at hunting and gathering. Children in farming communities play at animal tending and plant cultivation. Children in modern Western cultures play at games that involve reading and numbers, and they play with computers and other modern forms of technology.

Going beyond Groos, I would add that children are naturally motivated to play not just at the skills that are most prominent and valued among adults around them, but also, even more intensely, at new skills that lie at the culture's cutting edge. Because of this, children typically learn to use new technology faster than do their parents. From an evolutionary perspective, that is no accident. At a gut, genetically based level, children recognize that the most crucial skills to learn are those that will be of increasing importance in the future—the skills of their own generation, which may be different from those of their parents' generation. The value of this attraction to the new is especially apparent in modern times, when technology and the skills required to master that technology change so rapidly.

Human Sociability, and the Natural Drive to Share Information and Ideas

In Mitra's demonstrations in India, curiosity led children to approach and manipulate the computer, playfulness led them to become skilled at using it, and *sociability* caused the new knowledge and skills to spread like wildfire from child to child.[18] Because of their natural sociability and capacity for language, children's minds are networked with those of all their friends. When one child in Mitra's study made a discovery, such as how to download documents on the computer, that discovery spread quickly to the whole group of children nearby, and then some child in that group, who had a friend in another group, carried the spark of new knowledge to that other group, where a new brush fire was ignited, and so on, through the roughly three hundred children who at various times used the outdoor computer. Each discovery by one child became the discovery of all the children in the network. As I write this, philanthropists are working on the One Laptop per Child project as a means of bringing literacy and stores of knowledge to the whole world. According to Mitra, however, we don't need one laptop per child. Children learn more when they share a computer and learn from one another.

Other research confirms Mitra's observation that children learn more together than alone. Earlier in this chapter I described two of Laura Schulz's experiments on the explorations of four-year-olds. Here is another one.[19] Schulz and her colleagues allowed four-year-olds to explore a toy that had two brightly colored gears that both moved when a switch was turned on to operate a motor hidden inside the toy. The question posed by the experimenter to motivate the children's exploration was this: What caused each gear to turn? More specifically, did the motor turn gear A, which then turned gear B; or was the reverse true; or did the motor independently turn both gears? The children could solve this puzzle by removing one gear at a time to see what happened with the other gear when the switch was turned on, but they had to discover this strategy on their own. Schulz and her colleagues found that children exploring in pairs were far more likely to solve the puzzle than were children exploring alone. In pairs, they shared knowledge as they explored, so each child's insights became the insights of both.

We humans have many biological adaptations that cause us naturally, even automatically, to learn from others around us. One of these is reflexive *gaze following*. When we attend to another person our eyes move, automatically, reflexively, to gaze at the same spot at which the other person is gazing. This reflex helps us understand what the other person is thinking about or talking about. When a person says, "Oh, that is beautiful," our automatic gaze following helps us know immediately what *that* refers to.

Gaze following has been studied most fully in infants and toddlers. Beginning at about six months of age, babies tend to look at whatever their nearby caregiver is looking at.[20] This reflex ensures that babies generally see and pay attention to the same objects and events in their environment that their caregivers attend to, which may be the most important things to learn about in their culture. Gaze following also helps infants learn language. When a baby hears her mother enunciate a new word, maybe *mushroom*, the baby has a chance of learning what that word refers to if she is looking at the same object as her mother.[21]

No other animals exhibit gaze following to the extent that we humans do. In fact, the unique coloring of our eyes may be a special adaptation that came about through natural selection to enable us to follow each other's gazes and thereby understand each other better. The relatively dark blue or brown circular iris of the human eye is sharply set off by the bright white of the rest of the visible portion of the eyeball (the sclera), which makes it easy for others to see where we are looking. Other primates, including chimpanzees and bonobos, have dark sclera, which do not contrast with the iris. Chimpanzees and bonobos do engage in some gaze following and can learn through that means, but their gaze following is much less automatic than is humans'. It is also less accurate, because it depends entirely on seeing whole head movements, not eye movements.[22]

Of course, the greatest human adaptation for social learning is language. We learn language through linguistic play in infancy and early childhood, and use it to support most of our subsequent social learning. Language allows us to tell one another not just about the here and now but also about the past, future, faraway, and hypothetical—which no other animal can do. As the philosopher Daniel Dennett put it, "Comparing our brains with bird brains or dolphin brains is almost beside the point, because our brains are in effect joined together into a single cognitive system that dwarfs all others. They are joined by an innovation that has invaded our brain and no others: language."[23]

Listen to the everyday conversation of people of any age, in the same detached frame of mind that you might use in studying beings from another planet, and you will be amazed by the power of language and by the amount of information exchanged every minute. As children grow older, their use of language becomes ever more sophisticated, and the ideas they exchange and develop in their conversations do, too. For a master's thesis in education, Rhonda Goebel recorded and analyzed natural, everyday conversations among students at a school in Illinois that was modeled after the Sudbury Valley School.[24] Below is a snippet from one of those conversations. It's unedited, and like most unedited conversations it's a little hard to follow without seeing the gestures that accompany the words, but you can make it out. As you read it, think about the complex ideas these young people are presenting in relatively few words, and what they might be learning, with no teacher or textbook to guide them and no test to judge them. Latrice (age sixteen), Pete (twelve), Deena (fourteen), and Bethany (fifteen) are talking about Latrice's desire to abolish the fur industry (all names are pseudonyms).

> PETE: *Let's say like this, a farmer has a pasture of cows and he has some pigs, and that's his living. . . . I think that's just what the farmer does. That's his living, that's his business.*

LATRICE: *We're not talking about the meat industry. We're talking about the fur industry. They're two different things.*

DEENA: *You can eat meat to live if you want to.*

LATRICE: *But you're wearing it as a coat to say, "Aren't I special?"*

PETE: *I wouldn't do it.*

BETHANY: *I don't understand what you're arguing about.*

LATRICE: *We're arguing on the point that Pete says people wearing furs, people having fur farms, that's their business and it's their choice if they want to. Which is completely absurd because it's not their choice to take another animal's life. I don't think it should be their choice.*

PETE: *You don't think it should be, but it is.*

BETHANY: *It's just his opinion.*

LATRICE: *Pete, under the law that is true, but under the law it also says, in Illinois now, animal cruelty is a felony. Isn't it kind of absurd that you can have a fur farm and gas them and break their necks and electrocute them, and that's not considered cruelty? Everything used to be according to the law. It used to be somebody's personal business to own another human as a slave, as property. It used to be only the men's business to vote. . . . The law is just what's currently said. That doesn't determine what's right or wrong. . . . Obviously, you have a strong opinion, and I'm expecting something to back it up.*

The conversation then moved into related realms concerning the purpose of laws, the difference between laws and morality, and the question of what kinds of freedoms should or should not be permitted in a democracy. These are ordinary kids talking with one another, but they're grappling with abstract intellectual and moral concepts and challenging one another to think and express themselves more clearly. Kids "just talking." It occurs all the time and is a powerful vehicle of education, especially for kids past the age of about eleven or twelve, who are as motivated to explore one another's minds through language as four-year-olds are to explore toys with their hands.

How Schools Thwart Children's Educative Instincts

Why don't school lessons ignite enthusiasm and spread insights in the same wildfire way that Mitra observed among impoverished children in India playing at public computers? It is not hard to think of probable answers. Children in school are not free to pursue their own interests, or to pursue those interests in their self-chosen ways. Children in school are more or less continuously evaluated, and the concern for evaluation and pleasing the teacher (or, for some, rebellion against pleasing the teacher) often overrides and subverts the possibility of developing genuine interests. Children in school are often shown one and only one way to solve a problem and are led to believe that other ways are incorrect, squelching the potential for exciting discoveries. And as Mitra himself has pointed out, the segregation of children by age in schools prevents the diversity in preexisting skills and knowledge that seems to be a key to self-directed learning from others.[25]

Curiosity, playfulness, and meaningful conversation are all thwarted in school, because they require freedom. Psychologist Susan Engel and her colleagues conducted an observational study of kindergarten and fifth-grade classrooms in the United States and found that children in neither grade expressed much curiosity relevant to anything that they were required to study.[26] When children asked questions, they asked about rules and requirements, such as how much time they had to finish a task, not about the subject itself. Questions about the subject were asked almost entirely by teachers, and the students' task was to guess at the answers the teachers were looking for. When students did seem to show a spark of interest, the teacher often cut the interest off, so as not to fall behind on the assignment.

For example, while working at tracing letters on a worksheet, two kindergarten children paused to look at some Popsicle sticks with short riddles printed on them, which happened to be lying on the table. When the girls began trying to read and figure out the riddles, which genuinely interested them, the teacher took the sticks away and said, "Let's put these away for now, so you can finish your letters." As another example, during a fifth-grade lesson on the Egyptians' early use of wheels to pull weights, the teacher gave small groups of children a slab of wood, some blocks to transport on the slab, a string, some small wooden wheels, a ruler, and a worksheet telling them what to do with these objects. When one group began experimenting with the objects in a manner not specified by the worksheet, the teacher said, with no apparent irony in her voice, "Kids, I'll give you time to experiment at recess. Now it's time for science."

And that, pretty much, is what school is all about—suppressing curiosity and enthusiasm so students can complete assignments in a timely manner. It's no wonder that the longer children are in school, the less interested they become in the subjects taught. The decline in interest over successive grades in school has been shown in many large-scale research studies, especially for science, but also for other subjects and for schoolwork in general.[27] One study, however, suggests that the decline is not inevitable.[28] In that study, students in fifth through eighth grade in various public schools in Israel were assessed for their interest in science. Students in traditional public schools showed the typical decline in interest, but those in so-called democratic public schools did not. In fact, in the democratic schools interest in science tended to increase from year to year. By eighth grade, students' interest in science was substantially and significantly greater in the democratic than in the standard schools. "Democratic" schools in Israel are not nearly as democratic or tolerant of self-directed learning as the Sudbury Valley School, but they do permit much more freedom in curricula than do traditional schools. In Israeli democratic schools, teachers might allow students to experiment in science classes, not merely follow the steps listed in a workbook.

7

THE PLAYFUL
STATE OF MIND

ABOUT THIRTY YEARS AGO, a team of research psychologists headed by James Michaels at Virginia Polytechnic and State University conducted a simple experiment in a real-world setting. They hung around the pool hall in a university student center and watched friendly games of eight ball. At first they observed unobtrusively and counted the percentage of successful shots that each player made, in order to categorize players as experts or novices. They then moved in closer and began watching in a way that made it obvious to the players that they were evaluating their performances. They did this for multiple players over multiple games. Here's what they found: close observation caused the experts to perform even better than they did without observation, but it had the opposite effect on the novices. All in all, the average success rate of the experts rose from 71 percent up to 80 percent under observation, while that for novices fell from 36 percent to 25 percent.[1]

Other experiments, using a wide variety of tasks, have produced similar results. When research subjects believe their performance is being observed and evaluated, those who are already skilled become better and those who are not so skilled become worse. The debilitating effects of being observed and evaluated have been found to be even greater for mental tasks, such as solving difficult math problems or generating good rebuttals to the views of classical philosophers, than they are for physical tasks, such as shooting pool.[2] When the task involves creative thought or the learning of a difficult skill, the presence of an observer or evaluator inhibits almost all participants.[3] The higher the status of the evaluator, and the more consequential the evaluation, the greater the inhibition of learning.

There is every reason to believe that this principle, that evaluation facilitates the performance of those who are already skilled and inhibits that of learners, applies to students in school. Schools are presumably places for learning and practice, not for experts to show off. Yet, with their incessant monitoring and evaluation of students' performances, schools seem to be ideally designed to boost the performances of those who are already good and to interfere with learning. Those who have somehow already learned the school tasks, maybe at home, generally perform well in this setting, but those who haven't tend to flounder. Evaluation drives a wedge between those who already know how and those who don't, pushing the former up and the latter down. Evaluation has this pernicious effect because it produces a mind-set that is opposite from the playful state of mind, which is the ideal state for learning new skills, solving new problems, and engaging in all sorts of creative activities.

This chapter is about the power of play. I'll begin by discussing four general conclusions from psychological research that, in my interpretation, all illustrate the educative power of play. Then I'll present a definition of play and explain how each of the defining characteristics contributes to play's power.

The Power of Play: Four Conclusions

The four conclusions discussed here—each of which is supported by numerous experiments—are well known to research psychologists who study learning and performance, but not so well known to educators. Taken as a whole, they show that learning, problem solving, and creativity are worsened by interventions that interfere with playfulness and improved by interventions that promote playfulness.[4]

Pressure to Perform Well Interferes with New Learning

This is the conclusion supported by research such as that described in the chapter introduction. An easy way to apply pressure to perform well in a research study is to observe and evaluate the performance in a way that is obvious to the performer. Dozens of experiments have shown that such pressure worsens performance in those who are not yet highly skilled at a task or who are just beginning to learn it. People "just playing" at pool, or at math, or at coming up with clever rebuttals to arguments, do better than those who are trying to impress an evaluator—unless they are already highly skilled at the task.

Pressure to Be Creative Interferes with Creativity

Psychologist Theresa Amabile has devoted a distinguished career, mostly at Brandeis University, to studying creativity. In a typical experiment she would ask groups of people—sometimes kids, sometimes adults—to do a creative task, such as to paint a picture, make a collage, or write a poem, within a certain time period. Each experiment involved some sort of manipulation aimed at increasing the participants' motivation. She would tell some but not others that their product would be evaluated and ranked for creativity, or that it would be entered into a contest, or that they could receive a reward for creative work.

When the projects were completed, she would have them all evaluated for creativity by a panel of judges who did not know about the experimental manipulations. Creativity is hard to define, but the judges showed significant consistency in their evaluations. They gave highest rankings to projects that were original and surprising yet also somehow satisfying, meaningful, and coherent.

The overriding result of the experiments was this: any intervention that increased the incentive to be creative had the effect of reducing creativity.[5] In experiment after experiment, the most creative products were made by those who were in the non-incentive condition—the ones who worked under the impression that their products would not be evaluated or entered into contests and who were not offered any prizes. They thought they were just creating the product for fun. In the terminology of this chapter, they were playing.

If you want to increase the degree to which people will pull hard on a rope, or persist at some boring, repetitive task, such as shelling beans or copying sentences, you can succeed by giving them an incentive to perform better. If you enter them into a contest, or watch them conspicuously, or pay them well for excellent performance, their performance improves. But creativity doesn't work that way. High incentive seems to foul up rather than improve the process. You can't become creative by simply trying really, really hard. Creativity is a spark that comes when mental conditions are just right, and high incentive seems to mess up those conditions.

As Amabile herself points out, her findings are no surprise to people who make their living by being creative. Many highly successful novelists, playwrights, artists, musicians, and poets have written, or stated in interviews, that to think and produce creatively, they must forget about pleasing an audience, or pleasing critics, or winning prizes, or earning royalties. All such thoughts stifle creativity. Instead they must focus fully on the product they are trying to create, as if creating it for its own sake. For example, when the eminent novelist John Irving was asked whether he worried, when writing, about whether a book would sell, he responded, "No, no, oh no. You can't, you *can't!* . . . When you're writing, *only* think about the book."[6]

Inducing a Playful Mood Improves Creativity and Insightful Problem Solving

In an experiment performed after most of Amabile's classic studies, Paul Howard-Jones and his colleagues demonstrated a way to improve artistic creativity. In their experiment, young children were asked to produce collages, which were then assessed for creativity by a panel of judges. Before producing the collage, some of the children were put into a playful mood by allowing them twenty-five minutes of free play with salt dough. The other children spent that twenty-five-minute period at a nonplayful task, copying text. The result was that those in the play condition made collages that were judged to be significantly more creative than did those in the nonplay condition.[7]

Other researchers—most notably psychologist Alice Isen, who is now at Cornell University—have studied the effect of mood on the ability to solve insight problems. Insight problems require some kind of creative leap, which allows the person to see the problem differently than before. Such problems often seem impossible up until the moment of insight, after which the solution seems obvious. A classic example of such a problem, used in countless psychological experiments after its development in the 1940s, is Duncan's candle problem.

In this task, research participants are given a small candle, a book of matches, and a box of tacks and are asked to attach the candle to a bulletin board in a way that the candle can be lit and will burn properly. They are allowed to use no objects other than those they are given. The trick to solving the problem is to realize that the tacks can be dumped out of the box and the box can then be tacked to the bulletin board and used as a shelf on which to mount the candle. In the typical test situation, most people, including students at elite colleges, fail to solve this problem within the allotted time period. They fail to see that the tack box can be used for something other than a container for tacks. In Isen's experiment, some of the college student participants watched a five-minute clip from a slapstick comedy film before being presented with the candle problem. A second group saw a five-minute serious film about mathematics, and a third group saw no film. The results were dramatic. Seventy-five percent of the students who saw the comedy, compared to only 20 percent and 13 percent of the students in the other two groups, respectively, solved the problem successfully.[8] Just five minutes of humor, which had nothing to do with the candle problem, made the problem solvable for the majority of participants.

In other experiments, Isen and her colleagues showed that mood manipulations can improve insight in many other situation as well, including situations that could have life-or-death significance. In one such experiment, the researchers presented real physicians with a case history of a difficult-to-diagnose liver disease. The case included some misleading information, which created a barrier to identifying the relevant information and arriving at the correct solution. Mood manipulation was accomplished by giving some of the doctors a little bag of candy before presenting them with the problem. Consistent with Isen's expectations, those who got the bag of candy arrived at the correct diagnosis more quickly than those who didn't. They reasoned more flexibly, took into account all of the information more readily, and were less likely to get stuck on false leads than were those who had not received candy.[9]

Isen and other theorists who refer to her work describe such experiments as showing that a "positive mood" improves creative, insightful reasoning. I would be more specific and suggest that the particular type of positive mood that is most effective is a *playful* mood. I suspect that the slapstick movie led college students to feel, "Hey, this experiment is about having fun, not a test," and I suspect that the little bag of candy had a similar effect on the physicians. Of course, the real trick for a physician is to maintain that mood during the serious business of real diagnosis.

A Playful State of Mind Enables Young Children to Solve Logic Problems

In experiments conducted in England, M. G. Dias and P. L. Harris found that young children could solve logic problems in the context of play that they seemed unable to solve in a serious context.[10] The problems were syllogisms, the classic type of logic problem originally described by Aristotle. A syllogism requires a person to combine the information in two premises to decide whether a particular conclusion is true, false, or indeterminate (cannot be determined from the premises). Syllogisms are generally easy when the premises coincide with concrete reality, but are more difficult when the premises are counterfactual (contradictions to reality). The prevailing belief at the time that the British researchers conducted these experiments was that the ability to solve counterfactual syllogisms depends on a type of reasoning that is completely lacking in young children.

Here's an example of a counterfactual syllogism the researchers used:

All cats bark (major premise). *Muffins is a cat* (minor premise). *Does Muffins bark?*

Previous research—including research by the famous Swiss developmental psychologist Jean Piaget—had shown that children under about ten or eleven years old regularly fail to solve such syllogisms correctly—that is, they fail to give answers that logicians take as the correct answers. When the British researchers put syllogisms like this to young children in a serious tone of voice, the children answered as Piaget and others would expect. They said things like, "No, cats go *meow,* they don't bark." They acted as if they were unable to think about a premise that did not fit with their concrete, real-world experiences. But when the researchers presented the same problems in a playful tone of voice, which made it clear that they were talking about a *pretend* world, children as young as four years old regularly solved the problems. They said, "Yes, Muffins barks."

Think of it: four-year-olds in play easily solved logic problems that they were not supposed to be able to solve until they were about ten or eleven years old. In fact, subsequent experiments showed that, to a lesser degree, even two-year-olds solved such problems when presented in a clearly playful manner.[11] I'll explain later why these results should not be as surprising as they seemed to many people. But perhaps you can already see why they shouldn't.

ALL OF THESE FINDINGS tell us something about the power of play. Learning, creativity, and problem solving are facilitated by anything that promotes a playful state of mind, and they are inhibited by evaluation, expectation of rewards, or anything else that destroys a playful state of mind. But this raises a new, big question: What exactly is play, and what makes it such a powerful force for learning, creativity, and problem solving?

What Is Play?[12]

Play is a concept that fills our minds with contradictions when we try to think deeply about it. Play is serious, yet not serious; trivial yet profound; imaginative and spontaneous, yet bound by rules and anchored in the real world. It is childish, yet underlies many of the greatest accomplishments of adults. From an evolutionary perspective, play is nature's way of ensuring that children and other young mammals will learn what they must to survive and do well. From another perspective, play is God's gift that makes life on earth worthwhile.

It is not easy to define play, but it is worth our while to spend some time attempting to do so, as play's defining characteristics are strong clues for explaining its educative power. Here are three general points about play that are worth keeping in mind.

The first point is that the characteristics of play all have to do with motivation and mental attitude, not with the overt form of the behavior itself. Two people might be throwing a ball, or pounding nails, or typing words on a computer, and one might be playing while the other is not. To tell which one is playing and which one is not, you have to infer from their expressions and the details of their actions something about why they are doing what they are doing and their attitude toward it.

The second point toward definition is that play is not necessarily all or none. Play can blend with other motives and attitudes, in proportions ranging anywhere from zero up to 100 percent. For that reason, the adjective *playful*, which is understood as something that can vary by degrees, is often more useful than the noun *play*, which tends to be interpreted as all or none. People can, to varying degrees, bring a "playful attitude" or "playful spirit" to whatever activity they are doing. In general, pure play (activity that is 100 percent playful) is more common in children than in adults. In adults, playfulness most often blends with other attitudes and motives having to do with adult responsibilities. We don't have metrics for these things, but I would estimate that my behavior in writing this book is about 80 percent play. That percentage varies from time to time as I go along; it decreases when I worry about deadlines or how critics will evaluate it, and it increases when I'm focused only on the current task of researching or writing.

The third point is that play is not neatly defined in terms of some single identifying characteristic. Rather, it is defined as a confluence of several characteristics. People before me who have studied and written about play have, among them, described quite a few such characteristics, but they can all be boiled down, I think, to the following five: (1) play is self-chosen and self-directed; (2) play is activity in which means are more valued than ends; (3) play has structure or rules that are not dictated by physical necessity but emanate from the minds of the players; (4) play is imaginative, nonliteral, mentally removed in some way from "real" or "serious" life; and (5) play involves an active, alert, but non-stressed frame of mind.[13]

The more fully an activity entails all of these characteristics, the more inclined most people are to refer to that activity as play. By "most people" I don't mean just scholars. Even young children are most likely to use the word *play* to label activities that most fully contain these five characteristics. These characteristics seem to capture our intuitive sense of what play is. Notice that all of the characteristics have to do with the motivation or attitude the person brings to the activity. Let me elaborate on these characteristics, one by one, and expand a bit on each by pointing out some of its implications for thinking about the educative value of play.

Play Is Self-Chosen and Self-Directed

Play is, first and foremost, an expression of freedom. It is what one *wants* to do as opposed to what one is *obliged* to do. That is perhaps the most basic ingredient of most people's commonsense understanding of play. In one research study, for example, kindergartners identified as "play" only those activities that were voluntary—the things they did at recess—and as "work" all of the activities that were part of the school curriculum, including those that were designed to be enjoyable, such as finger painting, running relay races, and listening to stories.[14]

The joy of play is the ecstatic feeling of liberty. Play is not always accompanied by smiles and laughter, nor are smiles and laughter always signs of play; but play is always accompanied by a feeling of *Yes, this is what I want to do right now.* Players are free agents, not pawns in someone else's game. Players not only choose to play or not to play, but they also direct their own actions during play. As I will argue soon, play always involves rules of some sort, but all players must freely accept the rules, and if rules are changed, then all players must agree to the changes. That is why play is the most democratic of all activities. In social play (play involving more than one player), one player may emerge for a period as the leader, but only at the will of all the others. Every rule a leader proposes must be approved, at least tacitly, by all of the other players. The ultimate freedom in play is the freedom to quit. Because the players want to keep the game going, and because they know that other players will quit and the game will end if they are not happy, play is a powerful vehicle for learning how to please others while also pleasing oneself. I referred to this in earlier chapters, and will elaborate further in Chapter 8.

This point about play being self-chosen and self-directed is ignored by, or perhaps unknown to, adults who try to take control of children's play (and thereby ruin it). Adults can play with children, and in some cases can even be leaders in children's play, but to do so requires at least the same sensitivity that children themselves show to the needs and wishes of all the players. Because adults are commonly viewed as authority figures, children often feel less able to quit, or to disagree with the proposed rules, when an adult is leading than when a child is leading. And so the result often is something that, for many of the children, is not play at all. When a child feels coerced, the play spirit vanishes and all of the advantages of that spirit go with it. Math games in school and adult-led sports—with their adult rules—are not play for those who feel they have to participate. Adult-led games can be great fun for kids who freely choose them, but can seem like punishment for kids who haven't made that choice.

What is true for children's play is also true for adults' sense of play. Research studies have shown repeatedly that adults who have a great deal of freedom as to how and when to do their work commonly experience that work as play, even—in fact, especially—when the work is difficult. In contrast, people who must follow others' directions, with little creative input of their own, rarely experience their work as play.[15] Moreover, dozens of research studies have shown that when people *choose* to perform some task, they perform it more fully and effectively than when they feel compelled by others to perform it.[16] When compelled, they tend to do the minimum necessary to meet the requirements. I'm sure these findings come as no great surprise to you; social scientists sometimes go to considerable lengths to prove the obvious. It is interesting, though, that people so often forget these obvious points when thinking about children. Everyone, regardless of age, prefers freedom and self-direction to rigid control by others. When we compel children to "learn" in school, they are inclined to do the least possible learning that they can get away with, just as adults are in similar circumstances.

Play Is Motivated by Means More Than Ends

Many of our actions are "free" in the sense that we don't feel that other people are making us do them, but are not free, or at least not experienced as free, in another sense. These are actions that we feel we must do to achieve some necessary or desired goal. We scratch an itch to get rid of the itch, flee from a tiger to avoid getting eaten, study an uninteresting book to get a good grade on a test, work at a boring job to get money. If there were no itch, tiger, test, or need for money, we would not scratch, flee, study, or do the boring work. In those cases we are not playing.

To the degree that we engage in an activity purely to achieve some end, or goal, separate from the activity itself, that activity is not play. What we value most, when we are not playing, are the results of our actions. The actions are merely means to the ends. When we are not playing, we typically opt for the shortest, least effortful means of achieving our goal. The nonplayful student, for example, does the least studying that she can to get the "A" that she desires, and her studying is focused directly on the goal of doing well on the tests. Any learning not related to that goal is, for her, wasted effort.

In play, however, all this is reversed. Play is activity conducted primarily for its own sake. The playful student enjoys studying the subject and cares little about the test. In play, attention is focused on the means, not the ends, and players do not necessarily look for the easiest routes to achieving the ends. Think of a cat *preying* on a mouse in contrast to a cat *playing* at preying on a mouse. The former takes the quickest route for killing the mouse. The latter tries various ways of catching the mouse, not all efficient, and lets the mouse go each time so it can try again. The preying cat enjoys the end; the playing cat enjoys the means. (The mouse, of course, enjoys none of this.) Another way of saying all this is to say that play is *intrinsically* motivated (motivated by the activity itself), not *extrinsically* motivated (motivated by some reward that is separate from the activity itself).

Play often has goals, but the goals are experienced as an intrinsic part of the game, not as the sole reason for engaging in the game's actions. Goals in play are subordinate to the means for achieving them. For example, constructive play (the playful building of something) is always directed toward the goal of creating the object the player has in mind. But notice that the primary objective in such play is the *creation* of the object, not the *having* of the object. Children making a sand castle would not be happy if an adult came along and said, "You can stop all your effort now. I'll make the castle for you." That would spoil their fun. Similarly, children or adults playing a competitive game have the goal of scoring points and winning, but if they are truly playing, it is the process of scoring and trying to win that motivates them, not the points themselves or the status of having won. If someone would just as soon win by cheating as by following the rules, or get the trophy and praise through some shortcut that bypasses the game process, then that person is not playing.

Adults can test the degree to which their work is play by asking themselves this: "If I could receive the same pay, the same prospects for future pay, the same amount of approval from other people, and the same sense of doing good for the world for *not* doing this job as I am receiving for doing it, would I quit?" If the person would eagerly quit, the job is not play. To the degree that the person would quit reluctantly, or not quit, the job is play. It is something that the person enjoys independently of the extrinsic rewards received for doing it.

B. F. Skinner—the famous behavioral scientist whose views dominated psychology during the mid-twentieth century—developed an entire psychology built on the idea that all behavior is done to achieve desired ends, or rewards, or what Skinner called "reinforcers." Psychology has moved beyond that narrow view, but a variation of it still dominates among economists. Economists tend to see us as rational accountants, whose reasoning is geared toward achieving the maximum amount of money or goods with the minimum amount of effort. Modern economic theory, like old-fashioned Skinnerian psychology, works rather nicely for explaining how to get people (and rats) to do things they don't want to do, but falls apart entirely as soon as we turn our attention to play. Since play, to some degree, infuses most of what we humans do, Skinnerian psychology and modern economic theory have limited utility for understanding human behavior.

Researchers have shown that rewards in some cases actually *reduce* the likelihood that a person will engage in an activity, by instilling the idea that the activity is work rather than play. Of course, Mark Twain, who demonstrated more understanding of human behavior than any behavioral scientist I know, told us about that principle long ago. Tom Sawyer got his friend Ben to whitewash the fence not by paying him for it, but by acting as if Ben should pay *him* for the privilege. In a classic experiment conducted in the early 1970s, a group of researchers at the University of Michigan did the reverse of what Tom Sawyer did—they turned a previously enjoyable activity into work for a group of preschool children by rewarding them for it.[17] Initial observations showed that all of the children enjoyed drawing with colored felt-tip pens; they spent a good portion of their free time doing that. In the experiment, the children were divided into three groups. Those in the *expected-reward* group were told in advance that they would receive an attractive "good player" certificate for drawing a picture with felt-tip pens. Those in the *unexpected-reward* group were asked to draw a picture and then were given the certificate as a surprise afterward. Those in the *no-reward* group were asked to draw a picture and received nothing. The experiment was conducted in such a way that the children in each group did not know what was happening with the other groups.

The experiment had two significant results. First, those in the expected-reward group produced significantly *worse* drawings than did those in the other two groups, as judged by evaluators who did not know which group the drawings came from. Second, those in the expected-reward group spent only about half as much time drawing with felt-tip pens, in subsequent free-play sessions, as did those in the other two groups. No differences were found between the children in the no-reward and unexpected-reward groups. The researchers interpreted these results as evidence that the expected reward had caused children in that group to reframe their view of drawing with felt-tip pens. The children came to see such drawing as something one does for a reward rather than as something fun to do for its own sake. Therefore, when they had to draw, they put less effort into it (only enough to get the reward), and they tended to avoid drawing when no reward was available. The unexpected reward didn't have this effect, because that reward could not have served as a motivator. Those children did not know they would get a certificate, so they could not have said to themselves, "I'm only drawing this picture to get the certificate." Dozens of follow-up experiments, with adults as well as with children, have produced similar results using a wide variety of activities and rewards.[18]

The implications of such findings are pretty obvious. It is possible to ruin play by focusing attention too strongly on rewards and outcomes. This happens in competitive games when the goal of winning overtakes that of simply enjoying the game. When a game becomes primarily a means of proving oneself to be better than someone else, or of supporting the team's felt "need" to win, it becomes something other than play. All sorts of play can be ruined when rewards are made to appear to be the main reason for engaging in the activity. I suspect that many more of us would play in the realms of history, mathematics, science, and foreign languages were it not for our schools' attempts to encourage them through rewards and punishments, turning those potentially enjoyable activities into work.

Play Is Guided by Mental Rules

Play is freely chosen activity, but it is not free-form activity. Play always has structure, derived from rules in the player's mind. This point is really an extension of the attention to means in play. The rules of play are the means. To play is to behave in accordance with self-chosen rules. The rules are not like rules of physics, nor like biological instincts, which are automatically followed. Rather, they are mental concepts that often require conscious effort to keep in mind and follow.

A basic rule of constructive play, for example, is that you must work with the chosen medium in a manner aimed at producing or depicting some specific object or design. You don't pile up blocks randomly; you arrange them deliberately in accordance with your mental image of what you are trying to make. Even rough-and-tumble play (playful fighting and chasing), which may look wild from the outside, is constrained by rules. An always-present rule in play fighting, for example, is that you mimic some of the actions of real fighting, but you don't really hurt the other person. You don't hit with all your force (at least not if you are the stronger of the two); you don't kick, bite, or scratch. Play fighting is much more controlled than real fighting; it is always an exercise in restraint.

Among the most complex forms of play, rule-wise, is what play researchers call sociodramatic play—the playful acting out of roles or scenes, as when children are playing "house," or acting out a marriage, or pretending to be superheroes. The fundamental rule here is that you must abide by your and the other players' shared understanding of the role you are playing. If you are the pet dog in a game of "house," you must walk around on all fours and bark rather than talk. If you are Wonder Woman, and you and your playmates believe that Wonder Woman never cries, then you refrain from crying, even when you fall down and hurt yourself.

To illustrate the rule-based nature of sociodramatic play, the Russian psychologist Lev Vygotsky wrote about two actual sisters—ages seven and five—who sometimes *played* that they were sisters.[19] As actual sisters, they rarely thought about their sisterhood and had no consistent way of behaving toward each other. Sometimes they enjoyed each other, sometimes they fought, and sometimes they ignored each other. But when they were playing sisters, they always behaved according to their shared stereotype of how sisters should behave. They dressed alike, talked alike, walked with their arms around each other, talked about how similar they were to each other and how different from everyone else, and so on. Much more self-control, mental effort, and rule following was involved in playing sisters than in being sisters.

The category of play with the most explicit rules is that called formal games. These include games such as checkers and baseball, with rules that are specified, verbally, in ways designed to minimize ambiguity in interpretation. The rules of these games commonly are passed along from one generation of players to the next. Many formal games in our society are competitive, and one purpose of the formal rules is to make sure the same restrictions apply equally to all competitors. Players of formal games, if they are true players, must adopt these rules as their own for the period of the game. Of course, except in "official" versions of such games, players commonly modify the rules to fit their own needs and desires, but each modification must be agreed upon by all players.

The main point here is that every form of play involves a good deal of self-control. When not playing, children (and adults, too) may act according to their immediate biological needs, emotions, and whims, but in play they must act in ways that they and their playmates deem appropriate to the game. Play draws and fascinates the player precisely because it is structured by rules the player herself or himself has invented or accepted.

The student of play who most strongly emphasized play's rule-based nature was the above-mentioned Vygotsky. In an essay on the role of play in development, originally published in 1933, Vygotsky commented on the apparent paradox between the idea that play is spontaneous and free and the idea that players must follow rules:

> The . . . paradox is that in play [the child] adopts the line of least resistance—she does what she most feels like doing because play is connected with pleasure—and at the same time she learns to follow the line of greatest resistance by subordinating herself to rules and thereby renouncing what she wants, since subjection to rules and renunciation of impulsive action constitute the path to maximum pleasure in play. Play continually creates demands on the child to act against immediate impulse. At every step the child is faced with a conflict between the rules of the game and what she would do if she could suddenly act spontaneously. . . . Thus, the essential attribute of play is a rule that has become a desire. . . . The rule wins because it is the strongest impulse. Such a rule is an internal rule, a rule of self-restraint and self-determination. . . . In this way a child's greatest achievements are possible in play, achievements that tomorrow will become her basic level of real action and morality.[20]

Vygotsky's point, of course, is that the child's desire to play is so strong that it becomes a motivating force for learning self-control. The child resists impulses and temptations that would run counter to the rules because the child seeks the larger pleasure of remaining in the game. To Vygotsky's analysis, I would add that the child accepts and desires the rules of play only because he or she is always free to quit if the rules become too burdensome. With that in mind, the paradox can be seen to be superficial. The child's real-life freedom is not restricted by the rules of the game, because the child can at any moment choose to leave the game. That is another reason why the freedom to quit is such a crucial aspect of the definition of play. Without that freedom, rules of play would be intolerable. To be required to act like Wonder Woman in real life would be terrifying, but to act like that in play—a realm you are always free to leave—is great fun.

Play Is Imaginative

Another apparent paradox of play is that it is serious yet not serious, real yet not real. In play one enters a realm that is physically located in the real world, makes use of props in the real world, is often about the real world, is said by the players to be real, and yet in some way is mentally removed from the real world.

Imagination, or fantasy, is most obvious in sociodramatic play, where the players create the characters and plot, but it is also present to some degree in all other forms of human play. In rough-and-tumble play, the fight is a pretend one, not a real one. In constructive play, the players say they are building a castle, but they know it is a pretend castle, not a real one. In formal games with explicit rules, the players must accept an already established fictional situation that provides the foundation for the rules. For example, in the real world bishops can move in any direction they choose, but in the fantasy world of chess they can move only on the diagonals.

The fantasy aspect of play is intimately connected to play's rule-based nature. Because play takes place in a fantasy world, it must be governed by rules that are in the minds of the players rather than by laws of nature. In reality, one cannot ride a horse unless a real horse is physically present, but in play one can ride a horse whenever the game's rules permit or prescribe it. In reality, a broom is just a broom, but in play it can be a horse. In reality, a chess piece is a carved bit of wood, but in chess it is a bishop or a knight that has well-defined capacities and limitations for movement that are not even hinted at in the carved wood itself. The fictional situation dictates the rules of the game; the actual physical world within which the game is played is secondary. Through play the child learns to take charge of the world and not simply respond passively to it. In play the child's mental concept dominates, and the child molds available elements of the physical world to meet that concept.

Play of all sorts has "time-in" and "time-out," though that is more obvious for some forms of play than others. Time-in is the period of fiction. Time-out is the temporary return to reality—perhaps to tie one's shoes, or go to the bathroom, or correct a playmate who hasn't been following the rules. During time-in one does not say, "I am just playing," any more than does Shakespeare's Hamlet announce from the stage that he is merely pretending to murder his stepfather.

Adults sometimes become confused by the seriousness of children's play and by children's refusal, while playing, to say that they are playing. They worry needlessly that children don't distinguish fantasy from reality. When my son was four years old he was Superman for periods that sometimes lasted more than a day. During those periods he would deny vigorously that he was only pretending to be Superman, and this worried his nursery school teacher. She was only partly mollified when I pointed out that he never attempted to leap off of actual tall buildings or stop real railroad trains and that he would acknowledge that he had been playing when he finally did declare time-out by removing his cape. To acknowledge that play is play is to remove the magic spell; it automatically turns time-in into time-out.

An amazing fact of human nature is that even two-year-olds know the difference between real and pretend.[21] A two-year-old who turns a cup filled with imaginary water over a doll and says, "Oh oh, dolly all wet," knows that the doll isn't really wet. It would be impossible to teach such young children such a subtle concept as pretense, yet they understand it. Apparently the fictional mode of thinking, and the ability to keep that mode distinct from the literal mode, is innate to the human mind. That innate capacity is part of the inborn capacity for play.

The fantasy element of play is often not as obvious, or as full-blown, in adults' play as in children's play. That is one reason why adults' play is typically not of the 100 percent variety. Yet, I would argue, fantasy occupies a big role in much if not most of what adults do and is a major element in our intuitive sense of the degree to which adult activities are play. An architect designing a house is designing a real house. Yet, the architect brings a good deal of imagination to bear in visualizing the house, imagining how people might use it, and matching it with some aesthetic concepts she has in mind. It is reasonable to say that the architect builds a pretend house, in her mind and on paper, before it becomes a real one. A scientist, generating hypotheses to explain known facts, uses imagination to go beyond the facts themselves. Einstein referred to his own creative achievements in mathematics and theoretical physics as "combinatorial play," and he famously claimed that his understanding of relativity came to him by imagining himself chasing a beam of light and catching up to it, and imagining the consequences.[22] Geniuses often seem to be those who somehow retain, into adulthood, the imaginative capacities of small children. In all of us, the capacity for abstract, hypothetical thinking depends on our ability to imagine situations we haven't actually experienced and to reason logically based on those imagined situations. This is a skill every normal child exercises regularly in play.

When I say that my writing this chapter is about 80 percent play, I am taking into account not just my sense of freedom about doing it, my enjoyment of the process, and the fact that I'm following rules (about writing) that I accept as my own, but also the fact that a considerable degree of imagination is involved. I'm not making up the facts, but I am making up the way of stringing them together. Furthermore, I am constantly imagining how they will fit into the whole structure I am trying to build, one that does not yet exist as concrete reality.

So, fantasy is moving me along in this, much as it moves a child along in building a sand castle or pretending to be Superman.

Play, then, is a state of mind that promotes imagination. In a playful mood, the college students in Isen's experiments could imagine the tack box serving as a shelf on which to mount a candle. In a playful mood, the four-year-olds in Dias and Harris's experiments could imagine and think about a world in which all cats bark. In a playful mood, without external incentives to disrupt them, the participants in Amabile's experiments could imagine creative ways to produce drawings, collages, poems, or stories. In a playful mood, Einstein could imagine the relativity of motion and time. What a crime it is that we deprive children of play in school, and then we expect them to think hypothetically and be creative!

Play Is Conducted in an Alert, Active, but Non-Stressed Frame of Mind

This final characteristic of play follows naturally from the others. Because play involves conscious control of one's own behavior, with attention to process and rules, it requires an active, alert mind. Players do not just passively absorb information from the environment, or reflexively respond to stimuli, or behave automatically in accordance with habit; they have to think actively about what they are doing. Yet, because play is not a response to external demands or immediate biological needs, the person at play is relatively free from the strong drives and emotions that are experienced as pressure. And because the player's attention is focused on process more than outcome, and because the realm of play is removed from the serious world where consequences matter, the player's mind is not distracted by fear of failure. The mind at play is alert, but not stressed.

The mental state of play is what some researchers call "flow."[23] Attention is attuned to the activity itself, and there is reduced consciousness of self and time. The mind is wrapped up in the ideas, rules, and actions of the game and relatively impervious to outside distractions.

Many researchers who do not consider themselves to be studying play have described this state of mind as the ideal state for learning and creativity. In my mind, they are studying play.

A few years ago, on the basis of research like what I described in the first section of this chapter, psychologist Barbara Fredrickson developed what she calls the "broaden and build theory of positive emotions."[24] According to her theory, positive emotions *broaden* our perception and range of thought, which allows us to see what we didn't see before, put ideas together in new ways, experiment with new ways of behaving, and in these ways *build* our repertoire of knowledge, ideas, and skills. In contrast, negative emotions narrow our perception and thought to focus almost exclusively on the most salient source of distress—the fearsome tiger, the hated enemy, the evaluator, or the negative consequences of failure. Such distress also activates our autonomic arousal system, which facilitates performance on tasks that require a burst of physical energy and a narrow focus on the goal, but interferes with creativity, learning, and reflection. From an evolutionary perspective, negative emotions, especially fear and anger, arose to deal with emergencies, and emergencies are not the proper occasions for trying out new ways of thinking and behaving. In an emergency, you want to use methods of coping that are already habitual, not experiment with new ones.

Fredrickson's theory captures nicely much of what I have said in this chapter. But I would call it "the broaden and build theory of *playfulness.*" Or, to be more complete, maybe "the broaden and build theory of playfulness and *curiosity.*" The positive states of mind that broaden and build, in most if not all of Fredrickson's examples, are states that generate play and exploration.

The Power of Play Lies in Its Triviality

People often think of play as frivolous or trivial, and they are right. As I have explained, play is activity conducted for its own sake rather than to achieve serious real-world goals such as food, money, praise, escape from a tiger, or an addition to one's résumé. It is activity that takes place at least partly in a fantasy world. So it is indeed trivial! But here is the most delicious of play's paradoxes: the enormous educative power of play lies in its triviality.

Play serves the serious purpose of education, but the player is not deliberately educating himself or herself. The player is playing for fun; education is a by-product. If the player were playing for a serious purpose, it would no longer be play and much of the educative power would be lost.

Because the child at play is not worrying about his or her future, and because the child at play suffers no real-world consequence for failing, the child at play is not afraid of failure. The playing child feels free to try things out in a pretend world that would be too risky or impossible to try in the serious world. Because the child at play is not seeking approval from adult judges, the child is unhampered by evaluation concerns. Fear and concerns about evaluation tend to freeze the mind and body into rigid frames, suitable for carrying out well-learned habitual activities but not for learning or thinking about anything new. In the absence of concern about failure and others' judgments, children at play can devote all their attention to the skills at which they are playing. They strive to perform well, because performing well is an intrinsic goal of play, but they know that if they fail there will be no serious, real-world consequences.

Play is trivial, but not easy. Much of the joy of play lies in the challenges. A playful activity that becomes too easy loses its attraction and ceases to be play. The player then modifies the activity to make it harder or moves on to something different. Toddlers who have mastered the art of two-legged walking move on to more advanced forms of locomotor play, such as running, leaping, and climbing. Young animals similarly challenge themselves by playing at increasingly more difficult skills as they develop. In one study, wild goat kids that could already run well on flat ground were observed to concentrate their running play on steep slopes, where running was more difficult.[25] Similarly, young monkeys playfully swinging from branch to branch in trees choose branches that are far enough apart to stretch their skills, but sufficiently low to the ground that they would not be badly hurt if they fell.[26] Teenagers playing video games move from one level of difficulty to another in the game. There would be no thrill in always playing at the same level. Einstein's combinatorial play continuously challenged his mental abilities and pushed them to new heights. When children are free to play, they play naturally at the ever-advancing edges of their mental or physical abilities.

Another aspect of play that suits it well for its educative functions is repetitiveness. Most forms of play involve repetition. A cat playfully stalking a mouse keeps releasing the mouse in order to stalk it again. A baby playfully babbling keeps repeating the same syllables or the same sets of syllables, sometimes altering the sequence slightly, as if deliberately practicing their pronunciation. A toddler playing at walking may keep walking back and forth, over the same route. A young child playfully reading may "read" the same (memorized) little book, over and over again. All sorts of structured games, such as tag or baseball or twenty questions, involve repetition of the same actions or processes over and over. One of the defining characteristics of play is the focus on means rather than ends, and repetitiveness is a corollary of that characteristic. The player produces the same action repeatedly in order to get it right.

But the repetition is not rote. Because the repetition derives from the player's own will, each repetitive act is a creative act. If each act looks just like the previous one, that is because the player is deliberately striving for exact repetition. Most often, however, each "repeated" act is different in some systematic way from the previous one; the player is deliberately varying the act in some way to fit the game or to experiment with new ways of doing the same thing. A side effect of such repetition is the perfection and consolidation of the newly developing skill. The repetition in play may sometimes lead parents and other observers to think that nothing new is being learned, but if that were true the child would stop and do something else.

A CONCLUDING THOUGHT: Imagine that you had omnipotent powers and were faced with the problem of how to get young humans and other young mammals to practice the skills they must develop to survive and thrive in their local conditions of life. How might you solve that problem? It is hard to imagine a more effective solution than that of building into their brains a mechanism that makes them want to practice those very skills and that rewards such practice with the experience of joy. That, indeed, is the mechanism that natural selection has built, and we refer to the resultant behavior as play. Perhaps play would be more respected if we called it something like "self-motivated practice of life skills," but that would remove the lightheartedness from it and thereby reduce its effectiveness. So, we are stuck with the paradox. We must accept play's triviality in order to realize its profundity.

Nearly three hundred years ago the English poet Thomas Gray wrote, "Where ignorance is bliss, 'Tis folly to be wise." I'd reverse his words and say, "Where knowledge and skill are bliss, 'Tis wise to be folly."

8

THE ROLE OF PLAY IN SOCIAL AND EMOTIONAL DEVELOPMENT

PLAYING WITH OTHER CHILDREN, away from adults, is how children learn to make their own decisions, control their emotions and impulses, see from others' perspectives, negotiate differences with others, and make friends. In short, play is how children learn to take control of their lives.

Lessons from Informal Sports

Imagine an old-fashioned sandlot game of baseball. A bunch of kids of various ages show up at a vacant lot, hoping they'll find others to play with. Some come on foot, others by bicycle; some alone, some with friends. Someone brings a bat, another brings a ball (which may not be an actual baseball), and several have fielders' gloves. There are enough people for a game, so they decide to play. The two reputably best players serve as captains, and they choose sides. They lay out the bases—hats, Frisbees, or any objects of suitable size. There aren't enough players to fill all the positions, so they improvise. No adult is present to tell the kids what to do or to settle disputes; they have to work everything out for themselves. This way of playing baseball is actually *play*. It is an activity chosen and directed by the players themselves and done for its own sake, not for some external reward.

Now imagine a Little League game. It's played on a manicured field, which looks like a smaller version of the fields where professional games are played. Most kids are driven there, partly because it's far from home and partly because their parents are behind this activity. Many parents stay for the game, to show their support for their young players. The teams are predetermined, part of an ongoing league. Each team has an adult coach, and an adult umpire calls balls, strikes, and outs. An official score is kept, and over the course of the season wins and losses are tracked to determine the championship team. Some of the players really want to be there; others are there because their parents coaxed or pushed them into it.

The informal, self-directed way of playing baseball or any other game contains valuable lessons that formal, adult-directed games do not. Here are five such lessons, among the most valuable that anyone can learn in life.

Lesson 1: To keep the game going, you have to keep everyone happy. The most fundamental freedom in all true play is the freedom to quit. In an informal game, nobody is forced to stay, and there are no coaches, parents, or other adults to disappoint if you quit. The game can continue only as long as a sufficient number of players choose to continue. Therefore, everyone must do his or her share to keep the other players happy, including the players on the other team.

This means that you show certain restraints in the informal game beyond those dictated by the stated rules, which derive instead from your understanding of each player's needs. You don't run full force into second base if the second baseman is smaller than you and might get hurt, even though it might be considered good strategy in Little League (where, in fact, a coach might scold you for *not* running as hard as possible). This attitude is why children are injured less frequently in informal games than in formal sports, despite parents' beliefs that adult-directed sports are safer.[1] If you are pitching, you pitch softly to little Johnny, because you know he can't hit your fastball. You also know that even your teammates would accuse you of being mean if you threw your fastest pitches to someone so young. But when big, experienced Jerome is up, you throw your best stuff, not just because you want to get him out but also because anything less would be insulting to him. The golden rule of social play is not, *Do unto others as you would have them do unto you.* Rather, it is, *Do unto others as they would have you do unto them.* The equality of play is not the equality of sameness, but the equality that comes from granting equal validity to the unique needs and wishes of every player.

To be a good player of informal sports you can't blindly follow rules. Rather, you have to see from others' perspectives, to understand what others want and provide at least some of that for them. If you fail, you will be left alone. In the informal game, keeping your playmates happy is far more important than winning, and that's true in life as well. For some children this is a hard lesson to learn, but the drive to play with others is so strong that most eventually do learn it if allowed plenty of opportunity to play—plenty of opportunity to fail, suffer the consequences, and then try again.

Lesson 2: Rules are modifiable and player-generated. Because nothing is standardized in an informal game, the players have to make up and modify rules to adapt to varying conditions. If the vacant lot is small and the only ball available is a rubber one that carries too well, the players may decide that any ball hit beyond the lot's boundary is an automatic out. This causes the players to concentrate on placing their hits, rather than smashing them. Alternatively, the strongest players may be required to bat one-handed, with their nondominant hand, or to bat with a broomstick rather than an actual bat. As the game continues and conditions change, the rules may evolve further. None of this happens in Little League, where the official rules are inviolable and interpreted by an adult authority. In the formal game, the conditions must fit the rules rather than the other way around.

The famous developmental psychologist Jean Piaget noted long ago, in a classic study of children playing marbles, that children acquire a higher understanding of rules when they play under their own direction than when they are directed by adults.[2] Adult direction leads to the assumption that rules are determined by an outside authority and thus not to be questioned. When children play just among themselves, however, they come to realize that rules are merely conventions, established to make the game more fun and more fair, and can be changed to meet changing conditions. For life in a democracy, few lessons are more valuable.

Lesson 3: Conflicts are settled by argument, negotiation, and compromise. In the informal game, the players not only make and modify the rules, but also act as umpires. They decide whether a hit is fair or foul, whether a runner is safe or out, whether the pitcher is or isn't being too mean to little Johnny, and whether Julio should have to share his brand-new glove with someone on the other team who doesn't have a glove. Some of the more popular players may have more pull in these arguments than others, but everyone has a say. Everyone who has an opinion defends it, with as much logic as he or she can muster, and ultimately consensus is reached.

Consensus doesn't necessarily mean complete agreement. It just means that everyone *consents;* they're willing to go along with it for the sake of keeping the game going. Consensus is crucial if you want the game to continue. The need for consensus in informal play doesn't come from some highfalutin moral philosophy; it comes from practical reality. If a decision makes some people unhappy, some of them may quit, and if too many quit, the game is over (as noted under Lesson 1).

You learn in informal games that you must compromise if you want to keep playing. If you don't have a king who decides things for you, you have to learn how to govern yourselves.

Once I was watching some kids play an informal game of basketball. They were spending more time deciding on the rules and arguing about whether particular plays were fair than they were playing the game. I overheard a nearby adult say, "Too bad they don't have a referee to decide these things, so they wouldn't have to spend so much time debating." Well, is it too bad? In the course of their lives, which will be the more important skill—shooting baskets or debating effectively and learning how to compromise? Kids playing sports informally are practicing many things at once, the least important of which may be the sport itself.

Lesson 4: There is no real difference between your team and the opposing team. In an informal game, the players know from the beginning that their division into two teams is arbitrary and serves only the purpose of the game. New teams are chosen each time. Billy may have been on the "enemy" team yesterday, but today he is on your team. In fact, teams may even change composition as the game goes along. Billy may start off on the opposing team, but may move over to yours, for balance, when two of your teammates go home for supper. Or if both teams are short of players, Billy may catch for both. The concept of "enemy" or "opponent" in informal sports lies very clearly in the realm of play, not reality. It is temporary and limited to the game itself. In that sense the informal game resembles a pure fantasy game in which Billy pretends to be an evil giant trying to catch and eat you.

In contrast, in formal league sports, teams remain relatively fixed over a series of games, and the scores, to some degree, have real-world consequences—such as trophies or praise from adults. The result is development of a long-lasting sense of team identity and, with it, a sense that "my team is better than other teams"—better even in ways that have nothing to do with the game and may extend to situations outside of the game. A major theme of research in social psychology and political science concerns ingroup-outgroup conflict. Cliques, gangs, ethnic chauvinism, nationalism, wars—these can all be discussed in terms of our tendency to value people we see as part of our group and devalue those we see as part of another group. Formal team sports feed into our impulse to make such group distinctions, in ways that informal sports do not.[3] Of course, enlightened coaches of formal sports may lecture about good sportsmanship and valuing the other team, but we all know how much good lecturing does for children—or for adults, for that matter.

Lesson 5: Playing well and having fun really are *more important than winning.* "Playing well and having fun are more important than winning" is a line often used by Little League coaches after a loss, rarely after a win. But with spectators watching, with a trophy on the line, and with so much attention paid to the score, one has to wonder how many of the players believe that line, and how many secretly think that Vince Lombardi had it right. The view that "winning is the only thing" becomes even more prominent as one moves up to high school and then to college sports, especially in football and basketball, which are the sports American schools care most about. As they move up the ladder from children's leagues to high school to college to professional, an ever smaller number make the teams. The rest become spectators for the rest of their lives, growing fat in the stands and on the couch—*unless* they learn to play informally.

In informal sports, playing well and having fun really are more important than winning. Everyone knows that; you don't have to try to convince anyone with a lecture. And you can play regardless of your level of skill. The whole point of an informal game is to have fun and stretch your own skills, sometimes in new and creative ways that would be disallowed or jeered at in a formal game. You might, for example, try batting with a narrow stick, to improve your eye. You might turn easy catches in the outfield into difficult over-the-shoulder catches. If you are a better player than the others, these are ways to self-handicap, which make the game more interesting for everyone. In a formal game, where winning matters, you could never do such things; you would be accused of betraying your team. Of course you have to be careful about when and where to make these creative changes in your play, even in the informal game. You have to know how to do it without offending others or coming across as a show-off. Always, in informal play, you have to consult your inner social guide.

In my experience, both as a player and observer, players in informal sports are much more intent on playing beautifully than on winning. The beauty may lie in new, creative ways of moving that allow you to express yourself and stretch your physical abilities while still coordinating your actions to mesh with those of others. The informal game, at its best, is an innovative group dance, in which the players create their own moves, within the boundaries of the agreed-upon rules, while taking care not to step on each other's toes. I've played formal games, too, where varsity championships were at stake, and those were not creative dances. If stepping on toes helped you win those games, you stepped on them.

WHICH IS BETTER TRAINING for real life, the informal game or the formal one? The answer seems clear to me. Real life is an informal game. The rules are endlessly modifiable and you must do your part to create them. In the end, there are no winners or losers; we all wind up in the same place. Getting along with others is far more important than beating them. What matters in life is how you play the game, how much fun you have along the way, and how much joy you give to others. These are the lessons of informal social play, and they are far, far more important than learning the coach's method for throwing a curveball or sliding into second base. I'm not against formal sports for kids who really want them, but such sports are no substitute for informal play when it comes to learning the lessons we all must learn to live a satisfying life.

In an essay about informal sports as they are played at the Sudbury Valley School, Michael Greenberg, a former student at the school, presented some of these same thoughts more poetically than I. He wrote, in part:

> In all the years of playing very physical games like football, soccer, and basketball [at Sudbury Valley], there has never been an injury beyond a minor cut or bruise. People play all these sports in their regular clothes without any of the standard protective equipment that is normally required. How can this be explained when people wearing protective pads injure each other with alarming frequency? Because in a regimented, performance-oriented way of looking at sports (or life), making sure you don't hurt someone becomes less important than winning. So it doesn't matter how much you talk about "sportsmanship" or how many safety pads you wear, people are going to get hurt. When you approach sports (or life) as a fun, exciting process, as something that is done for the sheer joy and beauty of doing it, then not hurting someone, not impairing their ability to enjoy the same process, becomes a top priority. . . . To participate in an activity where the clash of unequal bodies is transformed through teamwork, pursuit of personal excellence, responsibility, and restraint into a common union of equal souls in pursuit of meaningful experience has been one of the most profound experiences of my life. I am sure it has had a similar effect on others.[4]

Lessons from Sociodramatic Play

Children learn valuable social lessons in all sorts of free social play, not just in informal sports. As illustration, here's a real example of the kind of imaginative play that researchers refer to as *sociodramatic* play, where children adopt roles and act out story lines together. All over the world, such play predominates among children in the age range of three to six.

Annie (age five years, eleven months) and Beth (five years, two months) were video-recorded by researchers Hans Furth and S. R. Kane as they played an imaginary game in the dress-up area of their after-school day-care center.[5] Annie started the game by saying, "Let's pretend that we had a ball tomorrow night and we had to get our stuff ready." Beth responded by picking up a dress and saying, "This was my dress," thereby demonstrating her implicit acceptance of the play idea and her eagerness to get the prop she wanted most. For the next twenty minutes, the two picked their clothing and accessories and discussed what would happen at the ball. Much of this time was spent haggling over who would play which role and who would get to use which props. They haggled over fancy items of clothing, a telephone, a table, a pair of binoculars, and where each would sleep the night before the ball. In each little argument, each girl gave reasons why she "needed" or "should have" that prop or role, but did so tactfully so as not to offend the other player.

Then, when Annie and Beth had come to a fairly satisfactory agreement on these issues, another little girl, Celia (age four years, nine months) came into the dress-up area from outdoors and asked to join them. They let her in, and then all three began a new round of negotiations about props and roles to include Celia. Each girl felt strongly about such matters as which clothes she would wear, what exactly would happen at the ball, and who was older and had higher status in the play. For the play to go on, they had to reach consensus on every major issue.

For example, Annie and Beth both thought that Celia, the youngest and smallest of the three, should be the "little sister," but Celia emphatically refused that role. To mollify her, Annie and Beth agreed that Celia could be the "big sister." Then, to preserve their relative status, Annie and Beth elevated themselves to the rank of mothers. There was some discussion of whether Celia could have two mothers, since "really, a person can have only one mother," which they resolved by deciding that one would be the stepmother. All three girls wanted to be named Gloria, which they decided was okay. All three girls wanted to marry the prince and become a queen. Beth and Annie acknowledged that in real life the prince could marry only one of them, but decided that "just for pretend" it would be okay for him to marry both of them. However, the idea of his also marrying Celia was too much for them to accept, even in their play, so they refused Celia's request that he marry her, too. To placate her, however, they elevated Celia still further to the role of "big sister princess."

These three girls were already skilled social players, and they were clearly becoming more skilled through the kind of practice that this play episode illustrates. Among the biggest lessons of such play are those of self-assertion, negotiation, and compromise. Each girl had to present her case skillfully to come as close as possible to getting what she wanted without upsetting the other players. In their manner of speech, the girls demonstrated that they understood the necessity of gaining consensus. For example, their proposals on how to play usually took the form of suggestions rather than demands. Most proposals ended with tag questions, such as "okay?" or "all right?" or "right?"

In their negotiations the girls frequently referred to certain rules that had become, by tradition, regular rules of play among the children in this day-care center. One was the finder's rule. Whoever first found or claimed a prop was generally the one who got to use it. However, an even higher rule, which could trump the finder's rule, was the fairness rule. It would not be right for one child to have all or most of the desired props; they had to be divided in a way that seemed at least reasonably fair to all. Players in all sorts of games are emphatic in their insistence on fairness, though they may disagree about the nature of that ideal state and how to reach it.

Another rule often invoked (not by this name) was the consistency rule. The play had to be internally consistent. For example, when Annie, who was eager for the ball to get under way, impulsively announced that the ball was about to begin, Beth reminded her that they had already decided that it wouldn't begin until the next day. They had to have a pretend night of sleep before the ball could begin. Annie understood and immediately conceded the point. The play also, to some degree at least, had to be consistent with the girls' understanding of how things are in the real world. Sometimes they could bend that rule, as when they decided that both Annie and Beth would marry the prince, but such bending required discussion, agreement, and, generally, acknowledgment that this was not how things worked in reality. As they played, the girls also affirmed and consolidated their understandings of certain conventions and rules in the real world. According to Furth and Kane's analysis, sociodramatic play is a means by which young children develop and exercise mental models of the society in which they live. In the researchers' words, children "construct society" through their play.

The three little girls were playing, doing what they wanted to do. But because what they wanted to do was to play an elaborate make-believe game with the other girls, they couldn't do *exactly* what they wanted to. They had to work out compromises and agreements with the others, and they had to control their impulses to cohere with the roles and story lines they had agreed upon. This is the magic of children's social play. By doing what they want to do, which is to play with other children, children learn to compromise and *not* do exactly what they want to do. Celia wanted to become a queen, but she was okay being "big sister princess." All of the girls wanted the most beautiful dress-up clothes, but they had to divide them up in a way that seemed fair enough to each of them. Annie at some point wanted the ball to start immediately—she was so eager for the prince to propose to her—but she had to control this impulse to maintain consistency with the narrative that the girls had already decided upon. All of this self-control and compromise occurred with no adult intervention. In fact, adult intervention would have ruined it. The children clearly enjoyed exercising their own power, intelligence, and capacity for self-restraint as they negotiated with one another, with no adult input at all.

I used this example of play because it was recorded and available, but there is nothing unique about it. Watch any group of little children playing together, who have had extensive experience at such play, and you will see amazing social minds at work. But watch from a distance, inconspicuously. If you watch boys you may find that they are not as tactful as Annie, Beth, and Celia in their negotiations, but they, too, generally figure out ways to meet one another's needs for the sake of the game.

It's not possible to conduct long-term experiments to see if children who are allowed more opportunity for play of this sort develop greater social skills than those who aren't, but correlational studies and short-term experiments, as well as common sense, strongly support this hypothesis. Children who engage in more sociodramatic play have, by various measures, been shown to demonstrate more empathy, and more ability to understand what another person thinks, knows, or desires, than do children who engage in less.[6] Moreover, several short-term experiments conducted in preschools have shown that when some children are provided with extra opportunity to engage in sociodramatic play and others are not, those in the extra-play groups later exhibit higher performance on various measures of social perspective-taking and ability to get along with others than do those in the control groups.[7]

Children's Play in the Holocaust

We turn now from the sweet scene of three little girls in the dress-up area of a playroom to terrible scenes—children in Nazi concentration camps. If play were a luxury, children here would not have played. But play is not a luxury. Play is children's means of making sense of their environment and adapting to it, as best they can, regardless of the type of environment. In the remarkable book *Children and Play in the Holocaust,* historian George Eisen, using diaries and interviews of survivors as evidence, described play among Jewish children in Nazi ghettos and concentration camps.[8]

In the ghettos, the first stage in concentration before prisoners were sent off to labor and extermination camps, parents tried desperately to divert their children's attention from the horrors around them and to preserve some semblance of the innocent play the children had known before. They created makeshift playgrounds and tried to lead the children in traditional games. The adults themselves played in ways aimed at psychological escape from their grim situation, if they played at all. For example, one man traded a crust of bread for a chessboard, because by playing chess he could forget his hunger. But the children would have none of that. They played games designed to confront, not avoid, the horrors. They played games of war, of "blowing up bunkers," of "slaughtering," of "seizing the clothes of the dead," and games of resistance. At Vilna, Jewish children played "Jews and Gestapomen," in which the Jews would overpower their tormenters and beat them with their own rifles (sticks).

Even in the extermination camps, the children who were still healthy enough to move around played. In one camp they played a game called "tickling the corpse." At Auschwitz-Birkenau they dared one another to touch the electric fence. They played "gas chamber," a game in which they threw rocks into a pit and screamed the sounds of people dying. One game of their own devising was modeled after the camp's daily roll call and was called *klepsi-klepsi,* a common term for stealing. One playmate was blindfolded; then one of the others would step forward and hit him hard on the face; and then, with blindfold removed, the one who had been hit had to guess, from facial expressions or other evidence, who had hit him. To survive at Auschwitz, one had to be an expert at bluffing—for example, about stealing bread or about knowing of someone's escape or resistance plans. Klepsi-klepsi may have been practice for that skill.

In play, whether it is the idyllic play we most like to envision or the play described by Eisen, children bring the realities of their world into a fictional context, where it is safe to confront them, to experience them, and to practice ways of dealing with them. Some people fear that violent play creates violent adults, but in reality the opposite is true. Violence in the adult world leads children, quite properly, to play at violence. How else can they prepare themselves emotionally, intellectually, and physically for reality? It is wrong to think that somehow we can reform the world for the future by controlling children's play and controlling what they learn. If we want to reform the world, we have to reform the world; children will follow suit. The children must, and will, prepare themselves for the real world to which they must adapt to survive.

Children's use of play to adapt to trauma has also been observed in other situations closer to home. For instance, a group of children who, unfortunately, had seen a man fall twenty feet to the ground and suffer serious injury outside their nursery school window were much distressed by this experience. For months afterward they played, on their own initiative, at such themes as falling, injury, hospitals, and death.[9] Children who have experienced terrorist attacks against them or their parents have likewise been observed to play at themes that involve reenactment coupled with some sort of soothing.[10] The soothing in their play may involve repair and mending of damages, protection and nurturance for those left behind, or the eventual triumph of good over evil.

Even children who have never experienced any particular trauma, beyond the little ones everyone experiences, often play at emotion-arousing, traumatic scenes. In doing so, they may be steeling themselves to deal with all sorts of unpredictable but inevitable unhappy and painful events. Researcher Gisela Wegener-Spöhring has described instances of such play among normal, well-adjusted kindergarteners in Germany.

For example, she described a scene of "whipping play," in which a popular boy sat bound in a chair while being whipped, with relatively hard blows with a leather strap, by his playmates.[11] To comfort him as he was being whipped, two girls gave him blocks as bananas to eat. The boys doing the whipping stopped occasionally to give him pretend drinks of water. This appeared to be highly enjoyable play for all of the participants, on the important life theme of pain and soothing for pain. According to Wegener-Spöhring, the only real violence related to this play occurred when the kindergarten teacher came over and stopped it, because she felt it was aggressive. Wegener-Spöhring contends that disruption of good play, when there is no good reason to do so, is always an act of violence and tends to produce a violent reaction. When the whipping game was forcibly stopped, the children's tempers turned bad. They began knocking over chairs and misbehaving in other ways, in apparent acts of rebellion.

The Value of "Dangerous" Play

Researchers who study play in animals have suggested that a major evolutionary purpose of play is to help the young learn how to cope with emergencies.[12] Juvenile mammals of all species deliberately and repeatedly put themselves into awkward, moderately dangerous, moderately frightening situations in their play. As they playfully gallop, leap, and chase one another around they continuously alternate between losing and regaining control of their bodily movements. When goat kids jump, for example, they twist and turn in ways that make it difficult to land. Young monkeys and apes playfully swinging in trees choose branches that are sufficiently far apart and high enough off the ground to create a degree of fear, but not so high that a fall would cause serious injury. Young chimpanzees seem especially to enjoy games of dropping freely from high branches and then catching onto lower ones at the last moment before hitting the ground.

Young mammals of nearly all species play chase games. They race after one another and take turns at being the pursued and the pursuer. For most species, the apparently preferred position in such chases is that of being pursued.[13] A typical game—for a pair of young monkeys, lambs, or squirrels, for example—starts with one youngster playfully attacking the other and then running off while looking back to be sure that the provoked playmate is pursuing. Observers of monkey play have noted that the chased animal generally shows more evidence of delight in the game—such as a broad playface (the monkey equivalent of a smile)—than does the pursuer.[14] Apparently, the reward for chasing is the opportunity to take a turn at being chased. When the pursuer catches and "tags" the other (typically with a playful nip), the erstwhile pursuer turns and joyfully becomes the pursued. Notice that the preferred position is the position of greatest vulnerability. The one who is running away has less control over what is happening, has less opportunity to stop and take a break, and is more vulnerable to falling and injury than is the one who is running after. The vulnerability itself seems part and parcel of the sense of thrill.

In addition to chasing games, young mammals, especially young males, engage in a great deal of playful fighting. Depending on the species, they butt heads, attempt to throw each other to the ground, attempt to pin each other, and try to give each other playful nips at specific target locations. Unlike in a real fight, in a play fight the larger and more skilled animal deliberately self-handicaps to avoid dominating the playmate. Detailed studies of juvenile rats play fighting suggest that for this species at least, each animal prefers to be in the subordinate position, which, again, offers the greatest physical and emotional challenge.[15] One rat will self-handicap to allow the playmate to get into the attack, on-top position and then will struggle to recover. Over time, the playmates alternate, so each can practice recovering from the vulnerable position.

Even casual observation shows that human children, like other young mammals, deliberately put themselves into fear-inducing, vulnerable positions in their play. They do this as they climb high in trees, dive off high towers or cliffs, leap over crevices from rock to rock, perform tricks on playground equipment, or skateboard down banisters. In their playful fighting, young children, like other young mammals, alternate between getting into and out of vulnerable positions.[16] The stronger partner self-handicaps, to allow the weaker partner to break free from being pinned and to allow that partner to get into the attack position, so both can experience the thrill of being in the vulnerable position and escaping from it. In all of this, young humans are much like the young of other mammals, and they are apparently learning the same crucial lessons.

Think about the universal pleasure of chasing games. The three-year-old girl squeals with almost unbearable joy as she flees from the terrible monster, in the form of her father or big brother, who threatens to catch her and eat her for breakfast. In every human chasing game I can think of, the preferred position is that of being chased. In nightmares and in real life, nothing is more terrifying than being chased by a predator or monster. But in play, nothing is more delightful.

The most universal and basic of all human chasing games is tag. Children everywhere play it, and the goal, always, is to spend as much time being chased, and as little time chasing, as possible. The punishment for being caught is that you become "it," and then you must serve time as chaser until you catch someone and can once again enjoy being chased. As children grow older they play increasingly sophisticated versions of tag, with rules that give additional structure to the game. A typical example is "fox and geese," which my childhood friends and I played on ice skates, on paths carved through the snow on frozen ponds in Minnesota. The preferred position always was to be a goose, not the fox. If you were caught, you had to be the fox until you caught someone and could again be a goose. Hide-and-seek and dodgeball are not exactly chasing games, but they, too, follow the rule: the preferred position is to be pursued. Punishment for being found, or for being hit by the ball, is that you have to be a pursuer.

Even formal team sports, such as soccer, American football, basketball, and hockey, can be understood as complex versions of tag. The joy lies in running across a field or court—kicking or carrying or dribbling a ball, or pushing a puck, toward some goal—while a horde of "enemies" chase after you. Baseball, too, is a form of tag. The batter, after hitting the ball, tries to run around a specified loop, from one safe point to another, while the other team tries to tag him out. In all such games, the teams alternate between offense and defense, and the preferred position is offense, in which you are chased as you run through "enemy" ground.

In many such vigorous activities, children are testing their own fear as well as their physical prowess. The combination of fear and joy is the feeling we call thrill. In such play children must be in charge of their own activities, because only they know how to dose themselves with the right amount of fear. Children swinging on swing sets or climbing trees or ropes know how high to go to generate the level of fear that for them creates excitement but not terror. No parent, coach, or gym teacher can ever make that judgment for them. In the "whipping game" described by Wegener-Spöhring, the boy being whipped would have signaled the whipping to stop if it became too painful. In all forms of playful fighting and chasing, each child has the right to call time-out or to quit if the emotional or physical challenge becomes too great. Without that right, the activity is no longer play.

In our culture today, parents and other adults overprotect children from possible dangers in play. We seriously underestimate children's ability to take care of themselves and make good judgments. In this respect, we differ not just from hunter-gatherer cultures (as described in Chapter 2), but from all traditional cultures in which children played freely. Our underestimation becomes a self-fulfilling prophecy—by depriving children of freedom, we deprive them of the opportunities they need to learn how to take control of their own behavior and emotions.

The Decline of Empathy and the Rise of Narcissism

As I discussed in Chapter 1, the decline of children's free play since about 1955 has been accompanied by a continuous rise in anxiety, depression, and feelings of helplessness in young people. Related to these findings, there has also been an increase in narcissism and decline in empathy.

Narcissism refers to an inflated view of the self, which tends to separate the self from others and prevent the formation of meaningful two-way relationships. Since the late 1970s, it has been assessed in normative groups of college students using the Narcissistic Personality Inventory (NPI), a questionnaire designed to tap the degree to which people are primarily concerned about themselves versus the degree to which they are concerned about others. *Empathy* is more or less the opposite of narcissism. It refers to a tendency to connect emotionally with others, to see things from others' point of view, and to feel sympathy for others' misfortunes. It has been assessed in normative groups of college students since the late 1970s with a questionnaire called the Interpersonal Reactivity Index. Scores on these questionnaires reveal a significant rise in narcissism over the years and a significant decline in empathy.[17] The questionnaire scores are apparently valid measures; they correlate with real-world behaviors. For example, people who score high on narcissism have been found to overrate their own abilities compared to those of others, to lash out angrily in response to criticism, and to commit white-collar crimes at higher rates than the general population.[18] Those who score low on empathy are more likely than the average person to engage in bullying and less likely to volunteer to help people in need.[19]

From all I have said in this chapter, it should be no mystery why a decline in play would be accompanied by a rise in emotional and social disorders. Play is nature's way of teaching children how to solve their own problems, control their impulses, modulate their emotions, see from others' perspectives, negotiate differences, and get along with others as equals. There is no substitute for play as a means of learning these skills. They can't be taught in school. For life in the real world, these lessons of personal responsibility, self-control, and sociability are far more important than any lessons that can be taught in school.

In addition to the correlational evidence and logical arguments linking a decline in play to a stunting of emotional and social development, there is also experimental evidence. We obviously can't conduct long-term experiments in which human children are deliberately deprived of play. However, such experiments can and have been conducted with animals. In some experiments, for example, rhesus monkeys have been raised with just their mothers and then compared to other rhesus monkeys who were raised more normally, with access to peers as well as mothers.[20] Monkey mothers interact in many ways with their young, but they do not play with them, so those in the former group were deprived of play throughout their development. Not surprisingly, when tested as young adults, they were found to be abnormal in many ways. They showed excessive fear and excessive aggression. When placed in a novel environment, which would elicit a small degree of fear in a normal monkey, these monkeys reacted with terror and did not adapt to the environment over time as a normal monkey would. When placed with peers, they failed to respond appropriately to the other animals' social signals and invitations. When a peer attempted to groom them, for example, they would lash out aggressively rather than accept the friendly overture. They also failed to show appropriate aggression-reducing signals in the presence of other monkeys and were therefore attacked more often than normal monkeys.

Similar experiments have been conducted with rats, with similar results. Rats raised without peer playmates exhibit abnormally high levels of both fear and aggression in various behavioral tests.[21] In one set of experiments, some otherwise peer-deprived young rats were allowed to interact for an hour per day with a playful peer while others were allowed to interact for an hour per day with a peer that had been rendered nonplayful by injection of the drug amphetamine.[22] Amphetamine knocks out the play drive in young rats without knocking out other social behaviors. The result was that rats with experience playing with a peer behaved much more normally in adulthood than did those with the same amount of exposure to a nonplayful peer. Apparently the essential interactions between young rats for normal emotional and social development occur in play. In other experiments, play-deprived young rats showed abnormal patterns of brain development. Without play, neural pathways running from frontal areas of the brain—areas known to be crucial for controlling impulses and emotions—failed to develop normally.[23]

It may seem cruel to raise young monkeys, and even young rats, in conditions where they cannot play freely with peers, for the sake of science. But if that is cruel, then what can we say about our current "normal" practice of depriving human children of free play with other children for the sake of protecting and educating them? It's cruel indeed, and dangerous.

What About Video Games?

The one form of play that hasn't declined in recent decades is video games. Some people blame such games, along with television, for the decline in outdoor play. They argue that television programming and video play are so seductive that they hold children at the screen and keep them from other activities. I understand the argument and see why it is compelling to some, but it doesn't fit well with my own observations or with researchers' findings from systematic surveys.

At Sudbury Valley, students can play and explore in whatever ways they like for as long as they like. All of them have unlimited access to computers and television, and almost all of them play and enjoy video games. But most of them also spend lots of time playing and exploring in the fields and woods outdoors. Surveys of game players in the general population, likewise, indicate that kids who are free to play outdoors as well as with video games usually, over time, choose a balance between the two.[24] Those who seem to become addicted to the games are generally those for whom other satisfying forms of play are not available.[25] Video-game play appears to compete much more with television watching than with outdoor play for children's free time. Overall, according to surveys, gamers do not play outdoors any less than do nongamers, but they do watch less television.[26] In fact, one recent large-scale study of factors promoting outdoor play among children in Holland revealed—to the surprise of some—that children who had a computer or a television in their own room played outdoors significantly *more*, not less, than did otherwise comparable children who had neither in their room.[27]

It seems to me that the decline in children's outdoor play has been caused primarily by the rise of parental fears and by other societal changes (described in Chapter 10) that have reduced children's opportunities to play freely outdoors. The increased video play seems to have come about for two reasons. First, the games really are fun and are becoming more so all the time as the technology and thought that goes into producing them has advanced. Second, as kids are more and more monitored and controlled by adults in the real world, the virtual world has emerged as a place where many of them can still be free. The nine-year-old may not be allowed to walk to the corner store by himself, but he is allowed to enter into and explore freely an exciting virtual world filled with all sorts of dangers and delights.

When kids are asked, in focus groups and surveys, what they like about video games, they generally talk about freedom, self-direction, and competence.[28] In the game, they make their own decisions and strive to meet challenges that they themselves have chosen. At school and in other adult-dominated contexts they may be treated as idiots who need constant direction, but in the game they are in charge and can solve difficult problems and exhibit extraordinary skills. In the game, age does not matter—skill does. In these ways, video games are like all other forms of true play. Far from contributing to the generational rise in anxiety, depression, and helplessness, video games appear to be a force that is helping to relieve those afflictions. This seems to be especially true in recent times, with the emergence of so-called massively multiplayer online role-playing games, such as *World of Warcraft*, which are far more social than previous video games and offer endless opportunities for creativity and problem solving.[29]

In these online games, players create a character (an avatar) that has unique physical and psychological traits and assets, and as that character, enter an extraordinarily complex and exciting virtual world simultaneously occupied by countless other players, who in their real-life forms may be anywhere on the planet. Players go on quests within this virtual world, and along the way they meet other players, who might become friends or foes. Players may start off playing solo, avoiding others, but to advance to the higher levels they have to make friends and join with others in mutual quests. Making friends within the game requires essentially the same skills as making friends in the real world. You can't be rude. You have to understand and abide by the etiquette of the culture you are in. You have to learn about the goals of a potential friend and help that individual to achieve those goals. Depending on how you behave, players may put you on their *friends* list or their *ignore* list, and they may communicate positive or negative information about you to other players. The games offer players endless opportunities to experiment with different personalities and ways of behaving, in a fantasy world where there are no real-life consequences for failing.

Players in these games can also form special-interest groups called *guilds*. To join, players must fill out an application, much like a job application, explaining why they would be valuable members. Guilds typically have structures similar to companies in the real world, with leaders, executive boards, and even recruitment personnel. Such games are in many ways like the imaginative sociodramatic games of preschool children, but played in a virtual world, with communication by online text, and raised up many notches in sophistication to fit the interests and abilities of the older children, teenagers, and adults who play them. Like all sociodramatic games, they are anchored in an understanding of the real world, and they exercise concepts and social skills that are relevant to that world. A study commissioned by the IBM Corporation concluded that the leadership skills exercised within these games are essentially the same as those required to run a modern company in the real corporate world.[30]

Much of the early research on video games was motivated by fears that the violent content in some of the games would increase young people's violent behavior in the real world. For those who have taken the trouble to examine it seriously, that research has quelled the initial fears.[31] There is no evidence that killing animated characters on a screen increases a person's likelihood of harming people in real life. In fact, some studies suggest that the pretend violence of video games helps young people learn to control and regulate their emotions, perhaps in much the same way that "dangerous" outdoor play does. One study, for example, revealed that college students who regularly played violent video games felt *less* hostility, and also less depression, after a frustrating mental task than did college students who rarely or never played such games.[32] I have to admit that I personally cannot play video games, or watch movies, that include graphic depictions of violence, because I find them revolting. But nothing in the research literature leads me to argue that there is any moral virtue in my avoiding such games and movies. I never forbade my children from such pretend violence, and they have grown up to be completely nonviolent, morally virtuous citizens.

More recently, researchers have begun to pay attention to the *positive* effects of video games. Several experiments have shown that playing fast-paced action video games can quite markedly increase players' scores on tests of visuospatial ability, including components of standard IQ tests.[33] Other studies suggest that depending on the type, video games can also increase scores on measures of working memory (the ability to hold several items of information in mind at once), critical thinking, and problem solving.[34] In addition, there is growing evidence that kids who previously showed little interest in reading and writing are now acquiring advanced literacy skills through the text-based communication in online video games.[35] And as I already mentioned, there is at least some evidence that playing high-action, emotion-arousing games helps young people learn to regulate their emotions in stressful situations. To date there has been little formal study of the social benefits of video games, but many anecdotal reports attest to such benefits, and what research has been done suggests that frequent video game players are, on average, better adjusted socially than their nonplaying peers.[36]

The route to getting our kids outdoors is not to throw away the computer or the television set, no more than it is to throw away the books we have in our homes. These are all great sources of learning and enjoyment. Rather, the route is to make sure kids have real opportunities to play freely outdoors, with other kids, without interference from adults. Kids in today's world need to become highly skilled with computers, just as hunter-gatherer kids needed to become highly skilled with bows and arrows or digging sticks. To develop such skills, they need freedom and opportunity to play with computers, the primary tools of today. But for healthy development, they also need freedom and opportunity to play outdoors, away from the house, with other kids. The key words here are *freedom* and *opportunity*—not coercion.

9

FREE AGE MIXING: A KEY INGREDIENT FOR CHILDREN'S CAPACITY FOR SELF-EDUCATION[1]

ONE MORNING AT the Sudbury Valley School, a remarkable scene unfolded before my eyes in the playroom.[2] A thirteen-year-old boy and two seven-year-old boys were creating, purely for their own enjoyment, a fantastic story involving heroic characters, monsters, and battles. The seven-year-olds gleefully shouted out ideas about what would happen next, while the thirteen-year-old, an outstanding artist, translated the ideas into a coherent story and sketched the scenes on the blackboard almost as fast as the younger children could describe them. The game continued for at least half an hour, which was as long as I permitted myself to watch before moving on to observe in other parts of the school. What a privilege, I thought, to be sole witness to an artistic creation that I know could not have been produced by seven-year-olds alone and almost certainly would not have been produced by thirteen-year-olds alone. The unbounded enthusiasm and creative imagery of the seven-year-olds I watched, combined with the advanced narrative and artistic abilities of the thirteen-year-old they played with, provided just the right chemical mix for this creative explosion to occur.

Daniel Greenberg, the visionary of Sudbury Valley whom I introduced in Chapter 5, has long contended that age mixing is the "secret weapon" that allows the school to succeed as an educational institution.[3] Likewise, Sugata Mitra has claimed that age mixing is a key to children's rapid learning from publicly available computers, in his studies of minimally invasive education in India (discussed in Chapter 6).[4] And as we have seen, anthropologists who have studied hunter-gatherer cultures have suggested that age mixing is vital to children's self-education in those cultures (Chapter 2).[5]

The free mingling of children who differ broadly in age is a key element to children's abilities to educate themselves successfully, on their own initiatives. Children learn by observing and interacting with others who are older and younger than they are. Yet education professors have paid almost no attention to the educative value of free age mixing; they are hooked on the idea that education is controlled by teachers and that it occurs most efficiently in settings where the students are all at the same level. They rarely, if ever, think about the idea that children can learn from one another in settings where they differ widely in age, skills, and levels of understanding.

From a historical perspective, and certainly from an evolutionary perspective, the segregation of children by age is an oddity—I would say a tragic oddity—of modern times. Children in hunter-gatherer cultures educated themselves through play and exploration with other children, and they necessarily did so in broadly age-mixed groups (as discussed in Chapter 2). Hunter-gatherer bands were small, and births were widely spaced, so children rarely would have had more than one or two potential playmates close in age. A typical group playing or exploring together might consist of half a dozen kids ranging in age from four to twelve, or seven to seventeen. The same was most likely true over the 99 percent or so of our species' history when we were all hunter-gatherers.[6]

Going back even further in our evolutionary history, age mixing among the young was also most likely the norm for our prehuman ancestors. Our great-ape relatives, including chimpanzees, bonobos, and gorillas, all live in small social groups, and females give birth to young one at a time. Therefore, play among young great apes normally involves individuals that differ considerably in age.[7] These observations suggest that the last common ancestors that we share with the great apes also lived in conditions in which same-age peers were rare. It would seem that our play instincts, and our self-educative instincts, evolved over millions of years, going back at least to our split from the lineages leading to the other great apes, under conditions in which most social interactions among the young were age-mixed.

After the development of agriculture, beginning roughly 10,000 years ago, people began to live in larger social groups, and a greater food supply allowed births to be more closely spaced. This development increased the opportunities for interactions among children close in age (hereafter called same-age interactions). Still, age mixing remained (and remains) the norm in traditional, non-Western, non-schooled societies, in part because children in such societies are expected to care for their younger siblings, which generally means including them in their playgroups.[8] Not until the large-scale expansion of compulsory, age-graded schooling, beginning about a hundred years ago in Western societies, were large numbers of children required to spend significant amounts of time in age-segregated settings.

Within the past three or four decades, in the United States and many other Western and Westernized nations, the degree of age segregation imposed on children has increased further, to a startling degree. Many children today spend not only their school hours, but also most if not all of their out-of-school time in settings where they have little opportunity to play with children who differ from them by more than a year or two in age. The decline in the size of nuclear families, the weakening of extended family ties, fears about negative influences that older children might have on younger ones, the decline in free neighborhood play, the increased amounts of time spent at school, and the proliferation of after-school programs and other adult-directed, age-segregated activities for children have conspired to reduce greatly children's opportunities to get to know others who are several years older or younger than them. The graded school model has commandeered our culture's thought about childhood. Many people today, including many psychologists who study child development, seem to think it is natural for children to interact with only two categories of people: same-age peers and adult caregivers or teachers.[9]

The Sudbury Valley School is one of the few settings in modern North America where age mixing of a degree comparable to that in hunter-gatherer societies and other traditional societies persists. The students, who number from about 130 to 180 and range in age from four to the late teens, are free all day to interact with whom they please, and they spend a good portion of their time interacting with students who are much older or younger. To document the extent of age mixing at Sudbury Valley, my research colleague Jay Feldman toured the school buildings and grounds fourteen times over the course of several weeks and recorded the membership of every group of two to seven students who were interacting with one another. When we analyzed those results, we found that more than half of the social interactions among students spanned age gaps greater than two years, and a quarter of them spanned gaps greater than four years.[10] We found that age mixing was especially common in play; it was less common in serious conversations. In a subsequent long-term qualitative study, Feldman and I documented and analyzed nearly two hundred separate scenes involving social interactions between adolescents (which we defined as age twelve and older) and younger children (defined as less than twelve years old and more than four years younger than the oldest adolescent in the interaction).[11]

What do children gain from interacting freely with children who differ from them in age? That is what the rest of this chapter is about.

I begin by examining the benefits to the younger children in age-mixed groups and then turn to the benefits to the older ones. Most of the examples come from observations at Sudbury Valley, but some are from the work of other researchers who have observed age-mixed interactions in non-Western societies or in special experimental settings in Western schools where students in different grades are allowed limited opportunities to interact.

The Value of Free Age Mixing for Younger Children

In age-mixed groups, the younger children can engage in and learn from activities that would be too complex, difficult, or dangerous for them to do on their own or only with others their own age. They can also learn simply from watching the more sophisticated activities of older children and overhearing their conversations. And they can receive emotional support and care beyond what age-mates could provide. These benefits may in some ways seem obvious, but here I'll elaborate to show how valuable such opportunities are to children's physical, social, emotional, and intellectual development.

Playing in the Zone of Proximal Development

Imagine two four-year-olds trying to play a game of catch. They can't do it. Neither can throw the ball straight enough or catch it well enough to make the game work. They soon tire of running after the ball and give up. Now imagine a four-year-old and an eight-year-old playing the same game. The older child can lob the ball gently into the hands of the younger one and can leap and dive to catch the younger one's wild throws. Both players can enjoy this game and learn from it, as they extend their throwing and catching skills. In a world of just four-year-olds there is no catch, but in a world that includes eight-year-olds as well as four-year-olds, catch becomes possible and enjoyable for all. The same is true for countless other activities.

In the 1930s, Lev Vygotsky—the Russian psychologist introduced in Chapter 7—coined the term *zone of proximal development* to refer to the set of activities a child cannot do alone or with others of the same ability but can do in collaboration with others who are more skilled.[12] He suggested that children develop new skills and understanding largely by collaborating with others within their zones of proximal development. Extending Vygotsky's idea, the Harvard psychologist Jerome Bruner and his colleagues introduced the term *scaffolding* as a metaphor for the means by which skilled participants enable novices to engage in a shared activity.[13] The scaffolds consist of the reminders, hints, encouragement, and other forms of help that lift the child up to a higher form of activity. In the above example, playing catch is in the zone of proximal development for the four-year-old, and the eight-year-old erects scaffolds by throwing gently and by running to catch wild throws.

In the educational literature, Vygotsky's and Bruner's concepts are used most often to describe interactions between children and their parents or teachers. Feldman's and my observations, however, suggest that the concepts apply even better to age-mixed interactions among children, where nobody is officially teacher or learner, but all are simply having fun. Older children are closer in energy level, activity preferences, and understanding to the younger children than are adults, so it is more natural for them to behave within the younger ones' zones of proximal development. Moreover, because older children do not see themselves as responsible for the younger children's long-term education, they typically do not provide more information or help than the younger ones want or need. They do not become boring or condescending.

In age-mixed play, where abilities differ considerably, scaffolding occurs continuously and naturally, often unconsciously, as a way of pulling the younger children up to a level that makes the game fun for all.

Here are some examples that Feldman and I observed in the realm of physical play at Sudbury Valley. In a game of four square, the teenage players hit the ball hard into the squares of the older players, but hit it very gently into the square occupied by Ernie (age four), and they modified the rules so Ernie could catch and throw the ball rather than hit it.[14] In a wrestling game, three boys (ages eight to eleven) all attacked Hank (age eighteen), who responded by throwing them around in ways well calibrated to their abilities and sizes. Clint, the oldest of the attackers, was tossed the farthest; Jeff, the youngest, was tossed the shortest distance. Hank seemed to know precisely how far to throw each boy so as to induce maximal thrill without terrorizing or hurting anyone. In an exuberant bout of "boffing" (fencing with padded swords), Sam (age seventeen) adjusted his fencing maneuvers to accord with the skills and style of each member of the horde of six- to ten-year-olds who attacked him, thereby presenting each with a challenge without overpowering any of them. In a game of basketball, Ed (an athletic fifteen-year-old) rarely shot, but spent much time dribbling while the gang of eight- to ten-year-olds who made up the opposing team tried to steal the ball from him. Then he would pass to his single teammate, Daryl (age eight), and encourage him to shoot.

In each of these cases, the teenagers adjusted their play to allow the younger children to engage in, enjoy, and learn from the game. On the basketball court, for example, Ed permitted his young teammate to play a higher level of basketball than the latter otherwise could, by setting him up for shots under the basket and telling him when to shoot. But none of the teenagers' adjustments to accommodate the younger players were sacrifices. The older players clearly enjoyed the younger ones, and they played in ways that stretched their own skills as well as those of their young playmates. Hank's wrestling prowess and Sam's fencing ability were exercised fully, even as they practiced restraint, in fending off multiple young attackers. For Ed, shooting and scoring would have been too easy, no fun for anyone, but dribbling through a crowd of short, scrappy defenders and setting up his young teammate to shoot was a great, fun way to exercise his dribbling, passing, and play-making abilities.

We also saw many instances of scaffolding of mental skills at the school, the most obvious of which occurred in age-mixed card games and board games. Most children under about age nine cannot play complex games of this type with age-mates (though there are exceptions). They lose track of rules; their attention wanders; the game, if it ever begins, quickly disintegrates. But at Sudbury Valley, students younger than this regularly play such games with older students. The older students accept them into the game because they enjoy the younger ones, or because they need them in order to have enough players. The younger ones are able to play because the older ones remind them of what they have to do. "It's your turn." "Hold your cards up, so people can't see them." "Try to keep track of what cards have already been played." "Whoa, before you discard that, look around and see what's down on the table." Such reminders might sometimes be presented in an annoyed tone of voice, or preceded by "Hey, blockhead"—especially if the one helped is capable of being more attentive—but they are helpful nevertheless. Older children offer the help because they must, to keep the game going. In playing such games, the younger children exercise very basic mental skills, such as paying attention, remembering, and thinking ahead. These are the foundation skills that go into what we commonly call intelligence.

Young students at Sudbury Valley typically learn the three R's without formal instruction, and our observations of age-mixed interactions have helped us understand how that occurs. At any given time of day at the school, it is possible to find older and younger children collaborating on activities that involve numbers, reading, or writing. In card games, board games, and computer games in which scores are kept, older children teach younger ones how to compute scores, a process that usually involves addition and sometimes subtraction or more complex calculations. In games involving written words, older children read the words aloud to those who can't yet read, and they tell younger ones how to spell words that the latter wish to type or write. In the process, the younger ones learn to recognize the most frequently used words, which carries them well along the way toward reading.

According to staff members at the school, students are learning to read and write (or, more precisely, type) earlier now than they did when Feldman and I made most of our observations, primarily because of the increased popularity of computer games, e-mail, Internet social networking, and texting. Children of all ages are involved in a great deal of play and exploration in which the typed word is the primary mode of communication, so they are learning to read and type in much the same natural way by which they earlier learned to understand and produce oral speech.

Experimental innovations in more conventional schools have likewise provided evidence that age mixing can promote the acquisition of literacy skills. In one study, James Christie and Sandra Stone compared the behavior of kindergarteners in a classroom over two separate years.[15] During the first year, the classroom was age-mixed, including kindergarteners, first graders, and second graders. During the second year, the same classroom, with the same teacher, was kindergarten only. The classroom contained a set of play centers that remained constant over the two years, and the researchers videotaped the activity during free-play periods. In the age-mixed condition, the kindergarteners played most often in groups that included at least one and usually more than one first or second grader, and as a consequence, were often drawn by the older children into play that involved reading and writing. On a per-pupil basis, the kindergarteners engaged in nearly four times more reading and six times more writing in the age-mixed condition than in the same-age condition.[16] Most of this literacy behavior occurred in the context of sociodramatic play. For example, in play cooking children would read recipes, in playfully putting a baby to bed they would read bedtime stories, and in a play birthday party they would write labels on presents.

In another study, researcher Kay Emfinger videotaped free play among children ranging from four to ten years old at an age-mixed summer enrichment program.[17] She found many instances in which the older children exposed younger ones to numerical concepts that would have been beyond the latter's abilities to understand or use alone. For example, in one scene an older child explained to a younger one how to give exactly seven drops of medicine—by counting them, one through seven—to a sick doll. In another, an older child explained to a younger one, in a game of store, how much it would cost to purchase two items when one cost $10 and the other $5, and how much change to give for a $20 bill. Such concepts are far more meaningful to children in the context of their own, self-directed sociodramatic play, where they understand exactly how the concepts apply, than in the more abstract and less voluntary realm of typical classroom instruction.

At Sudbury Valley the youngest students are four years old, but research elsewhere shows that children younger than this also benefit from age-mixed play. Two- and three-year-olds are generally incapable of collaborative social play with others their own age. Instead, they engage in what is called parallel play; they play side by side, paying some attention to one another, but not merging their play into a socially combined activity.[18] In an age-mixed environment, however, older companions erect scaffolds that draw such toddlers into truly social play. Even four-year-olds are capable of raising the play level of three-year-olds. Two separate experiments, in different preschools, showed that three-year-olds engaged in much more social play, and less parallel play, when mixed with four-year-olds than when grouped just with other three-year-olds.[19]

In another study, conducted in thirty-six Mayan households in a Mexican village, researcher Ashley Maynard unobtrusively filmed pairs of siblings playing together in the normal context of the older child's responsibility to care for the younger one. She focused on pairs in which the younger child was two years old and the older one was anywhere from three to eleven. The children played at such everyday activities as making pretend tortillas, caring for baby dolls, and selling products at a make-believe store. According to Maynard, every play episode was also a teaching and learning episode, as the older children always helped the younger ones play in more advanced ways than they could have alone. Even the three-year-olds helped by providing models of more advanced actions, which the two-year-olds observed and imitated. In general, the older the play partner, the more skilled that partner was in increasing the complexity and sociability of the two-year-old's play.[20]

By the age of eight, these children were remarkably sophisticated guides for their younger siblings. They gave verbal explanations of how to play specific roles, provided them with appropriate props, helped them physically with difficult maneuvers, and modified their own activities in ways that allowed the two-year-olds to respond appropriately.

In one scenario, eight-year-old Tonik and two-year-old Katal played together at giving a baby doll a bath. Katal wanted to do the washing herself and Tonik enabled her to do so by demonstrating the process, providing her with a glass of water to pour over the doll, and giving her step-by-step verbal instructions on the appropriate way to wash a baby.

Learning by Observation

In an age-mixed environment, children learn from older children by watching and listening, even when they are not directly interacting with them. Through observing the activities of older children, younger ones get some idea of how those activities are done and become inspired to try them. Through hearing the more sophisticated language and thoughts of older children, younger ones expand their own vocabularies and improve their own thinking.

Part of the natural process of growing up is to look ahead, at those who are further along but not so far along as to be out of reach. Five-year-olds aren't particularly interested in emulating adults, who are too much in a different world. But five-year-olds do very much want to be like the cool eight- and nine-year-olds they see around them. If those eight- and nine-year-olds are reading and discussing books, or playing computer games, or climbing trees, or collecting Magic the Gathering cards, then the five-year-olds want to do that, too. Similarly, eight- and nine-year-olds look to young teens as models; young teens look to older teens; and older teens look to adults. This all occurs naturally in an age-mixed environment, such as Sudbury Valley. People don't have to establish themselves deliberately as models for younger children; they simply are.

In a small study of how and why children learn to read at Sudbury Valley, which two of my undergraduate students and I conducted years ago, some children told us that they became motivated to read primarily by observing older students reading and talking about what they had read. As one student put it, "I wanted the same magic they had; I wanted to join that club." Feldman's and my more formal research at the school focused on joint participation, not observational learning, but we could not help but notice that often when a group of students was doing something interesting, others—usually younger—would be watching intently. Sometimes the watching led to subsequent imitation of the watched activity. Here's an example from my own notebook of observations.

> As I sat near the school's playground I watched two ten-year-old girls easily and nonchalantly perform the trick of walking upright down the slide. A six-year-old girl nearby watched them more intently than I, and then she climbed the ladder and started gingerly to walk down the rather high and steep slide herself. This was clearly a challenge for the little girl. She walked with knees bent and hands down, ready to grab the rails if she lost balance. I also noticed that the two older girls remained next to the slide and looked on with a degree of apprehension, ready to catch her, but not too obviously so, if she should fall. One said, "You don't have to do it, you can just slide," but the little girl continued walking, slowly, and beamed with pride when she made it to the bottom. Shortly after that, the two older girls began climbing a nearby tree, and the younger girl followed them in that activity too. The little girl was clearly motivated to do, with effort, what the older girls could do with ease.

In our study of age-mixed interactions between adolescents and younger children, we noticed that the period of combined play was often preceded by a period in which the younger student watched the older one. The watching appeared to motivate the subsequent combined activity. Bridget (age seven), for example, watched Maggie (age twelve) play solitaire. When Maggie finished, Bridget asked her how to play. Maggie set out the cards, explained the rules, and helped the younger girl play a full game, occasionally pointing out where a card went. In another example, Scott (age thirteen) was making up and singing funny rap songs, with a golf club as a pretend microphone, while Noah (age seven) looked on laughing and giggling. Finally, Scott invited Noah into his play. He said, "Give me a beat." When Noah responded that he didn't know what that meant, Scott explained and demonstrated the process. Noah then copied Scott's "beat" sounds while Scott made up another rap.

In their graduation theses, in formal interviews, and in informal conversations, many of the school's students and graduates have talked about interests they developed from watching older students at the school. Among these are playing musical instruments, creating minia-ture objects from clay, cooking, developing film, programming com-puters, writing plays, and performing such physical feats as traversing the entire exterior of the main school building by clinging to footholds and handholds in the building's granite walls, without ever touching the ground. As anthropologist Irenäus Eibl-Eibesfelt has pointed out, based on his observations in many parts of the world, age mixing in a community over time permits the development of a child culture, in which each new "generation" of children acquires specific skills and knowledge from the older children and then passes them on to the next generation. [21] The first child who ever climbed around the outside of the school building at Sudbury Valley without touching the ground started a new cultural tradition, which continued to challenge new stu-dents decades later.

Younger children don't blindly mimic older ones. Rather, they watch, think about what they see, and incorporate what they learn into their own behavior in ways that make sense to them. Because of this, even the mistakes and unhealthy activities of older children can provide positive lessons for younger ones. One of the first students to do all of his primary and secondary education at Sudbury Valley—who was there throughout the 1970s, when the school still had a smoking room—told his father that he was glad he had hung around the teenagers in the smoking room when he was a young child.[22] By observing and listening to those older kids he learned a great deal, including the lessons that tobacco is addictive and that he did not want to jeopardize his own health and longevity by smoking. By the time he was a teenager and might have been tempted to smoke, he had long overcome any tendency to see smoking as "cool."

David Lancy is an anthropologist who has observed children playing and learning in many societies throughout the world, including traditional societies in Liberia, Papua New Guinea, and Trinidad. He is author of *The Anthropology of Childhood* and coauthor of *The Anthropology of Learning in Childhood,* in the latter of which he wrote, "The single most important form of learning is observation."[23] Very little explicit teaching occurs in traditional societies. Children in such societies do practice skills through active participation with more-skilled others, and some verbal instruction may accompany those activities, but most often children first learn about culturally relevant activities and skills by watching and overhearing their elders.

Lancy and a number of other anthropologists have suggested that Western schools—by indoctrinating students with the idea that learning occurs through top-down verbal instruction from a teacher and that copying others is cheating—may be teaching children *not* to learn through observation. By way of illustration, Lancy told me of a recent experience he had while skiing in Utah. A boy of about eleven years old, who had apparently never used a Poma lift before, approached this unusual type of ski lift without paying attention to how others were using it. When it was his turn to board, he held up the whole line of skiers behind him while he asked someone to teach him how to use the lift. In any non-Western culture, according to Lancy, a child in a similar situation would have had the sense to hold back and learn by watching how others did it. It is far more efficient to learn a task like riding a Poma lift by observation than by verbal instruction.

Indeed, there is some experimental evidence that children in the United States pay less attention to what is going on around them, and thereby learn less through observation, than do children in traditional non-Western cultures. In one such experiment, Maricela Correa-Chávez and Barbara Rogoff compared the observational learning of children in a traditional Mayan culture in Guatemala with that of middle-class European-American children in California.[24] The procedure was to bring pairs of siblings into the laboratory and to teach one child how to build a certain interesting toy (a moving mouse or a jumping frog) while the other one sat nearby and was given a different toy to play with. Then, in the crucial test, the child who had not been taught to build the toy, but who could have learned by observation, was asked to build it. The result was that the untaught Guatemalans demonstrated significantly more understanding of how to build the toy than did the untaught Americans. Moreover, within the Guatemalan group, those from the most traditional Mayan families learned more, through observation, than did those from the more Westernized families.

Receiving Care and Emotional Support

The prominent educational philosopher Nel Noddings has long argued that care is essential to education.[25] Children must feel safe and cared for in order to devote themselves fully to exploring and learning, and children learn best from those with whom they have caring, trusting relationships. Whether or not one agrees with all of Noddings's ideas about the relationship of care to education, it is hard to argue with the general idea that children are better off when surrounded by people who care for them than when surrounded by people who don't.

At Sudbury Valley, the continuous presence of older children, who know the younger ones well and care for them—in the context of the moral environment established by the school's democratic procedures— helps to ensure that young children feel safe and secure. In our tours of the school, we saw countless instances of older students exhibiting care and affection toward younger ones. For example, at almost any time of day, we could find young children sitting on teenagers' laps or snuggling next to them on a couch. In some cases the teenager was reading to, talking with, or playing with the young child, but in other cases the teen was engaged in his or her own activity and the child appeared to be there just for comfort and closeness. We also saw many instances of young children approaching older ones for help, advice, or approval, and most often the latter responded in ways that satisfied the child's needs or wishes. We observed teenagers helping young children find lost objects, reminding them to put away their toys, teaching them skills in the context of joint play, complimenting them on their creations, and resolving squabbles among them. As part of his research, Feldman identified thirty instances in which a younger student asked an older student for advice, instruction, or some other form of help, and in twenty-six of those cases the older student complied, usually gladly.[26] All this occurred even though the teenagers at the school have no formal responsibility to care for young children. They do so because they want to and because they find the young children's requests to be irresistible.

There is no way a single kindergarten or elementary school teacher, or even two of them, in a standard classroom of thirty or so students, could possibly provide the direct care and comfort to each child that the older students provide to the young ones at Sudbury Valley. The fact that the older ones care for the younger ones because they want to, not because they have to, makes the care all the more meaningful.

Almost no research has been conducted on the possible care and support that older students might provide for younger ones in conventional schools. A rare exception is a study by Jeffrey Gorrell and Linda Keel of a tutoring program at a university laboratory school, in which eighth graders tutored first graders three times a week for twenty-minute sessions.[27] The researchers report that at first the tutors spent most of their tutoring time trying to keep their young charges on task, but by the end of the first month the relationships became more playful and affectionate. The first graders began sitting on their tutors' laps and there was a marked increase in such signs of affection as hand-holding, kissing, head-patting, and good-natured banter. According to the researchers, the relationships that best satisfied the emotional needs and desires of the first graders were also the most successful in meeting the academic goals of the tutoring program. The little kids learned better from the older ones after they had established emotionally meaningful relationships with them than they did before. It's noteworthy that Gorrell and Keel's study was conducted roughly three decades ago—today such signs of affection would be outlawed in most conventional schools.

The Value of Free Age Mixing for Older Children

The advantages of age mixing go in both directions. By interacting with younger children, older ones practice leadership and nurturance, and they gain the experience of being the mature one in relationships (which is especially important for children without younger siblings). Older children also gain deeper understandings of concepts by teaching younger ones, which forces them to think about what they do or do not know. And just as older children inspire younger ones to engage in more complex or sophisticated activities than they otherwise would, younger children inspire older ones to engage in more creative activities than they otherwise would. Here I'll examine briefly each of these three categories of benefits for the older children; to a considerable degree, they are simply the flip sides of the benefits to the younger ones.

Learning to Nurture and Lead

At Sudbury Valley older children teach games to younger ones, adapt their athletic play so as to include younger ones, sometimes add structure to the younger ones' fantasy games, encourage them in their artwork and other projects, read to them, comfort them, hold them on their laps, help them find lost objects, help them settle disputes, and caution them about dangers. In such ways they practice the kinds of skills needed to be good parents, caregivers, and leaders. They do all this eagerly and willingly, not because they have to, but because something in them, which is part of human nature and is encouraged by the school's democratic, caring ethos, tells them that these are the appropriate ways to behave toward younger children.

We also observed scenes at the school in which older children discussed appropriate ways to behave toward younger ones or reprimanded younger children for failing to treat still younger ones kindly. In one scene, for example, three girls (ages six to eight) rather rudely excluded four-year-old Linda, who wanted to join them in folding origami papers. Nancy, age ten, who was reading nearby, happened to see this. She put down her book, went over to the three girls, and said, "How would you feel if you were pushed away like that?" The three girls then gave the four-year-old an origami paper and showed her how to fold it. In another scene, Sabrina (age seventeen) scolded Melinda (age eleven) for failing to put away the dress-up clothes that had been left out by the younger children with whom Melinda had been playing. Melinda responded that she wasn't responsible for the clothes because the other children, not she, had brought them out and worn them. Sabrina told her that it was still her responsibility because she (Melinda) knew the school rules and the younger children looked up to her as an example. Reprimands such as these seem to be much more effective when they come from older children than when they come from adults.

Feldman also documented several long-term friendships between teenagers and much younger students at the school.[28] In such cases the teenager seemed to take special pride in the younger one, almost as if the latter were his or her child, or a special niece or nephew, and seemed, consciously or not, to be practicing for parenthood. For example, Shawn, who at age nineteen was the oldest student at the school, spent a good deal of time with Rex (age five) and Jordan (age six). Shawn owned a special, gigantic set of Lego blocks, with which he would build extraordinary constructions that the younger children admired. Often he would leave this set in the playroom so that others could play with it, and on such occasions he would put Rex and Jordan "in charge," to be sure that the set wasn't misused and that the blocks were put away at the end. Rex and Jordan took this responsibility seriously and seemed proud that Shawn would trust them in this way. In the year after he graduated, Shawn visited the school three times, and on each occasion made a special point of visiting Rex and Jordan.

Consistent with our observations at Sudbury Valley, cross-cultural research suggests that the presence of much younger children elicits the nurturing instinct in older children and stimulates its growth. In a review of cross-cultural observations of children's social interactions, anthropologist Beatrice Whiting concluded that boys and girls every-where demonstrate more kindness and compassion toward children who are at least three years younger than they do toward those closer to their own age.[29] In a study conducted in a subsistence farming com-munity in Kenya, Carol Ember found that boys (ages eight to sixteen) who helped their mothers care for younger children and infants at home—because they had no sisters who could do this traditionally feminine task—were on average kinder, more helpful, and less aggres-sive in their interactions with their own peers than were boys without such babysitting experience.[30]

Further evidence that young people learn to be kind and caring through interactions with younger children comes from research in conventional schools. Studies of cross-age tutoring programs reveal that the experience of tutoring younger children leads the tutors to score higher on measures of responsibility, empathy, and helpfulness toward others.[31]

Even more impressive are findings coming from the Roots of Em-pathy program, founded by Mary Gordon in Toronto. Gordon devel-oped the program after years of working with abusive parents and abused children and observing that children who grew up unloved and surrounded by violence often became unloving and violent parents. The idea behind her new program was to bring real babies and their mothers (and sometimes their fathers) into school classrooms so that children from all backgrounds could gain experience looking at ba-bies, talking about babies, and thinking about what it is like to be a baby. The idea was that this would help set children on the road to be-coming, ultimately, better parents. She found, through experience, that her program also had a remarkable, more immediate effect on the classrooms that participated. The children who had this experience—of a monthly visit from a baby and parent—became kinder and more compassionate with one another. Bullying declined. Kids who had previously been teased and taunted for being different were now in many cases admired for their differences. The exposure to the infant and the discussions of the thoughts and feelings the infant evoked served as a powerful force for the spread of compassion throughout the classroom, an effect that lasted the whole month, from one baby visit to the next.

Here's a story from Gordon's book about her program.[32] The toughest and meanest-looking student in one eighth-grade class was a boy named Darren, who was two years older than the others because he had been held back. He was already growing a beard, had a tattoo on his partially shaved head, and was intimidating to all around him. Darren's mother had been murdered in front of his eyes when he was four years old, and he had lived in a series of foster homes. His defense against such pain and loneliness was to look and act tough. But the six-month-old baby who had been brought to the classroom and the discussions about the baby melted him. The mom had brought along a Snugli, a soft carrier trimmed with pink brocade, which she used to hold the baby close to her. Near the end of the class visit, after the class had spent forty minutes observing and talking about the baby, the mother asked if anyone wanted to try on the Snugli. To everyone's dismay, Darren raised his hand. With the Snugli strapped on, he then asked the mom if she would put the baby in it. With, I imagine, considerable apprehension, the mother did just that. Darren then sat quietly for several minutes in the corner rocking, while the baby snuggled contentedly into his arms and chest. When it was time for the baby and mother to leave, Darren asked the mother and the instructor, "If a person has never been loved, can he still be a good father?"

The Roots of Empathy program has now spread throughout Canada and made inroads into a number of other countries. Kimberly Schonert-Reichl, a psychology professor at the University of British Columbia, has conducted controlled studies purporting to show that the program significantly reduces aggression and increases kindness, not only on the day of the baby's visit, but throughout the school year.[33] In the age-segregated environment that we create with conventional schools, contrived means of bringing older children and younger ones into contact may be essential if we want to build up children's capacity for empathy and compassion.

Learning Through Teaching

Teaching, whether it occurs formally in a classroom or informally in our daily interactions with one another, challenges us intellectually. When we try to explain a concept to another person, we have to turn our sometimes rather vague understanding into words that are so clear that the other person, who may know nothing about the concept, can understand it. To do this we have to think deeply about the concept and sometimes even change our initial understanding of it. Teaching and learning have been described as bidirectional activities, in which the "teacher" and "learner" learn from each other.[34] Such bidirectionality occurs especially in cases where the status or authority difference between teacher and learner is not too great, so the latter feels comfortable questioning and challenging the former. Several studies of cross-age tutoring in conventional schools have shown that the tutors' as well as the tutees' understanding of the tutored concepts increases.[35]

When older children explain concepts to younger ones, they often articulate ideas that are at the edge of their own understanding. For example, the eight-year-old who explained the steps in bathing a baby to her two-year-old sister, in their doll play, may have been putting those steps into words, and thinking about them in a structured way, for the first time. Likewise, children helping others learn to read or to use numbers in the context of play are most likely making certain phonetic or numeric concepts clearer to themselves as they explain them and answer the younger ones' questions.

At Sudbury Valley, Feldman and I saw many instances of back-and-forth discussions between older and younger students that seemed to expand the understanding of both individuals. For example, when older students taught strategy games, such as chess, to younger ones, the questions asked by the younger children often led the older ones to stop and think before answering. They had to reflect on their own understanding of why one move was better than another before they could answer. They had to turn their gut understanding, acquired from experience, into conscious, clear verbal statements. It seems likely that such reflection made them more aware of what they knew and didn't know, which would lead them ultimately to a better understanding of the game.

We also saw such bidirectional teaching and learning in cases where younger students asked older ones for advice outside of the context of play. In one instance, for example, eight-year-old Eric was complaining to fourteen-year-old Arthur about how two other boys (ages nine and ten), who were his off-and-on friends, had been bothering him by calling him names. Arthur suggested to Eric that he should bring a complaint to the school's Judicial Committee. Eric challenged this by replying, "They have freedom of speech." Arthur, after some thought, replied that freedom of speech meant that they had the right to say those things, but that Eric also had the right not to hear them. In this case, the back-and-forth exchange may well have led Arthur, as well as Eric, to think about the school's concepts of personal rights and freedoms more deeply than he had before.

The Creativity-Enhancing Effects of Younger Children

Just as younger children are inspired to engage in the advanced activities they see among older children, the older ones are inspired to engage in the creative and imaginative activities they see among younger ones. In our formal study at Sudbury Valley, we found that teenagers initiated a bit more than half of the interactions between teenagers and younger children, in cases where there was a clear initiator.[36] They joined young children in playing with paints, clay, or blocks, or in make-believe games, or in exuberant, creative chase games—all activities that most teenagers elsewhere in our culture would have abandoned. Even when they weren't playing directly with them, the mere presence of younger children and their playthings seemed to inspire the older students to play more creatively than they otherwise would. Through such continued play, many students at the school become excellent artists, builders, storytellers, and creative thinkers. Many of the graduates go on to careers that require a high degree of creativity,[37] and I suspect that their age-mixed play experiences are part of the reason.

We also observed that even nominally competitive games, such as card or board games, were played in more creative, lighthearted ways when the players differed widely in age and ability than when they did not. There is no pride to be gained by the older, more skilled player in beating a much younger one, and the younger one has no expectation of beating the older one in an even match, so they play to have fun, to stretch their skills, and to experiment with creative moves rather than to win. In age-mixed games of chess, for example, the older, more skilled player might try out novel and risky openings, deliberately get into difficult positions, or play at lightning speed in order to make the game interesting and fun. As I discussed in Chapter 8, the lighthearted, playful attitude is more conducive to learning new skills and thinking creatively than is the serious attitude of competition or proving one's worth.

I'VE DESCRIBED HOW free age mixing allows younger children to engage in and learn from activities that would be too difficult for them to do alone; learn from and be inspired by older ones through watching and listening to them; and receive more care and emotional support than they otherwise would. I've also described how free age mixing allows older children to practice and develop their nurturing and leadership skills and capacities; learn through teaching; and engage in more playful, creative, and artistic activities than they otherwise would. When we segregate children by age, in school and in other settings, we deprive them of all of these powerful learning opportunities.

In emphasizing the value of age-mixed interactions, I do not mean to disparage the value of same-age interactions. For many purposes, people with relatively equal abilities make better playmates and conversational partners than do those with unequal abilities. They have more in common and have more to talk about, and the relatively serious and sometimes competitive interactions among them can motivate them to greater heights of performance. When children are not institutionally segregated by age, they spend much time with others who differ considerably from them in age, but they spend even more time with others who are close in age. It is no surprise that best friends, at Sudbury Valley as well as elsewhere, are usually relatively close in age.

My focus here has been on the value of free age mixing in bringing people together who differ in ability. Before closing, however, I should mention that another value of free age mixing is that it can bring together people who are similar in ability. It allows a person who is ahead of or behind his or her age-mates in some realm to find equal partners among older or younger children. The child who is awkward at climbing can play at scrambling up rocks and trees with younger children without being left behind, and in that way can improve his climbing ability. The talented eleven-year-old guitar player, whose musical ability is beyond that of her age-mates, can jam with teenagers who are at her level. The young chess prodigy can play serious, challenging games with older players who are at his same level of skill. What is most important for optimal development is an environment in which children are free to choose whom they interact with, so they can be with older, younger, or same-age others in accordance with their self-perceived needs, which vary from hour to hour and day to day.

10

TRUSTFUL PARENTING IN OUR MODERN WORLD

IN THE SPRING OF 2008, on a sunny Sunday, Lenore Skenazy dropped off her nine-year-old son at Bloomingdale's in midtown Manhattan. She gave him a handful of quarters, $20 for emergencies, a map, a Metrocard, and permission to get home on his own. To get to their house in the borough of Queens, he would have to take the subway and transfer to a bus, a route he had taken many times before with his mom. When he got home he was pleased as punch. He had been begging for this opportunity to prove that he could get home on his own using public transportation, and now he had done it. He glowed with his new sense of maturity.

Skenazy, who was then a columnist for the *New York Sun,* wrote about her son's adventure. Within hours after the column appeared, the media had labeled her "America's Worst Mom." In a rare show of unity, all of the women on ABC television's *The View* soundly condemned her decision. The more polite of the other fourth-grade moms at the playground said, according to Skenazy, things like, "Well, that's fine, and I'll let my son do that too . . . when he's in college." Skenazy used this incident as a trigger to write the wonderfully funny book *Free-Range Kids,* in which she diminishes parental fears by showing how ridiculous so many of them are.

Now, I don't mean to one-up Skenazy—whom I've gotten to know and admire greatly—in the America's worst parent competition, *but . . .* when he was thirteen, my son went to London for two weeks by himself. I must admit, that was back in 1982, when it was easier to be a trustful parent than it is today. He had approached his mom and me in the spring, when he was still twelve, with this proposal. He would earn all the money for the trip himself, so we couldn't use cost as an excuse to stop him. He would plan the whole trip himself—in fact, he had already planned much of it. He wanted to prove to himself that he could organize and do something this complicated without adult help. He also wanted to see certain castles and museum treasures, which he had been reading about and which were prominent in the Dungeons and Dragons games he played. He had never been abroad. Neither, for that matter, had his mom or I.

We hesitated, "not because of your age," we explained, "but because of your diabetes." He had (and, of course, still has) Type I diabetes. He had been testing his own sugar levels, giving himself insulin injections, and regulating his diet appropriately ever since his diabetes first appeared, at age nine. He was as disciplined as any adult diabetic I have ever known. Yet, it is dangerous for anyone with insulin-dependent diabetes to travel alone. There's always the risk of insulin-induced hypoglycemia, in which you lose judgment and even consciousness. What if that happened while he was away, in a strange place, and nobody helped him?

To all this, he said, "I'll always have diabetes. If you're telling me that I can't travel alone because of diabetes, you're telling me that I'll never be able to travel alone. I don't accept that. I'm not going to let diabetes prevent me from doing what I want to do. When I'm older I'll travel alone and you won't be able to stop me. If it's not age you're concerned about, then what's the difference between my traveling now and my traveling when I'm eighteen, or thirty, or fifty?" His logic, as always, was impeccable.

We finally relented. We fulfilled our parental obligation to nag only by making him promise to do something that he no doubt had the good sense to do anyway—to wear his medic alert medallion everywhere, so if he did have an insulin reaction people could read it and see that he was diabetic and needed help. He spent the rest of that spring and all summer working and earning all the money he needed for the trip. He earned most of it through a job at a small restaurant, which he secured on his own. At first he washed dishes, but when they saw what a good worker he was, they promoted him to working the grill and coordinating the kitchen. That itself was a wonderful growth experience. By October, he was ready to take his adventure. He was then thirteen years old. Because he was a student at Sudbury Valley, taking time off from school was no problem. Everyone there understood that this trip was a valuable educational experience, so they marked him as in attendance but on a field trip.

He was abroad for two weeks, saw countless castles, toured Westminster Abbey, spent days immersed in the treasures of the National Gallery and other museums, and took walking tours all over London. He also took a side trip to Oxford for a Moody Blues concert, another to Cardiff to walk the hills and see Cardiff Castle, and another to Paris with a fifteen-year-old young lady he had met on the plane to London. All in all, it was an amazing set of experiences that led him to new heights in confidence about his ability to run his own life. Diabetes diashmetes.

Now, I'll be the first to admit that my son wasn't just any thirteen-year-old kid. Had he been less responsible and less capable of thinking things through, his mother and I probably would have said no. To be a trustful parent is *not* to be a negligent parent—you have to know your child. But responsibility does not grow in a vacuum. If you want responsible kids, you have to allow them the freedom to be responsible, and that, sadly, is much harder to do today than it was in 1982; and in 1982 it was harder than in years before that.

Today it would be almost impossible for parents to allow their child to have such an adventure, no matter how responsible he or she might be. For starters, working as a cook in a restaurant, where he earned the money for the trip, is now illegal (in my home state of Massachusetts) for anyone under sixteen years old. On the matter of social pressure, even in 1982 our decision raised a few eyebrows. Imagine how your friends and relatives would react if you, a parent today, made such a decision.

But at other times and places people might have wondered more about our hesitation than about our final decision. As Skenazy says in the introduction to her book, "[Our great-great-grandparents] sent *their* sweet children out on slow, rusty steamers to the New World with only a couple of rubles and a hard salami."[1] As another example, on the basis of her extensive observations of young children on the Marquesan island of 'Ua Pou, in the South Pacific, researcher Mary Martini wrote the following:

> Thirteen members of a stable play group were observed daily for four months and less systematically for another two. . . . Children ranged from two to five years old. They played several hours a day without supervision while their siblings attended school nearby. They organized activities, settled disputes, avoided danger, dealt with injuries, distributed goods, and negotiated contact with passing others—without adult intervention. They avoided adults, probably because adults disrupted their play. The play area was potentially dangerous. A strong surf broke on the boat ramp. The large rocks on the shore were strewn with broken glass. The valley walls were steep and slippery. Children played on a high bridge and high, sharp, lava rock walls. Machetes, axes, and matches were occasionally left around and young children played with these. In spite of these dangers, accidents were rare and minor. Hitting, teasing, and scolding were frequent, but fistfights,

tantrums, and prolonged crying were rare. Disputes were frequent but were dissipated after a few minutes. Children did not seek adults or older children to settle conflicts or direct their play.[2]

When Martini asked parents about their children's playing with matches and machetes, she found that they would take those things away when they knew about it, because they were afraid the children would waste the matches and ruin the machetes, not because they were afraid the children would hurt themselves. According to Martini, the children on this island were remarkably well adjusted psychologically and socially. They didn't whine or demand adult attention as Western children so often do, and they were extraordinarily adept at solving their own problems as they arose. I'm not advocating that we emulate these Marquesans in our treatment of two- to five-year-olds, but we do have something to learn from them.

I doubt there has ever been a human culture, anywhere, at any time, that underestimates children's abilities more than we North Americans do today. Our underestimation becomes a self-fulfilling prophecy, because by depriving children of freedom, we deprive them of the opportunities they need to learn how to take control of their own behavior and emotions.

This chapter is about trustful parenting and what we can do, in our modern world, to make this style of parenting possible and normal again. What can we do, as individuals and collectively as a society, to restore children's birthrights to learn through free play, exploration, and independent adventure? What can we do to reverse the trend that has prevented so many children from practicing courage and developing the full level of emotional resilience needed for a happy, healthy, fulfilling life?

Three Styles of Parenting

As a prelude to addressing the questions above, I find it useful to distinguish among three general styles of parenting, each of which has dominated at specific times and places in human history. Although I present them as separate categories, they are not mutually exclusive; indeed, many parents today practice some combination of all three.

Trustful parenting is the style that most clearly allows the self-educative instincts to blossom. Trustful parents trust their children to play and explore on their own, to make their own decisions, to take risks, and to learn from their own mistakes. Trustful parents do not measure or try to direct their children's development, because they trust children to do so on their own. Trustful parents are not negligent parents. They provide not just freedom, but also the sustenance, love, respect, moral examples, and environmental conditions required for healthy development. They support, rather than try to direct, children's development, by helping children achieve their own goals when such help is requested. This parenting style predominated through the long stretch of human history when we were hunter-gatherers (as discussed in Chapter 2).

Trustful parenting sends messages to children that were consistent with the needs of children in hunter-gatherer bands, but are also consistent with the real needs of children today: *You are competent. You have eyes and a brain and can figure things out. You know your own abilities and limitations. Through play and exploration you will learn what you need to know. Your needs are valued. Your opinions count. You are responsible for your own mistakes and can be trusted to learn from them. Social life is not the pitting of will against will, but the helping of one another so that all can have what they need and most desire. We are with you, not against you.*

Hunter-gatherers who grew up this way usually became highly competent, cooperative, nondomineering, cheerful, valued members of their society. They contributed to their bands not because they felt forced to, but because they wanted to, and they did so with a playful spirit. One group of anthropologists summed all this up as follows: "The successful forager . . . should be assertive and independent and is so trained as a child."[3] Trustful parents today understand that today's successful adults, likewise, are assertive and independent and that children today should be so trained—"trained" not by directing them, but by allowing them to guide their own development and make their own discoveries about the world.

I refer to the other two parenting styles as *directive* styles, because they are oriented toward directing children's behavior and development rather than allowing children to direct themselves. These styles work against, rather than with, the child's will.

The *directive-domineering* style of parenting arose gradually with the rise of agriculture and reached its zenith during feudal and early industrial times. As discussed in Chapter 3, unquestioned obedience to lords and masters during this time often meant the difference between life and death, so the goal of parenting shifted from that of creating free and independent people to that of creating subservient beings. Rather than foster the child's will, directive-domineering parents attempted to quash that will and replace it with a willingness to abide by the wills of others. Physical beatings were a regular and widely approved means of suppressing the will.

In recent times, at least in some homes, psychological beatings have replaced physical beatings as the primary means of directive-domineering parenting. Regular inductions of guilt or shame, or threats of abandonment or withdrawal of love, can be even more powerful than the rod or whip in beating children into submission. But whatever its means, the goal of the directive-domineering parent is to turn the child into a servant. Yet history tells us that directive-domineering parenting has never been fully effective. Freedom is so strong a drive that it can never be fully beaten out of a person, regardless of age. Even in the humblest servant or the meekest child, free will continues to bubble below the surface, ready to boil over when the lid is loosened. That is why societies in which the masses are controlled by the few are never stable. In the long run, the directive-domineering style works no better in homes than it does in nations.

Today, at least in our culture, most people are repelled by the idea of beating children into submission, whether by physical or psychological means. In today's globalized, networked world, initiative, creativity, and self-assertion are generally valued. We see that blind obedience doesn't work as a style of life. Unskilled labor has declined, replaced by machines, and people must be creative self-starters to find ways to support themselves. People today espouse many of the same values as hunter-gatherers. Over the past century or two, with the decline in need for child labor and the return of democratic values, the directive-domineering style of parenting has continuously declined. For a while—peaking around the 1950s—trustful parenting seemed to experience a renaissance, but in the decades since then, this parenting style has been gradually replaced by a new kind of directive parenting, *directive-protective* parenting.

Directive-protective parents do not limit children's freedom in order to force them to labor in fields or factories, or to make them servile, as directive-domineering parents did. Rather, they limit freedom because they fear for their children's safety and futures and believe they can make better decisions for them than the children can for themselves. With all good intentions, directive-protective parents deprive their children of freedom at least as much as did the directive-domineering parents of the past. Directive-protective parents don't beat their children, but use all of the other powers they have as providers to control their children's lives. While trustful parents view children as resilient and competent, directive-protective parents view them as fragile and incompetent. While trustful parents believe that children develop best when allowed to play and explore on their own, directive-protective parents believe that children develop best when they follow a path carefully laid out for them by adults.

Reasons for the Decline in Trustful Parenting

Why did the rise in trustful parenting in the first half of the twentieth century begin to reverse itself in the middle of that century? In other words, what social changes over the past several decades have caused parents to be ever less trustful and ever more directive-protective in their relationships with their children? A full answer would describe a large number of interconnected changes in the social world, but here are the ones that seem to me to be most relevant:

Decline of neighborhoods and loss of children's neighborhood play groups. In the 1950s, most people—adults as well as children—knew their neighbors. This was partly because most women were home during the day and formed friendship networks, but men, too, tended to be home more than they are now. Workdays were shorter, on average, and people were home on weekends. Because people knew their neighbors, they trusted them. They weren't afraid to let their kids run freely in the neighborhood and socialize with everyone there. They also knew that their neighbors knew their kids and would keep an eye out for trouble. Today, in contrast, out-of-home work has come to dominate adult life for both men and women, and most adult friendships are formed at work rather than at home. A result is that parents are uncertain about the character of other people in the neighborhood, and this, of course, leads to distrust.

The biggest attraction for children to the outdoors, or to any place, is other children. So, when some parents begin to restrict their children from playing freely outdoors, the neighborhood becomes less inviting for other children. Moreover, the neighborhood may become truly less safe for any given child when fewer children are out there. There is safety in numbers. Children look out for one another and bring help if an injury occurs. (This is especially true if the playgroup includes a mix of older and younger kids.) And if child predators do exist, they are far less likely to prey on a child surrounded by witnesses than on a child alone. It's a vicious cycle: Fewer children outdoors means that the outdoors is less inviting and less safe than it was before, which results in still fewer children outdoors. To make neighborhoods inviting and safe once again for children's play, that cycle must be reversed.

Decline of local common sense about parenting, and rise of a worldwide network of fear. In the 1950s, most adults had more familiarity with and understanding of children than they do today. Families tended to be larger; extended families tended to live in the same town and share time together; and older children helped to care for younger ones. By the time people started their own families, they already had lots of experience with children. They knew firsthand something about child development. They knew something about children's competencies and the value of play and adventure for children. They were also part of a neighborhood network of other parents, who were friends and shared stories about their children. In contrast, people today often start families with little firsthand experience with children. Their ideas and information about childhood and parenting often come from what they read or hear from "experts" and the media.

The "experts" see it as their job to warn about dangers. Almost everything, to one authority or another, is a potential danger to children: knives, fire, germs, small toys (small enough to swallow), ticks and other biting insects, poisonous plants, ultraviolet sunlight, playground equipment, peers, older children and teenagers, and, of course, child abductors and predators (who, if you listen to the media, lurk behind every corner). If you listen to it all, and if you don't consider how small each risk really is, you begin to see the world as a terribly frightening place indeed. On all of these counts, some caution is called for. These dangers do exist and we should let our children know about them if they don't already. But when the fear becomes so great that we don't allow children to play and explore and take risks on their own, we prevent them from learning how to take care of themselves. That may be the greatest danger of all.

Some "experts" also seem to believe that we must protect our children's fragile self-esteem, so they will always think well of themselves. Parents respond by praising their children's smallest achievements, attending their games to cheer them on, and trying to arrange their kids' lives so they never fail. This, too, is part of the directive-protective parenting style. Most children recognize such continuous praise and support as false and shrug it off as one more annoyance they have to deal with from their parents. A few don't, however, and those are the ones we need to worry about. The "experts" also warn that we must protect children from their own foolishness. We read regularly of new data purporting to prove that children and especially adolescents are, for biological reasons, knuckleheads. It can't be true; if it were, we would not have survived as a species during all those tens of thousands of years when children were trusted, and when real dangers—such as predators—were much more prevalent than they are today.

The news media also are great purveyors of fear. Almost every day brings another story of a terrible thing that happened to a child some-where. If hundreds of thousands of children go outside to play without adult supervision and come home healthier, wiser, and braver, that is not news. But if one child somewhere is abducted, drowns, or is run over by an automobile, that news is broadcast throughout the state or even the world, depending on how lurid the story. The information parents receive does not reflect statistical reality, and it feeds into every parent's worst nightmares.

Increased uncertainty about future employment. The world of employ-ment is less stable now than it was a few decades ago. It's impossible to predict what jobs will be available in the future or what job skills will be required. Labor unions, which once helped to protect jobs, are largely a thing of the past. Companies and whole industries sprout up and dis-appear with unsettling frequency. A result of all this is that parents worry about their children's abilities to make a living more than they did in times past, and this contributes to their increased tendency to view childhood as a time of résumé building rather than a time of play. Somehow, parents believe, if they can get their children into the right adult-directed extracurricular or volunteer activities, get them to achieve high scores on tests, and get them into the most prestigious schools, they can protect their children's futures. They are wrong, of course, but the perception persists.

The reality is that the best protection against unemployment in uncertain times is having precisely those qualities people develop through self-directed experiences, not through the prodding of parents or teachers. Uncertain times require personal responsibility, independence of thought, self-initiative, self-assertion, flexibility, creativity, imagination, and willingness to take risks. These are the characteristics fostered by the trustful style of parenting and inhibited by the directive-protective style.

Rise in the power of schools and in the need to conform to schools' increasingly restrictive requirements.   Perhaps the most significant of all the contributors to the decline of children's freedom has been the continuous rise in the power of schools to interfere with the lives of children and families. School was an inhibitor of children's freedom in the 1950s, but it is even more so today. The school year is longer, the sanctions for missing days of school are greater, and the activities conducted at school are more rigidly controlled than in times past. Moreover, schools today extend their influence beyond the school walls and into family life far more than in times past (as discussed in Chapter 1). There are summer reading lists, for example, and parents are supposed to make sure their children get those books and read them. ("No, Mary, you can't read the book you want to read, because that's not the book you need to write a report on.") Homework is assigned even to the youngest students, and parents are often required to sign homework sheets and act as enforcers. Parents are regularly called in for conferences and made to feel guilty when their children misbehave in school or don't do well on tests. Parents are expected to play the role at home that teachers play at school, pushing and prodding their children to do the things the school system has decided they must do. Parents who complain about any of this are viewed as troublemakers.

Because I blog on play and learning for *Psychology Today,* I often read sad comments from parents about their children's experiences in school. Here's one that is quite typical, from the mother of a kindergartener at a public school that, she says, has the reputation of being "excellent." Her daughter's school day runs from 8 A.M. to 3 P.M., not counting the long bus ride each way, with no breaks except for one half-hour recess and a lunch period (at 10:40 A.M.!) in which a lady with a bullhorn quiets the children if they are too noisy. In addition, these five-year-olds are expected to do homework every night, supervised by a parent. The homework is real homework—math assignments, writing assignments, and the like. Here is what this mom says about the consequences:

> My daughter started school so excited and within two or three days was crying and asking to go back to preschool. That eventually passed, but the child that has emerged when she gets home is so different. She vacillates between anger and whininess. She yells at her younger sister, calls her a baby, and slams doors, or she clings to me and wants me to do everything for her. I know this is because of school. . . . Almost every parent I have talked to mentions some of the same, if not worse, for their child. Is this to be expected in any school? I feel powerless and stressed myself. When I talk to other parents, we are all afraid to be "that mom," for fear it will adversely affect our child even more. There is now a culture within the education system that keeps us quiet! We are constantly getting notes about what a child this age "is capable of doing" and that we need to "let them do it." Our children "will survive." Funny, I was hoping my child did more than survive. I guess thriving is no longer an option. I feel like a witness to a crime who is frozen and does nothing to stop it!

It's hard, if not impossible, to be a trustful parent in these conditions. The state, through its compulsory and increasingly prison-like schools, almost forces parents to be directive rather than trustful. You have to fight with your kids to get them to adapt to the school, and you have to fight with the school to try to get it to adapt in some small way to your kids.

Rise of a school-centric model of child development and parenting. In addition to its direct influence on families' lives, the school system has had an even more pervasive indirect influence. Increasingly, researchers, parents, and society at large have come to view all of childhood through the lens of schooling. Everyone categorizes children according to their grade in school. Most research studies of children are conducted in schools and focus on school issues and concerns. The result is a school-centric view of child development that distorts human nature.

In schools, learning is adult-directed, not child-directed. In schools, learning is considered to be sequential, along established pathways. You have to learn A before you learn B. In schools, children's companions are all the same age—there is no learning of skills through play with older kids, or of responsibility through play with younger ones. In schools, self-initiated play and exploration are disruptions. All these are components of the school-centric model of child development. As a result, people have come to believe that learning is fundamentally sequential and adult-directed, that the proper companions are other children of the same age, and that self-directed play and exploration are largely a waste of time for children beyond the age of four or five. Developmental psychology textbooks, for example, commonly refer to the preschool years as "the play years," as if play naturally stops or takes a backseat after that. We have allowed the schooling system to blind us to the natural ways of children.

The school-centric model of childhood has taken increasing hold over time and affected all aspects of children's lives. Playgrounds are no longer places where children go and play freely with one another, but are places of coaching and teaching, led by adults. Children are sorted there into age-segregated groups, just as they are in school. In the home many parents today, in implicit acceptance of the school-centric model, define themselves as teachers of their children. They look for "teaching moments," buy educational toys, and "play" and talk with their children in ways designed to impart specific lessons. No wonder parent-child interactions these days are often accompanied by lots of eye rolling and "whatevers" from the children. Home life begins to become as tedious as school.

It is not hard to see why parents buy into the school-centric model. They become convinced by the rhetoric that their children will fail at life if they don't get high grades in school and get into a top college. They begin to see themselves as competing with other parents to produce kids with the best résumés. As the school system becomes increasingly powerful, people's implicit conceptions of child development grow ever more to match the schooling model; and children, out of school as well as in, become ever less free, ever more controlled, and ever more deprived of self-initiated adventures. Sadly, in many cases, the assumption that children are incompetent, irresponsible, and in need of constant direction and supervision becomes a self-fulfilling prophecy. The children themselves become convinced of their incompetence and irresponsibility, and may act accordingly. The surest way to foster any trait in a person is to treat that person as if he or she already has it.

How to Become a More Trustful Parent

Many parents would like to adopt a more trustful style, but find it hard to do so. The voices of fear are loud and incessant, and the fears are never completely unfounded. Terrible accidents do happen; adult predators do exist; delinquent peers can have harmful influences; children and adolescents (like people of all ages) do make mistakes; and failure can hurt. We are also, by nature, conformists. It is hard to swim against the current and risk the negative judgments of parenting peers. Yet, some do, and if enough begin to swim upstream, the river may change its flow.

Suppose you are a parent who accepts the idea that all of life involves risks and that children need freedom in order to be happy, to learn how to be responsible, and to develop the character traits needed to deal with life's inevitable dangers and setbacks. How can you, despite the forces against you, despite the fearful voices in your head, become a more trustful parent and allow your children more freedom? Here are some suggestions.

Examine Your Own Values

What is a good life? What sorts of experiences make life worthwhile? The first step toward trustful parenting is to examine your own values and think about how they might apply to your children and your relationship with them. If freedom, personal responsibility, self-initiative, honesty, integrity, and concern for others rank high in your system of values, and if they represent characteristics you would like to see in your children, then you will want to be a trustful parent. None of these can be taught by lecturing, coercion, or coaxing. They are acquired or lost through daily life experiences that reinforce or suppress them. You can help your children build these values by living them yourself and applying them in your relationship with your children. Trust promotes trustworthiness. Self-initiative and all of the traits that depend on self-initiative can develop only under conditions of freedom.

Think back to your own childhood and recall your happiest moment. Where were you? What were you doing? Who, if anyone, was with you? More specifically, was an adult with you at that moment? Michael Thomas, a child psychiatrist and author, routinely poses these questions to audiences in his speaking engagements. When he asks whether an adult was present at their happiest childhood moment, typically about 10 percent raise their hand. For the other 90 percent, no adult was present. That, according to Thomas, suggests that our happiest moments are usually those that are fully our own, the result of our own doing, not something presented to us by powerful others.[4]

The memory that comes to me when I try this exercise is of a very early morning, in the spring, when I was ten or eleven years old. I had risen before dawn to get in two or three hours of fishing before school. I had ridden my bicycle in the dark, with fishing gear attached, to the dam on the river about two miles from home. I had gone alone; none of my friends wanted to get up that early. And there I was, line in the water, just me, the river, the early morning birds singing their springtime songs, the patches of lingering snow, maybe a fish nibbling, maybe not, while the sun began to peek above the horizon. It's hard to know precisely what it was about that moment that made it so striking; it was far from my first experience with sunrises or early morning fishing. But that morning I was suddenly filled with a sense of awe and wonder. I felt lifted above the mundane level of existence. I experienced what humanistic psychologists have long referred to as a "peak experience" and what religious people may mean when they talk about moments of insight into God's grace. There is no way I could have had that experience if an adult had been there with me. The adult, no matter how well meaning and respectful, would have interfered, simply by being there. I could not possibly have felt so tall if an adult were next to me.

Let Go of the Idea That You Determine Your Child's Future

If we value freedom and personal responsibility, we must respect our children's rights to chart their own lives. Our ambitions cannot be theirs, and vice versa. The self-charting begins in infancy. To learn responsibility, children must learn how to make their own decisions in the course of each hour, day, and year, and they can learn that only by practicing it. All loving, caring parents care about their children's futures, so it can be hard not to try to control them. But the attempt at control defeats its goals. When we try to determine our children's destinies, we prevent them from taking ownership of their own lives. When we try to pilot our children through the daily and weekly mazes of life, we prevent them from practicing their own piloting and learning from their own mistakes. When we offer our children advice they didn't ask for and don't need, we reduce the chance that they will ask us for advice when they do want and need it.

It is important to remind yourself, as a trustful parent, that your child is not you. What we call "reproduction" is not. It doesn't produce another you. You contribute a random half of your genes, your mate contributes a random half of his or hers, and then they combine and mix to produce what is genetically a whole new person, who may share some of your traits but who, for the most part, is not you at all. Nor is your child *yours*. Your child is its own being who, like every child, comes into the world designed to grow, learn, and chart a life course. You are simply part of the environmental substrate that your child uses to create himself or herself. Try to be a good substrate by providing what your child needs, but don't assume that it is your responsibility to direct your child's development.

Whether your child succeeds or fails is up to your child, not you, and the measure of success or failure must be your child's, not yours. The world is full of unhappy lawyers, doctors, and business executives, and many clerks and janitors are happy, fulfilled, and decent. Career success is not life success. You can be happy or unhappy in any profession, but you can't be happy, at least not for long stretches, if you feel that your life is not yours. These are truisms. They may sound trite. But too many people forget them when it comes to their child-care practices.

In a series of large-scale surveys, Sinuya Luthar and her colleagues at Columbia University found that high school students from affluent suburban families in the northeastern United States reported even more anxiety, depression, and illicit drug use than did those from impoverished inner-city neighborhoods.[5] Moreover, those who reported the most such problems were those who felt most pressured by their parents to achieve. The same studies also suggested that time with parents could have either negative or beneficial effects, depending on the nature of that time. Being carted around by parents from one activity to another was associated with greater anxiety and depression, but having regular family meals together was associated with less anxiety and depression. Emotional closeness with parents was valuable to the teens, but that closeness was hampered when the parents were more concerned with their children's achievements than with simply enjoying time together. Trustful parents enjoy their kids; they don't think of them as their "project."

Resist the Temptation to Monitor
Your Child's Activities

Trustful parents resist urges to be in continuous contact with their children, to monitor their activities, or to inquire about the details of their day. With modern technology, it is easy and tempting to track your child's every move. You can observe through hidden cameras, track the Web pages that your child visits, and insist on regular cell-phone reports of current whereabouts and activities. You can even use a global positioning device to know where your child is at every moment, as is done with prisoners. You might even justify such monitoring by convincing yourself that it demonstrates to your child that you care. But how would you like to be constantly monitored? How would you like it if someone—maybe your loving husband or wife—was watching, recording, and evaluating all of your private activities? The message sent by such monitoring is always, "I don't trust you."

But modern technology is not required to demonstrate such lack of trust. The method of constant, detailed inquiry does the trick as well. A trustful parent does not ask for detailed reports, from the child or anyone else, about hours spent away from the parent's gaze. Everyone has a right to privacy and opportunities to experiment without being judged. Inquiry that infringes on privacy only invites dishonesty and resentment.

Find or Create Safe Places and Opportunities
for Children to Play and Explore

As a trustful parent you do have some major responsibilities concerning your child. You can't navigate your child's ship, or even teach many navigation skills, but you can and do provide the pond. Realtors tell us that the main concern of most young families in finding their first home is the rank of the local public school on test scores and percentage who go on to college. But as a trustful parent, your concern will focus more on the quality of the neighborhood as a place to play. A neighborhood of huge houses and big yards and high test scores, but where there are no kids outside playing together, is not a good place for your child.

Look for a neighborhood where kids of all ages can be found intermingling, playing, exploring, and hanging out talking with one another. Your child will want to join them and will learn from them. More often than not, such a neighborhood is one where the homes are not stately, where homeowners would rather see dandelions and kids on their lawns than perfect carpets of grass, and where yards are not isolated from one another by fences and hedges. Ideally, it should also be a neighborhood with little or no through traffic, so the streets are safe for kids to cross or even play in. Such neighborhoods, though less common than they once were, do still exist, and more would exist if home buyers demanded them. Look also for a neighborhood where the parents themselves spend some leisure time outdoors and get to know other parents and their children. A large-scale study of factors contributing to children's outdoor play in four cities in Holland revealed that one of the most important factors was the cohesiveness of the neighborhood. The more fully the neighbors knew and trusted one another, the more hours their kids spent playing outdoors.[6]

If moving to a preexisting play-friendly neighborhood is not an option for you, you might work to improve your current neighborhood. A first step is to get to know other parents who live near you and bring them together to discuss common concerns. Many if not most parents will jump at such an opportunity, but someone needs to take the initiative. An immediate effect of such meetings will be to promote interfamily friendships, which all by themselves may spill over into children's friendships and more outdoor play. Through such meetings you might work with other parents to identify or develop a local place for kids to play, which even little kids can get to by foot, and maybe a rotating method to monitor that place if parents otherwise feel nervous about letting their kids go there without them. If there's no reasonable, existing place for such play, how about your own front yard?

Mike Lanza—founder of an online organization called Playborhood—built a neighborhood playground in his front yard. On his website, and in a recent book, he provides lots of practical advice for others who wish to do something similar.[7] The Lanzas' front-yard playground includes a sandbox, a nicely paved driveway with basketball hoop, an attractive fountain at toddler level to splash in, a picnic table with storage benches filled with toys and drawing and electronic equipment, a white board on a fence for artistic creations, and more. Mike and his family (which now includes three young boys) regularly eat meals at their front-yard picnic table as a way of attracting and meeting neighbors, and in various other ways they have let the kids and parents in the neighborhood know they are welcome to play or lounge in their yard anytime they wish, whether or not any of the Lanzas are there. In essence, they have put up a PLEASE TRESPASS sign!

According to Mike, this venture is far from a sacrifice on their part. Getting to know the neighbors and seeing kids having fun in their yard has added to the richness of their lives and given their children a constant supply of playmates. Mike deliberately designed the playground to be attractive to kids of all ages. He also built more play opportunities into the backyard, including an in-ground trampoline and a tree house. These, too, are open to the community, but it is the front-yard playground and the Lanzas' frequent presence there that initially draws neighbors to their house and leads them to feel comfortable playing there.

Of course, if you are a typical twenty-first-century American adult, you immediately conjure up all the possible negatives. What about liability if somebody gets hurt? What about vandalism or theft? What about town ordinances? Won't neighbors worry about noise or decline in property values? Mike has good answers to these questions and suggests ways that you might address them in your own community. The point is, start with a positive mind-set. Figure out what you want to do to create a healthy neighborhood—or, as Mike calls it, a healthy "playborhood"—for your children to grow up in, and then figure out a way to do it that works where you live. Include your closest neighbors in your thinking from the beginning, even those who don't have kids, so they are with you, not against you. Take their concerns seriously, not as barriers but as problems to be solved in your planning.

Enabling your kids to play freely and relatively safely with other kids is one of the most valuable things you can possibly do for them. If you are at the same time helping other kids, so much the better! People in various parts of the country have begun to follow the Lanzas' lead. The front-yard playground and picnic area have the potential to replace the old-fashioned and now almost extinct front porch as a neighborhood community builder. But the playground in your own yard should not be an excuse to keep your kids from wandering else-where. Especially as they get older, they need to move out to broader areas. Your yard or any other neighborhood playground is just a starting place for your kids' ever-expanding world of adventure.

With a little imagination and effort there are many other things you can do to enable more free play for your children. For example, you might lobby your local school to open up the gym for free play for a certain period of time every day after school. You might lobby the town park commission to hire a responsible teenager to monitor play areas in the park on weekends or after school, so children can play there without parents' feeling they have to be there with them. You might take family vacations with other families who have kids, so your kids can play with theirs while you and the other adults enjoy adult com-panionship. The nuclear family is a fine thing as a home base for raising children, but for healthy development, children need to explore beyond it, even when they are little.

Consider Alternatives to Conventional Schooling

To be a trustful parent, you may need to find an alternative to conven-tional schooling for your kids, an alternative that works with, rather than against, their desire and capacity to take charge of their own ed-ucation. I've already described the Sudbury Valley School as one such alternative. At the time I am writing this, there are at least twenty-two schools in the United States modeled after Sudbury Valley and at least fourteen in other countries.[8] These are all private schools, but their tuitions are far less than those of regular private schools. There are also many other nontraditional schools that, to varying degrees, permit much more play and self-direction than do conventional public and private schools.

Another alternative is homeschooling. In terms of numbers, homeschooling is the largest truly alternative schooling movement in the United States. The number of US children of school age (five to seventeen) who are homeschooled grew from about 850,000 in 1999 to an estimated two million or slightly more in 2011, or from about 1.7 percent to nearly 4 percent of the school-age population.[9] Not all parents who choose homeschooling do so primarily for the sake of their children's freedom. Roughly a third choose it for religious reasons,[10] and some no doubt choose it because they are unusually directive; they want to control their kids' schooling themselves rather than leave that task to others. Regardless of their initial motives, however, most homeschooling parents become increasingly relaxed, less directive, over time. Both they and their kids typically find the planned curriculum to be boring, so they begin to do more interesting things, usually initiated by the kids. With experience, homeschooling parents become increasingly trustful of their children's abilities to direct their own education, and some of them become *unschoolers*.

Unschooling is the category of home-based education most compatible with trustful parenting. The term was coined in the 1970s by the educational theorist and former teacher John Holt, in his magazine *Growing Without Schooling*. Defined most simply, unschooling is *not schooling*. Unschooling parents do not send their children to school, and at home they do not do the kinds of things that are done at school. They do not establish a curriculum, do not require particular assignments for the purpose of education, and do not test their children to measure progress. Instead, they allow their kids freedom to pursue their own interests and to learn, in their own ways, what they need to know to follow those interests. They believe that learning is a normal part of all of life, not something separate that occurs at special times and places.

For official record-keeping purposes, unschoolers are lumped in with homeschoolers, so nobody knows exactly how many there are. However, people in the homeschooling movement generally estimate that roughly 10 percent of homeschoolers are unschoolers, which seems reasonable based on the proportions I see at homeschooling conventions. That estimate would be higher, probably much higher, if so-called relaxed homeschoolers were also included. These are families who sort of have a curriculum for their kids but don't necessarily follow or enforce it.

Recently my colleague Gina Riley and I conducted a survey of 232 families who identify themselves as unschoolers. We are still analyzing the questionnaire responses, but some results are already clear.[11] More than a third of the families started off sending a child to school, but removed the child from school because of damaging effects the school seemed to be having on the child—such as depression, anxiety, anger, or loss of interest in learning. Nearly half of the families tried a more conventional form of homeschooling, with regular lessons at home, before moving on to unschooling. In essentially all of these cases the move from home lessons to unschooling occurred because the child and parents found the lessons to be tedious, stressful, or both, and to be unnecessary because the child was learning without them.

In response to our question about the main advantages of unschooling for their family, the majority talked about the positive effects it had on their children's happiness, assertiveness, or self-confidence; the positive effects it had on their children's curiosity and learning; and the positive effects it had on family closeness and family life in general. Many who previously had a child in school commented on what a relief it was not to have to schedule their personal lives around the school schedule. To our question about the disadvantages of unschooling, the most common response by far had to do with the stress or annoyance of having to explain and defend unschooling to relatives and others who were critical of their decision. Many also commented about having to overcome their own self-doubts about doing something so different from the norm. It can be difficult to swim against the current. That is one reason why many unschoolers have formed strong social networks with one another, both locally through community meetings and more broadly through Internet groups, in which they provide social support for one another.

Unschooling has been around long enough that there are now many adults who skipped all of what would have otherwise been their primary and secondary school years. So far no formal study has been conducted to see how they are faring, but many case examples can be found in articles, books, and blogs written by unschoolers. All in all, unschooling "ungraduates" seem to have no particular difficulty getting into colleges and doing well there if they choose that route, and no particular difficulty getting good jobs with or without college.

To give you just one example, I spoke recently with Kate Fridkis, a delightful twenty-five-year-old living in New York City who had never been to school until she entered college. Her parents chose unschooling for Kate and her brothers from the beginning, because they believed that learning should not be separate from life. Kate told me of all kinds of advantages that seemed to come to her because she was unschooled. She could follow her own interests and develop her own passions, which became many and diverse. She could go places and join activities that others couldn't, because they were in school. She could make friends with people of all ages, in many different contexts, without feeling that she had to confine herself to people her own age. She never had to adapt to a conformist school culture, which allowed her to enjoy and to feel no embarrassment about the ways she differed from others and allowed her to appreciate differences in others. At age fifteen she got a paying job at her synagogue as a lay clergy member, leading services for the whole congregation, which would have been impossible because of the time conflict if she had been in school.

Her experiences at the synagogue led her to develop a passionate interest in religion as a social phenomenon, which led her to study comparative religion in college and then to obtain a master's degree in the subject at Columbia University. She had no trouble adjusting to the academic demands of higher education. Her main disappointments as an undergraduate came from the immaturity and lack of intellectual interests among her classmates and the boring lectures she had to sit through. Today she is happily married, is a freelance writer with articles in a variety of prominent publications, works as a cantor at a synagogue, continues to pursue diverse interests for fun, and authors two popular blogs—one called "Skipping School" and the other (on body image) called "Eat the Damn Cake."

I don't think that unschooling is the answer for every family, or even for most, unless societal changes occur to help support it. It requires a considerable commitment of time and resources. Generally, at least one adult has to be home when the kids are young. Most often that adult is the mom, which means that she must be willing to forgo or postpone a career, or able to manage a career from home. Although unschooling parents don't direct their children's learning, they do make efforts to provide a rich learning environment for their children and to help them find ways to pursue their own interests. Unschooling also typically involves a lot of family togetherness, which may be wonderful for some families, but could be awful for others. Some kids need to be away from their parents more than is typically possible with unschooling, and some parents need more time away from kids. In our culture of relatively isolated nuclear families, where most adults work outside of the home, it can be hard to spend the day with kids and still have enough adult companionship. An advantage of Sudbury Valley or a similar school for self-directed learning is that it gives kids a chance to spend time in a stable setting separate from home, where there are rich opportunities for play, exploration, learning, and friendships that the parents don't need to provide or arrange. But for many families, according to their own reports, unschooling is a terrific option.

A Vision for the Future

I'm optimistic about the future of education. I'm optimistic that we as a culture will come to our senses and restore to children the freedom to take control of their own learning, so learning will once again be joyful, exciting, and an integral part of life rather than tedious, depressing, and anxiety provoking.

My optimism does not come from the education establishment. That establishment—including schools of education, the textbook and testing industries, and organizations of teachers and school administrators—is so entrenched in the status quo and its own self-interests that all it can do is push for more of the same. When it becomes clear that children aren't learning much of what is taught in school, the hue and cry from these sources is that kids must spend even more time in school and do more schoolwork at home. If two hundred hours of instruction on subject X does no good, let's try four hundred hours. If children aren't learning what is taught to them in first grade, then let's start teaching it in kindergarten. And if they aren't learning it in kindergarten, well, that could only mean that we need to start in prekindergarten! If children forget over summer vacation what little they learned during the previous school year, then let's abolish their summer vacation—and diminish further their possibilities for life outside of school.[12]

Almost everyone involved in the education enterprise considers himself or herself to be a "reformer," in tacit acknowledgment that the current system doesn't work. This has been true since the dawn of compulsory schooling. Some want to reform the system by nudging it one way (maybe by offering a few more choices and lightening up a little on the testing), while others want to reform it by nudging it the other way (with an even more standardized curriculum and more rigorous testing). This is the stuff of countless books and articles written by professors of education. But no one in the education establishment is willing to admit that coercive schooling doesn't work precisely because it is coercive and that the only meaningful reform is one that puts kids in charge of their own learning.

Instead, my optimism comes from what is happening outside the education establishment. I'm cheered by the ever-growing stream of people who are leaving coercive schooling for relaxed homeschooling, unschooling, Sudbury schooling, and other forms of education that allow children to control their own learning. The more oppressive the school system becomes, the more it is driving people away, and that is good.

The movement out of schools is also facilitated by the revolution in information technology. Today anyone who can get their hands on a computer with Internet access—even street kids in India—can access the world's entire body of knowledge and ideas, all beautifully organized and available through easy-to-use search engines. For almost anything you want to do, you can find instructions and video on the Internet. For almost any idea you want to think about, you can find arguments and counterarguments on the Internet, and even join a discussion about it. This is far more conducive to intellectual development than the one-right-answer approach of the standard school system. The idea that you have to go to school to learn anything or to become a critical thinker is patently ridiculous to any kid who knows how to access the Internet, and so it is becoming harder and harder to justify top-down schooling. And with text-based electronic communication becoming almost as commonplace as oral communication, more and more kids are learning to read and write on their own before they start school, which also prompts parents to question the necessity of coercive schooling. If Johnny can read before starting first grade, why send him to first grade?

At some point in the not-too-distant future, I predict, we'll reach a tipping point. Everyone will know at least one Kate Fridkis, who grew up not doing anything like standard schooling and who is doing just fine in life. People will begin to say things like, "Look at Kate, and Bob, and Mary Jane; none of them went to school and they're happy, productive, responsible citizens. Why should I send my kids to school if they are unhappy there?" People will begin to demand changes in the laws that make schooling compulsory or that define what schooling has to be, and this will enable more to leave the compulsory system without having to do the legal loop-de-loops that are now required and that keep many from even trying.

Like all major social changes, the key here is a shift in beliefs about what is normal and not normal. Not many years ago being homosexual was seen by almost everyone as abnormal—a sin or a disease, depending on whether you took a religious or a secular view. There are still some people who feel that way, but few of them are under the age of thirty. The norm has changed. Being homosexual is now largely seen as another normal human variation, like being left-handed. That change came about because some brave gay people took the plunge. They came out and declared pride in their sexual orientation. As more and more people discovered that some of their valued friends and relatives were homosexual, and that some of society's idols and heroes were, too, it became harder to condemn it or call it a sickness. There is an analogy here to what I think will happen in education. As more people meet adults who didn't go to a coercive school, or who don't send their kids to one, it will be ever harder to think of that decision as aberrant or abhorrent.

And there is another force working here, too—the natural human drive for freedom and self-determination. History tells us that when people see freedom as a viable option, they choose it. When adults see that coercive schooling isn't necessary for success in the culture, they will find it hard *not* to choose freedom for their kids, and the kids themselves will demand it. Children will no longer buy the argument that schooling is bad-tasting medicine that must be endured because it is necessary or good for them. As more people leave the coercive school system, a significant bloc of voters will begin to demand that some of the public education money that's been freed up be used to help support kids' self-directed learning, to provide educational *opportunities* rather than coercion. Think of what could be done with even a fraction of the roughly $600 billion of taxpayer money that is currently spent on coercive K–12 schools every year in the United States![13]

We do have a social obligation to provide rich educational opportunities for every child, regardless of his or her family background or income. There are many possible ways to do this. One possibility would be a system of voluntary, noncoercive schools—perhaps modeled after Sudbury Valley—where children could play, explore, and learn in an environment conducive to healthy intellectual, physical, and moral development. Per student, Sudbury schools cost only about half of what we now spend per student on coercive public schools, so this plan would result in great savings to taxpayers. Another possibility would be a system of community centers, open to everyone free of charge.

Imagine a center in your community where kids—and adults, too—could come to play, explore, make new friends, and learn. Computers, art supplies, athletic equipment, and science equipment would be available to play with. The public library might partner with it. Local people would offer classes—in music, art, athletics, math, foreign languages, cooking, business management, checkbook balancing, or anything else that people deemed fun, interesting, or important enough to study or practice in a structured way. There would be no requirements, no grades, no ranking or comparisons between people. Local theater and music groups could put on productions there, and people of all ages could form new groups depending on their interests. There would be a gymnasium for indoor play and, if possible, fields and woods for outdoor play and exploration. Children would come to the center, not because they have to, but because that is where their friends are and where there are so many exciting things to do. For parents who need child care during the day so they can work, the center might provide that, too, in an efficient way that capitalizes on the joy and benefit that older kids get out of helping to care for younger ones.

The center might be governed, town meeting style, by those who join and use it. Through democratic vote, the members would make major budgetary decisions and elect a board to oversee its operations. They might hire several adults, and maybe some teenagers, to help manage the daily activities. The members would decide democratically on rules of behavior in the center and a system for enforcing the rules. The price for joining would be agreement to follow the rules and, maybe an agreement to help out with some of the work in running it. Kids as well as adults would have a vote, and kids as well as adults would have to agree to the membership contract. All this could be done at a fraction of the cost of the community's present budget for coercive schools.

I'm only guessing here on the details of what might replace coercive schools. I suspect, and hope, that the details will vary considerably from community to community, depending on local needs and demands.

The decline in coercive schools and the rise in voluntary educational opportunities will be gradual, but eventually the coercive system will fade away. And then we will witness a full renewal of children's capacities for self-control and desire to learn, and an end to the epidemic of anxiety, depression, and feelings of helplessness that plague so many youth today.

ACKNOWLEDGMENTS

I SAID IN CHAPTER 1 that I've had hundreds of great teachers over the course of my life; I thank them all. They are bookended by Ruby Lou, wherever she may now be, and Danny Greenberg, whose pioneering work and ideas have inspired me and whose friendship has warmed me. I owe this book mostly to my dear son Scott, who turned me in this direction so long ago and has kept me on my toes ever since. And, of course, my dear wife Diane, who has filled my life with play and joy ever since we first said hello. There are so many other colleagues and friends and loved ones who deserve to be mentioned that I will stop now before I start, for fear of going on forever.

Specific to this book, I thank my wonderful agent, Jill Marsal, who found me through my blog, said she could see a book, and guided me through the proposal. I also thank Thomas (TJ) Kelleher, the executive editor who decided that the book is worth publishing and gave me an initial boost of encouragement, Collin Tracy, the production editor who skillfully shepherded the book through all of its various stages, and Antoinette Smith, who did the final copyediting so very well. I especially thank Tisse Takagi, the main editor for the book, for her excellent word pruning and all the other help she gave. You, dear readers, should thank her, too.

NOTES

NOTES TO CHAPTER 1

1. Clinton (2001).
2. Portions of this section and the next are adapted from Gray (2011a).
3. Chudacoff (2007).
4. Quoted by Johnson (1988).
5. Finkelhor et al. (2010).
6. Family, Kids, and Youth (2010). This survey was sponsored by IKEA Inc. and was overseen by Barbie Clarke, CEO of the marketing research group Family, Kids, and Youth.
7. See O'Brien and Smith (2002).
8. Clements (2004).
9. Hofferth and Sandberg (2001).
10. Hofferth (2009).
11. Clements (2004).
12. Family, Kids, and Youth (2010).
13. Comment posted in the "Readers Comments" section of P. Gray's February 24, 2010, *Psychology Today* blog essay; http://blogs.psychologytoday.com/blog/freedom-learn.
14. Twenge (2000); Twenge et al. (2010).
15. Newsom et al. (2003).
16. Data are from Tables 4 and 5 of Newsom et al. (2003). Because the scores for boys and girls on these items were similar and changed in similar ways, I have summarized the results by averaging the scores for the two sexes.
17. According to records kept by the Centers for Disease Control and Prevention, suicide rates among children and adolescents rose steeply between 1950 and 1995; then they declined gradually until 2003, apparently because of greater awareness and the development of programs aimed at preventing childhood suicide. More recent reports, however, indicate that adolescent and childhood suicide rates have been rising, again, since 2003. For rates by age group from 1950 to 2005, see www.infoplease.com/ipa/A0779940.html#axzz0zVy5PKaL. For a report of increased suicide since 2003, see Nauert (2008).
18. Twenge et al. (2004).

19. For evidence of a causal link between a helpless style of thinking and depression, see Abramson et al. (1989); Alloy et al. (2006); Weems & Silverman (2006); Harrow et al. (2009).

20. References in Twenge et al. (2004); Reich et al. (1997).

21. Luthar and Latendresse (2005).

22. Csikszentmihalyi and Hunter (2003).

NOTES TO CHAPTER 2

1. Lee and DeVore (1968).

2. Diamond (1997).

3. The date that we take as the beginning of human existence is arbitrary. The line of primates that led to our species split off from that which led to our closest ape relatives—chimpanzees and bonobos—about six million years ago (Corballis, 1999). By four million years ago, our ancestors were walking upright, and by two million to one million years ago they had much larger brains than did other apes, built fires, made tools, lived in social groups, and survived by hunting animals and gathering roots, nuts, seeds, berries, and other plant materials (Konner, 2002; Ridley, 2003).

4. Throughout this chapter my focus is on the variety of hunter-gatherer society that anthropologists refer to as *immediate-return* or *egalitarian* hunter-gatherers, or as *band* societies. These are societies in which people live in small bands that move from place to place within circumscribed territories to follow the available game and vegetation. They are contrasted with the category of hunter-gatherer society referred to as *delayed-return* or *non-egalitarian* hunter-gatherers, or as *collector societies*—typified by the Kwakiutl of the American northwest coast and the Ainu of Japan—which are relatively sedentary societies, where people exploit a particular local resource for food (commonly fish). Collector societies are in many ways more like primitive agricultural societies than like band hunter-gatherers. They are less prevalent than band societies, and archaeological evidence suggests that they originated more recently and are less likely than band societies to represent the predominant living conditions of our preagricultural ancestors (Kelly, 1995). In line with the practice of many anthropologists, when I use the term *hunter-gatherer*, unmodified, I am referring specifically to the band, egalitarian variety.

5. Portions of this and subsequent sections of this chapter are adapted from Gray (2009).

6. Ingold (1999).

7. Ingold (1999); Wiessner (1996).

8. Lee (1988), p. 264.

9. Boehm (1999).

10. For a good discussion of consensual decision-making in one hunter-gatherer society, see Silberbauer (1982). For a more general reference, see Kent (1996).

11. Gould (1969), p. 90. Although physical punishment of children appears to be rare in all hunter-gatherer cultures, it has been observed to occur to some

degree in at least some such cultures, including the Hazda of central Africa (Blurton Jones, 1993).

12. Gosso et al. (2005), pp. 218, 226.

13. Liedloff (1977), p. 90.

14. Guemple (1988), p. 137.

15. Thomas (2006), p. 198.

16. Ibid., pp. 198–199.

17. Bakeman et al. (1990).

18. For the survey, we identified ten anthropologists who, among them, had lived in and studied seven different hunter-gatherer cultures on three continents, and we questioned them extensively with a written questionnaire, about their observations of children's lives in the cultures they had studied (see Gray, 2009).

19. Draper (1976), pp. 210, 213.

20. Blurton Jones, Hawkes, and Draper (1994).

21. Hewlett et al. (2011).

22. Thomas (2006).

23. Draper (1976), pp. 205–206.

24. Hewlett et al. (2011).

25. Thomas (2006).

26. Liebenberg (1990).

27. Wannenburgh (1979), p. 41.

28. Thomas (2006), pp. 99–100.

29. Kaplan et al. (2000).

30. Walker et al. (2002).

31. Liebenberg (1990).

32. Kaplan et al. (2000).

33. Bock (2005); Kaplan et al. (2000).

34. Hewlett et al. (2011).

35. Draper (1988); Gosso et al. (2005); Turnbull (1961).

36. Gray and Feldman (2004).

37. Sutton-Smith and Roberts (1970).

38. Marshall (1976).

39. Turnbull (1982).

40. Ibid.

41. Bakeman et al. (1990); Eibl-Eibesfeldt (1989); Gosso (2005).

42. Hay and Murray (1982); Rheingold et al. (1976).

43. Bakeman et al. (1990); Wiessner (1982).

44. Turnbull (1982), p. 134.

45. Gould (1969), p. 120.

46. Liedloff (1977), p. 10.

47. Thomas (2006), pp. 216–217.

NOTES TO CHAPTER 3

1. Diamond (1997).

2. Sahlins (1972).

3. Shostak (1981), p. 10.

4. Woodburn (1968).

5. Draper (1988).

6. Bock and Johnson (2004).

7. Salamone (1997).

8. Chagnon (1977); Good and Chanoff (1991). Yanomami social organization was also undoubtedly affected by the slave raiding and genocide committed against them by Spanish, Dutch, and Portuguese invaders in the seventeenth century (Salamone, 1997).

9. Fajans (1997).

10. Quoted by Fajans (1997), p. 40.

11. Barry, Child, and Bacon (1959).

12. Gardner (1991).

13. Barry et al. (1959); DeVore et al. (1968); Gould (1969).

14. Ember and Ember (2005).

15. Gray (2009).

16. Thomas (1959), p. 152; Gould (1969), p. 128.

17. Orme (2001).

18. Ibid., p. 315.

19. Ensign (1921).

20. Gray (2009).

21. Weber (1904–1905/1958).

22. Mulhern (1959).

23. Greenleaf (1978), p. 57.

24. Quoted by Mulhern (1959), p. 383.

25. Mulhern (1959), p. 383.

26. Bernard (1836).

27. Melton (1988), p. 43.

28. Ibid., pp. 43–44.

29. Ibid., p. 186.

30. Miller (2000).

31. Bowles and Gintis (2000).

32. Melton (1988), p. 158.

33. Heywood (2001).

34. Melton (1988), pp. 531–532.

35. Quoted by Johnson (2000), p. 40.

36. Ensign (1921).

37. Bowles and Gintis (2000).

38. Ross (1901), p. 163.

39. Ibid., p. 164.

40. Ibid., p. 163.

41. Ibid., p. 174.

42. Kaestle (2000).

NOTES TO CHAPTER 4

1. Csikszentmihalyi and Hunter (2003).
2. Schneller (2002).
3. Clark (1977).
4. Einstein (1949), p. 19.
5. McMahon (2007); Oleck (2008); Pytel (2007).
6. Pytel (2007).
7. Education Portal (2007).
8. Gray (2011a); Twenge and Foster (2010); Twenge et al. (2008).
9. H. Smith (2000), pp. 62–63.
10. Merrell et al. (2008); J. D. Smith et al. (2004).
11. Gray (1993).
12. Mayes et al. (2009), p. 2; Pastor and Reuben (2008).
13. Ricaurte et al. (2005).
14. Gray (2010).

NOTES TO CHAPTER 5

1. Greenberg (1974).
2. Sudbury Valley School (1970), p. 18.
3. Ibid., p. 42.
4. Gray and Chanoff (1986).
5. Greenberg and Sadofsky (1992); Greenberg, Sadofsky, and Lempka (2005).
6. The comparison of Sudbury Valley to a hunter-gatherer band is adapted from Gray (2011b).
7. Ingold (1999).
8. Gray and Feldman (1997, 2004).
9. Gray (2009); Thomas (2006).
10. Gray (2009).
11. Sadofsky, Greenberg, and Greenberg (1994).
12. Gray and Chanoff (1986).

NOTES TO CHAPTER 6

1. Mitra (2003, 2005); Mitra and Rana (2001).
2. Mitra and Dangwal (2010).
3. Mitra (2004).
4. Aristotle (1963 translation).
5. Gordon (1999).
6. Inglis et al. (2001).
7. Roberts et al. (2007).
8. In one such experiment (by Renner, 1988), newborns, just one day old, were first shown one or the other of two similar checkerboard patterns and then were tested with both patterns in front of them to see which one attracted most

of their attention. The babies looked longer at the pattern they had not seen before. To exhibit such a preference, the newborns had to perceive the difference between the two and remember that difference over the seconds that separated one trial from the next.

9. Friedman (1972).

10. Baillargeon (2004, 2008).

11. Ruff (1986, 1989).

12. Schulz and Bonawitz (2007).

13. Bonawitz et al. (2011).

14. Hughes and Hutt (1979); Hughes (1978).

15. Groos (1898), p. 75.

16. Evidence for these species' difference in play is found in Burghardt (2005) and Fagen (1981).

17. Groos (1901).

18. Mitra and Rana (2001).

19. Schulz et al. (2007).

20. Brooks and Meltzoff (2002).

21. Ibid. (2008).

22. Okamoto-Barth et al. (2007); Tomonaga (2007).

23. Dennett (1994).

24. Goebel (2000).

25. Mitra (2005).

26. Engel (2006, 2009).

27. Eccles et al. (1993); Galton (2009); Harter (1981); Lepper et al. (2005); Osborne et al. (2003).

28. Vedder-Weiss and Fortus (2011).

NOTES TO CHAPTER 7

1. Michaels et al. (1982).

2. Allport (1920); Beilock et al. (2004).

3. Aiello and Douthitt (2001).

4. Much of the research that I cite in this chapter was conducted by people who don't use the term "play" or "playful" in describing their hypotheses and findings. They talk instead about "pressured" versus "unpressured" states of mind, or about positive moods versus negative moods, or about self-motivated tasks and goals versus those imposed by others. But from the perspective of this chapter, all such research is about play. Play is unpressured, self-motivated activity, conducted with a positive frame of mind.

5. Amabile (1996); Hennessey and Amabile (2010).

6. Amabile (2001).

7. Howard-Jones et al. (2002).

8. Isen, Daubman, and Nowicki (1987).

9. Estrada, Isen, and Young (1997).

10. Dias and Harris (1988, 1990).

11. Richards and Sanderson (1999).

12. A shorter version of this discussion of the defining features of play appeared in Gray (2009).

13. Particularly useful sources in generating this list of play's defining characteristics were Huizinga (1944/1955), Rubin et al. (1983), Smith (2005a), Sylva et al. (1976), and Vygotsky (1933/1978).

14. King (1982).

15. Kohn (1980); Kohn and Slomczynski (1990).

16. For an analysis of some of these studies, see Patall et al. (2008).

17. Lepper et al. (1973).

18. For a review of such experiments, see Lepper and Henderlong (2000).

19. Vygotsky (1933/1978).

20. Ibid., pp. 99–100.

21. Leslie (1994).

22. Einstein (1949).

23. Csíkszentmihályi (1990).

24. Fredrickson (2001, 2003).

25. Byers (1977).

26. Symons (1978).

NOTES TO CHAPTER 8

1. For a discussion of the high frequency of serious injuries in formal youth sports, see Hyman (2009).

2. Piaget (1932/1965).

3. For a classic study showing how formal team sports can create and exacerbate conflicts between groups of boys, see Sherif et al. (1961).

4. M. Greenberg (1992).

5. Furth (1996); Furth and Kane (1992).

6. Connolly and Doyle (1984); Elias and Berk (2002); Jenkins and Astington (1996); Newton and Jenvey (2011).

7. Burns and Brainerd (1979); Dockett (1998, described by Smith, 2005); Saltz, Dixon, and Johnson (1977).

8. Eisen (1988).

9. Brown et al. (1971).

10. Chazan and Cohen (2010).

11. Wegener-Spöhring (1994).

12. Spinka et al. (2001).

13. Suggested originally by Groos (1898) and more recently confirmed by others (see Fairbanks, 2000; Power, 2000). Exceptions, however, occur in the case of predatory animals, including wolves and dogs, where the preferred position in chase games is that of pursuer.

14. Power (2000), p. 194.

15. Pellis et al. (2010).
16. Aldis (1975), p. 187.
17. Konrath et al. (2011); Twenge and Foster (2010).
18. Blickle et al. (2006); Judge et al. (2006); Thomaes et al. (2009).
19. Konrath et al. (2011).
20. Herman et al. (2011).
21. Pellis and Pellis (2011); Bell et al. (2010).
22. Hall (1998); Einon et al. (1978).
23. Pellis and Pellis (2011).
24. For reviews, see Goldstein (2011) and Przybylski et al. (2010).
25. Przybylski et al. (2009).
26. Goldstein (2011).
27. Aarts et al. (2010).
28. McLeod and Lin (2010); Olson (2010); Przybylski et al. (2010); Yee (2006).
29. Barnett and Coulson (2010).
30. Reaves and Malone (2007).
31. Ferguson (2010).
32. Ferguson and Rueda (2010).
33. Green and Bavelier (2003); Spence and Feng (2010).
34. Akilli (2007).
35. Black and Steinhkuehler (2009).
36. Durkin and Barber (2002); Ferguson (2010); Olson (2010).

NOTES TO CHAPTER 9

1. This chapter is adapted, in considerable part, from an article I published in the *American Journal of Play* (Gray, 2011c).

2. My usual method to observe children at play is to sit some distance away, but close enough to see and hear them, while I pretend to read a book or magazine. I write notes as I watch and listen, if I can do so without being noticed, or I write the notes shortly thereafter.

3. D. Greenberg (1992).

4. Mitra (2005).

5. Gray (2009).

6. Gray (2009); Konner (1975).

7. Konner (1975).

8. Konner (2010), pp. 492–495. For examples, see Roopnarine et al. (994); Farver and Howes (1988).

9. One index of this implicit assumption is the paucity of research on children's age-mixed interactions. Recently I examined every issue of the two leading journals of developmental psychology—*Child Development* and *Developmental Psychology*—published from 2000 to 2010 (Gray, 2011c). I found a total of 213 articles concerned with interactions among children less than twenty-four months apart and only 19 that included interactions among children more than twenty-

four months apart. Of those nineteen, fifteen dealt exclusively with interactions among siblings and four dealt at least partly with interactions among nonsiblings. A more exhaustive survey of journals in education as well as psychology, and of databases in the social sciences, likewise revealed very few studies that involved age-mixed interactions among children.

10. Gray and Feldman (1997).

11. Ibid. (2004).

12. Vygotsky (1978).

13. Wood et al. (1976).

14. All the names of Sudbury Valley students in this chapter and elsewhere in the book are pseudonyms.

15. Christie and Stone (1999); Christie et al. (2002).

16. I calculated this from the numbers in Table 3 of Christie and Stone (1999), p. 122.

17. Emfinger (2009).

18. Originally established in a classic study by Parten (1932).

19. Goldman (1981); Mounts and Roopnarine (1987).

20. Maynard (2002); Maynard and Tovote (2010).

21. Eibl-Eibesfeldt (1982).

22. D. Greenberg (1987), p. 77.

23. Lancy et al. (2010), p. 5.

24. Correa-Chávez and Rogoff (2009).

25. Noddings (2005).

26. Feldman and Gray (1999).

27. Gorrell and Keel (1986).

28. Feldman (1997).

29. Whiting (1983).

30. Ember (1973).

31. Dearden (1998); Spencer (2006); Yogev and Ronen (1982).

32. Gordon (2005).

33. Schonert-Reichl et al. (2011).

34. LeBlanc and Bearison (2004).

35. Cohen et al. (1982); McKinstery and Topping (2003).

36. Gray and Feldman (2004).

37. Gray and Chanoff (1986); Greenberg et al. (2005).

NOTES TO CHAPTER 10

1. Skenazy (2009), p. xii.

2. Martini (1994), p. 74.

3. DeVore et al. (1968).

4. Ozment (2011).

5. Luthar and D'Avenzo (1999); Luthar and Latendresse (2005),

6. Aarts et al. (2010).

7. Lanza (2012). Also, Lanza's website at www.playborhood.com.

8. Sudbury schools are listed on the Sudbury Valley School website at www .sudval.org.

9. The US Department of Education (2008) estimated the number of home-schooled children to be 850,000 in 1999 and 1,508,000 in 2007. DOE data for subsequent years were not yet available, but Ray (2011) presents an educated estimate of 2,040,000 for 2010.

10. In a national survey of homeschooling families conducted in 2007, 36 percent said their most important reason for homeschooling was to provide religious or moral instruction (US Department of Education, 2008).

11. For a preliminary report on the survey results, see Gray (2012b).

12. For the case against summer vacation, see Von Drehle (2010). For the case against abolishing summer vacation, see Gray (2012a).

13. US Department of Education data, found at www.ed.gov.

BIBLIOGRAPHY

Aarts, M., Wendel-Vos, W., van Oers, H. A. M., van de Goor, I. A. M., & Schuit, A. J. (2010). Environmental determinants of outdoor play in children: A large-scale cross-sectional study. *American Journal of Preventive Medicine, 39,* 212–219.

Abramson, L. Y., Metalsky, G. I., & Alloy, L. B. (1989). Hopelessness depression: A theory-based subtype of depression. *Psychological Review, 96,* 358–372.

Aiello, J. R., & Douthitt, E. A. (2001). Social facilitation from Triplet to electronic performance monitoring. *Group Dynamics: Theory, Research, and Practice, 5,* 163–180.

Akilli, G. K. (2007). Games and simulations: A new approach in education? In D. Gibson, C. Aldrich, & M. Prensky (Eds.), *Games and simulations in online learning: Research and development frameworks* (pp. 1–20). Hershey, PA: Information Science.

Aldis, O. (1975). *Play-fighting.* New York: Academic Press.

Alloy, L. B., Abramson, L. Y., Whitehouse, W. G., Hogan, M. E., Panzarella, C., & Rose, D. T. (2006). Prospective incidence of first onsets and recurrence of depression in individuals at high and low cognitive risk for depression. *Journal of Abnormal Psychology, 115,* 145–156.

Allport, E. H. (1920). The influence of the group upon association and thought. *Journal of Experimental Psychology, 3,* 159–182.

Amabile, T. (1996). *Creativity in context: Update to the social psychology of creativity.* Boulder, CO: Westview Press.

———. (2001). Beyond talent: John Irving and the passionate craft of creativity. *American Psychologist, 56,* 333–336.

Aristotle. (1963 translation). D. E. Gershenson & D. A. Greenberg (translators). Metaphysica, liber A. *The Natural Philosopher, 2,* 3–55.

Baillargeon, R. (2004). Infants' physical world. *Current Directions in Psychological Science, 13,* 89–94.

———. (2008). Innate ideas revisited. *Perspectives in Psychological Science, 3,* 2–13.

Bakeman, R., Adamson, L. B., Konner, M., and Barr, R. (1990). !Kung infancy: The social context of object exploration. *Child Development, 61,* 794–809.

Barnett, J., & Coulson, M. (2010). Virtually real: A psychological perspective on massively multiplayer online games. *Review of General Psychology, 14,* 167–179.

Barry, H., Child, I., Bacon, M. K. (1959). The relation of child training to subsistence economy. *American Anthropologist, 61,* 51–63.

Beilock, S. L., Kulp, C. A., Holt, L. E., & Carr, T. H. (2004). More on the fragility of performance: Choking under pressure in mathematical problem-solving. *Journal of Experimental Psychology: General, 133,* 584–600.

Bell, H. C., Pellis, S. M., & Kolb, B. (2010). Juvenile peer play experience and the development of the orbitofrontal and medial prefrontal cortex. *Behavioral and Brain Research, 207,* 7–13.

Bernard, J. (1836/2007). "Though I was often beaten for my play": Excerpt from Autobiography of the Rev. John Bernard, *Collections of the Massachusetts Historical Society, v. 25.* Reprinted in Martin, J. (Ed.) (2007), *Children in colonial America.* New York: New York University Press.

Black, R. W., & Steinkuehler, C. (2009). Literacy in virtual worlds. In L. Christenbury, R. Bomer, & P. Smargorinsky (Eds.), *Handbook of adolescent literacy research,* 271–286. New York: Guilford.

Blickle, G., Schlegel, A., Fassbender, P., & Klein, U. (2006). Some personality correlates of white-collar crime. *Applied Psychology 55,* 220–233.

Blurton Jones, N. (1993). The lives of hunter-gatherer children. In M. E. Pereira & L. A. Fairbanks (Eds.), *Juvenile primates: Life history, development, and behavior,* 308–326. New York: Oxford University Press.

Blurton Jones, N., Hawkes, K., and Draper, P. (1994). Differences between Hazda and !Kung children's work: Affluence or practical reason? In E. S. Burch Jr. & L. J. Ellana (Eds.), *Key issues in hunter-gatherer research,* 189–215. Oxford: Berg.

Bock, J. (2005). What makes a competent adult forager? In B. S. Hewlett & M. E. Lamb (Eds.), *Hunter-gatherer childhoods: Evolutionary, developmental, and cultural perspectives,* 109–128. New Brunswick, NJ: Transaction.

Bock, J., & Johnson, S. E. (2004). Subsistence ecology and play among the Okavango Delta peoples of Botswana. *Human Nature, 15,* 63–81.

Boehm, C. (1999). *Hierarchy in the forest: The evolution of egalitarian behavior.* Cambridge, MA: Harvard University Press.

Bonawitz, E., Shafto, P., Gweon, H., Goodman, N. D., Spelke, E., & Schulz, L. (2011). The double-edged sword of pedagogy: Teaching limits children's spontaneous exploration and discovery. *Cognition, 120,* 322–330.

Bowles, S., & Gintis, E. (2000). The origins of mass public education. Ch. 33 in Roy Lowe (Ed.), *History of education: Major themes. Volume II: Education in its social context.* London: RoutledgeFlamer.

Brooks, R., & Meltzoff, A. N. (2002). The importance of eyes. How infants interpret adult looking behavior. *Developmental Psychology, 38,* 958–966.

———. (2008). Infant gaze following and pointing predict accelerated vocabulary growth through two years of age: A longitudinal growth curve modeling study. *Journal of Child Language, 5,* 207–220.

Brown, N. S., Curry, N. E., & Tittnich, E. (1971). How groups of children deal with common stress through play. In N. E. Curry & S. Arnaud (Eds.), *Play: The child strives toward self-realization.* Washington, DC: National Association for the Education of Young Children.

Burghardt, G. M. (2005). *The genesis of animal play: Testing the limits.* Cambridge, MA: MIT Press.

Burns, S. M., & Brainerd, C. J. (1979). Effects of constructive and dramatic play on perspective taking in very young children. *Developmental Psychology, 15,* 512–521.

Byers, J. A. (1977). Terrain preferences in the play behavior of Siberian ibex kids (*Capra ibex sibirica*). *Zeitschrift fur Tierpsychologie, 45,* 199–209.

Chagnon, N. (1977). *Yanomamo: The fierce people,* 2nd ed. New York: Holt, Rinehart & Winston.

Chazan, S., & Cohen, E. (2010). Adaptive and defensive strategies in post-traumatic play of young children exposed to violent attacks. *Journal of Child Psychotherapy, 36,* 133–151.

Christie, J. F., & Stone, S. J. (1999). Collaborative literacy activity in print-enriched play centers: Exploring the "zone" in same-age and multi-age groupings. *Journal of Literary Research, 31,* 109–131.

Christie, J. F., Stone, S. J., & Deitscher, R. (2002). Play in same-age and multiage grouping arrangements. In J. L. Roopnarine (Ed.), *Conceptual, social-cognitive, and contextual issues in the fields of play,* 63–75. Westport, CT: Ablex.

Chudacoff, H. P. (2007). *Children at play: An American history.* New York: New York University Press.

Clark, R. W. (1977). *Edison: The man who made the future.* New York: Putnam's Sons.

Clements, R. (2004). An investigation of the status of outdoor play. *Contemporary Issues in Early Childhood, 5,* 68–80.

Clinton, H. R. (2001). An idyllic childhood. In S. A. Cohen (Ed.), *The games we played: A celebration of childhood and imagination.* New York: Simon & Schuster.

Cohen, P. A., Kulik, J. A., & Kulik, C. (1982). Educational outcomes of tutoring: A meta-analysis of findings. *American Educational Research Journal, 19,* 237–248.

Connolly, J. A., & Doyle, A. (1984). Relation of social fantasy play to social competence in preschoolers. *Developmental Psychology, 20,* 797–806.

Corballis, M. C. (1999). Phylogeny from apes to humans. In M. C. Corballis & S. E. G. Lea (Eds.), *The descent of mind: Psychological perspectives on hominid evolution.* Oxford: Oxford University Press.

Correa-Chávez, M., & Rogoff, B. (2009). Children's attentions to interactions directed to others: Guatemalan Mayan and European American patterns. *Developmental Psychology, 45,* 630–641.

Csíkszentmihályi, M. (1990). *Flow: The psychology of optimal experience.* New York: Harper & Row.

Csíkszentmihályi, M., & Hunter, J. (2003). Happiness in everyday life: The uses of experience sampling. *Journal of Happiness Studies, 4,* 185–199.

Dearden, J. (1998). Cross-age peer mentoring in action. *Educational Psychology in Practice, 13,* 250–257.

Dennett, D. C. (1994). Language and intelligence. In J. Khalfa (Ed.), *What is intelligence?* Cambridge: Cambridge University Press.

DeVore, I., Murdock, G. P., and Whiting, J. W. M. (1968). Discussions, part VII: Are the hunter-gatherers a cultural type? In R. Lee & I. DeVore (Eds.), *Man the hunter*. Chicago: Aldine.

Diamond, J. (1997). *Guns, germs, and steel: The fates of human societies.* New York: Norton.

Dias, M. G., & Harris, P. L. (1988). The effect of make-believe play on deductive reasoning. *British Journal of Developmental Psychology, 6,* 207–221.

Draper, P. (1976). Social and economic constraints on child life among the !Kung. In R. B. Lee & I. DeVore (Eds.), *Kalahari hunter-gatherers: Studies of the !Kung San and their neighbors,* 199–217. Cambridge, MA: Harvard University Press.

———. (1988). Technological change and child behavior among the !Kung. *Ethnology, 27,* 339–365.

Durkin, K., & Barber, B. (2002). Not so doomed: Computer game play and positive adolescent development. *Applied Developmental Psychology, 23,* 373–392.

Eccles, J. S., Wigfield, A., Midgley, C., Reuman, D., MacIver, D., & Feldlaufer, H. (1993). Negative effects of traditional middle schools on students' motivation. *Elementary School Journal, 93,* 553–574.

Education Portal (2007). Published online at http://education-portal.com/articles/75_to_98_Percent_of_College_Students_Have_Cheated.html.

Eibl-Eibesfeldt, I. (1982). The flexibility and affective autonomy of play. *Behavioral and Brain Sciences, 5,* 160–162.

———. (1989). *Human ethology.* New York: Aldine de Gruyter.

Einon, D. F., Morgan, M. J., & Kibbler, C. C. (1978). Brief periods of socialization and later behavior in the rat. *Developmental Psychobiology, 11,* 231–225.

Einstein, A. (1949). Autobiography. In P. Schilpp, *Albert Einstein: Philosopher-scientist.* Evanston, IL: Library of Living Philosophers.

Eisen, G. (1988). *Children and play in the Holocaust: Games among the shadows.* Amherst: University of Massachusetts Press.

Elias, C. L., & Berk, L. E. (2002). Self-regulation in young children: Is there a role for sociodramatic play? *Early Childhood Research Quarterly, 17,* 216–238.

Ember, C. R. (1973). Feminine task assignment and the social behavior of boys. *Ethos, 1,* 424–439.

Ember, C. R., & Ember, M. (2005). Explaining corporal punishment of children: A cross-cultural study. *American Anthropologist, 107,* 609–619.

Emfinger, K. (2009). Numerical conceptions reflected during multiage child-initiated pretend play. *Journal of Instructional Psychology, 36,* 326–334.

Engel, S. (2006). Open Pandora's box: Curiosity in the classroom. Sarah Lawrence Child Development Institute Occasional Papers. Published online at www.slc.edu/media/cdi/pdf/ . . . /CDI_Occasional_Paper_2006_Engel.pdf.

———. (2009). Is curiosity vanishing? *Journal of the American Academy of Child and Adolescent Psychiatry, 48,* 777–779.

Ensign, F. C. (1921). *Compulsory school attendance and child labor.* Iowa City, Iowa: Athens Press.

Estrada, C. A., Isen, A. M., & Young, M. J. (1997). Positive affect facilitates integration of information and decreases anchoring in reasoning among physicians. *Organizational Behavior and Human Decision Processes, 72,* 117–135.

Fagen, R. (1981). *Animal play behavior.* New York: Oxford University Press.

Fairbanks, L. A. (2000). The developmental timing of primate play: A neural selection model. In Parker, S. T., Langer, J., & McKinney, M. L. (Eds.), *Biology, brains, and behavior: The evolution of human development,* 131–18). Santa Fe, NM: School of American Research Press.

Fajans, J. (1997). *They make themselves: Work and play among the Baining of Papua New Guinea.* Chicago: University of Chicago Press.

Family, Kids, and Youth. (2010). *Play Report: International Summary of Results.* Published online at www.fairplayforchildren.org/pdf/1280152791.pdf.

Farver, J., & Howes, C. (1988). Cross-cultural differences in social interaction: A comparison of American and Indonesian children. *Journal of Cross-Cultural Psychology, 19,* 203–215.

Feldman, J. (1997). *The educational opportunities that lie in self-directed age mixing among children and adolescents.* PhD dissertation, Department of Psychology, Boston College.

Feldman, J., & Gray, P. (1999). Some educational benefits of freely chosen age mixing among children and adolescents. *Phi Delta Kappan, 80,* 507–512.

Ferguson, C. (2010). Blazing angels or resident evil? Can violent video games be a force for good? *Review of General Psychology, 14,* 68–81.

Ferguson, C., & Rueda, S. M. (2010). The Hitman study: Violent video game exposure effects on aggressive behavior, hostile feelings, and depression. *European Psychologist, 15,* 99–108.

Finkelhor, D., Turner, H., Ormrod, R., & Hamby, S. L. (2010). Trends in childhood violence and abuse exposure: Evidence from two national surveys. *Archives of Pediatric and Adolescent Medicine, 164,* 238–242.

Fredrickson, B. L. (2001). The role of positive emotions in positive psychology: The broaden-and-build theory of positive emotions. *American Psychologist, 56,* 218–226.

———. (2003). The value of positive emotions. *American Scientist, 91,* 330–335.

Friedman, S. (1972). Habituation and recovery of visual response in the alert human newborn. *Journal of Experimental Child Psychology, 13,* 339–349.

Furth, H. G. (1996). *Desire for society: Children's knowledge as social imagination,* 149–173. New York: Plenum.

Furth, H. G., & Kane, S. R. (1992). Children constructing society: A new perspective on children at play. In H. McGurk (Ed.), *Childhood social development: Contemporary perspectives.* Hillsdale, NJ: Erlbaum.

Galton, M. (2009). Moving to secondary school: Initial encounters and their effects. *Perspectives on Education: Primary Secondary Transfer in Science, 2,* 5–21.

Gardner, P. M. (1991). Foragers' pursuit of individual autonomy. *Current Anthropology, 32,* 543–572.

Goebel, R. L. (2000). *Can we talk? Manifestations of critical thinking in young people's spontaneous talk.* Master's thesis, School of Education, DePaul University, Chicago.

Goldman, J. A. (1981). Social participation of preschool children in same- versus mixed-age groups. *Child Development, 32,* 644–650.

Goldstein, J. (2011). Technology in play. In Anthony D. Pellgrini (Ed.), *The Oxford handbook of the development of play,* 322–337. Oxford: Oxford University Press.

Good, K., & Chanoff, D. (1991). *Into the heart: One man's pursuit of love and knowledge among the Yanomami.* New York: Simon & Schuster.

Gordon, D. M. (1999). *Ants at work: How an insect society is organized.* New York: Free Press.

Gordon, M. (2005). *The roots of empathy: Changing the world child by child.* Toronto: Thomas Allen Publishers.

Gorrell, J., & Keel, L. (1986). A field study of helping relationships in a cross-age tutoring program. *Elementary School Guidance and Counseling, 24,* 268–276.

Gosso, Y., Otta, E., de Lima, M., Ribeiro, F. J. L., & Bussab, V. S. R. (2005). Play in hunter-gatherer societies. In A. D. Pellegrini & P. K. Smith (Eds.), *The nature of play: Great apes and humans,* 213–253. New York: Guilford.

Gould, R. A. (1969). *Yiwara: Foragers of the Australian desert.* New York: Charles Scribner.

Gray, P. (1993). Engaging students' intellects: The immersion approach to critical thinking in psychology instruction. *Teaching of Psychology, 20,* 68–74.

———. (2009). Play as the foundation for hunter-gatherer social existence. *American Journal of Play, 1,* 476–522.

———. (2010). ADHD and school: The problem of assessing normalcy in an abnormal environment. *Psychology Today, Freedom to Learn* blog, Published online at www.psychologytoday.com/blog/freedom-learn/201007/adhd-and -school-the-problem-assessing-normalcy-in-abnormal-environment.

———. (2011a). The decline of play and the rise of psychopathology in childhood and adolescence. *American Journal of Play, 3,* 443–463.

———. (2011b). The evolutionary biology of education: How our hunter-gatherer educative instincts could form the basis for education today. *Evolution: Education and Outreach, 4,* 28–40.

———. (2011c). The special value of children's age-mixed play. *American Journal of Play, 3,* 500–522.

———. (2012a). Doing more time in school: A cruel non-solution to our educational problems. *Psychology Today, Freedom to Learn* blog. Published online at www.psychologytoday.com/blog/freedom-learn/201205/doing-more-time -in-school-cruel-non-solution-our-educational-problems-0.

———. (2012b). (1) The benefits of unschooling: Report I from a large survey; (2) What leads families to unschool their children: Report II from a large survey; (3) The challenges of unschooling: Report III from a large survey. *Psychology Today, Freedom to Learn* blog. Three reports, published online beginning with www.psychologytoday.com/blog/freedom-learn/201202/the-benefits -unschooling-report-i-large-survey.

Gray, P., & Chanoff, D. (1986). Democratic schooling: What happens to young people who have charge of their own education? *American Journal of Education, 94,* 182–213.

Gray, P., & Feldman J. (1997). Patterns of age mixing and gender mixing among children and adolescents at an ungraded democratic school. *Merrill-Palmer Quarterly, 43,* 67–86.

———. (2004). Playing in the zone of proximal development: Qualities of self-directed age mixing between adolescents and young children at a democratic school. *American Journal of Education, 110,* 108–145.

Green, C. S., & Bavelier, D. (2003). Action video game modifies visual selective attention. *Nature, 423,* 534–537.

Greenberg, D. (1974). *Outline of a new philosophy.* Framingham, MA: Sudbury Valley School Press.

———. (1987). *Free at last: The Sudbury Valley School.* Framingham, MA: Sudbury Valley School Press.

———. (1992). Sudbury Valley's secret weapon: Allowing people of different ages to mix freely at school. In D. Greenberg (Ed.), *The Sudbury Valley School experience,* 3rd ed., 121–136. Framingham, MA: Sudbury Valley School Press.

Greenberg, D., & Sadofsky, M. (1992). *Legacy of trust: Life after the Sudbury Valley School experience.* Framingham, Massachusetts: Sudbury Valley School Press.

Greenberg, D., Sadofsky, M., & Lempka, J. (2005). *The pursuit of happiness: The lives of Sudbury Valley alumni.* Framingham, MA: Sudbury Valley School Press.

Greenberg, M. (1992). On the nature of sports at SVS, and the limitations of language in describing SVS to the world. In D. Greenberg (Ed.), *The Sudbury Valley School experience,* 3rd ed. Framingham, MA: Sudbury Valley School Press.

Greenleaf, B. K. (1978). *Children through the ages.* New York: McGraw-Hill.

Groos, K. (1898). *The play of animals.* New York: Appleton.

———. (1901). *The play of man.* New York: Appleton.

Guemple, L. (1988). Teaching social relations to Inuit children. In T. Ingold, D. Riches, & J. Woodburn (Eds.), *Hunters and gatherers 2: Property, power, and ideology,* 130–149. Oxford: Berg.

Hall, F. S. (1998). Social deprivation of neonatal, adolescent, and adult rats has distinct neurochemical and behavioral consequences. *Critical Reviews of Neurobiology, 12,* 129–162.

Harrow, M., Hansford, B. G., & Astrachan-Fletcher, E. B. (2009). Locus of control: Relation to schizophrenia, to recovery, and to depression and psychosis—a 15-year longitudinal study. *Psychiatry Research, 168,* 186–192.

Harter, S. (1981). A new self-report scale of intrinsic versus extrinsic orientation in the classroom: Motivational and informational components. *Developmental Psychology, 17,* 300–312.

Hay, D. F., & Murray, P. (1982). Giving and requesting: Social facilitation of infants' offers to adults. *Infant Behavior and Development, 5,* 301–310.

Hennessey, B., & Amabile, T. (2010). Creativity. *Annual Review of Psychology, 61,* 569–598.

Herman, K. N., Paukner, A., & Suomi, S. J. (2011). Gene X environment interactions in social play: Contributions from rhesus macaques. In A. D. Pellgrini (Ed.), *The Oxford handbook of the development of play,* 58–69. Oxford: Oxford University Press.

Hewlett, B. S., Fouts, H. N., Boyette, A. H., & Hewlett, B. L. (2011). Social learning among Congo Basin hunter-gatherers. *Philosophical Transactions of the Royal Society B, 366,* 1168–1178.

Heywood, C. (2001). *A history of childhood: Children and childhood in the West from medieval to modern times.* Oxford: Blackwell.

Hofferth, S. (2009). Changes in American children's time, 1997–2003. *International Journal of Time Use Research, 6,* 26–47.

Hofferth, S. L., & Sandberg, J. F. (2001). Changes in American children's time, 1981–1997. In T. Owens & S. L. Hofferth (Eds.), *Children at the millennium: Where have we come from, where are we going?* 193–229. New York: Elsevier Science.

Howard-Jones, P. A., Taylor, J. R., & Sutton, L. (2002). The effect of play on the creativity of young children during subsequent activity. *Early Child Development and Care, 172,* 323–328.

Hughes, M. (1978). Sequential analysis of exploration and play. *International Journal of Behavioral Development, 1,* 83–97.

Hughes, M., & Hutt, C. (1979). Heart-rate correlates of childhood activities: Play, exploration, problem-solving, and day-dreaming. *Biological Psychology, 8,* 253–263.

Huizinga, J. (1955; first German edition published in 1944). *Homo Ludens: A study of the play-element in culture.* Boston: Beacon Press.

Hyman, M. (2009). *Until it hurts: America's obsession with youth sports and how it harms our kids.* Boston: Beacon Press.

Inglis, I. R., Langton, S., Forkman, B., & Lazarus, J. (2001). An information primacy model of exploratory and foraging behavior. *Animal Behaviour, 62,* 543–557.

Ingold, T. (1999). On the social relations of the hunter-gatherer band. In R. B. Lee & R. H. Daly (Eds.), *The Cambridge encyclopedia of hunters and gatherers,* 399–410. Cambridge: Cambridge University Press.

Isen, A. M., Daubman, K. A., & Nowicki, G. P. (1987). Positive affect facilitates creative problem solving. *Journal of Personality and Social Psychology, 52,* 1122–1131.

Jenkins, J. M., & Astington, J. W. (1996). Cognitive factors and family structure associated with theory of mind development in young children. *Developmental Psychology, 32,* 70–78.

Johnson, D. (1998). Many schools putting an end to child's play. *New York Times,* April 7, A1, A18.

Johnson, R. (2000). Notes on schooling of the English working class, 1780–1850. In Roy Lowe (Ed.), *History of education: Major themes. Volume II: Education in its social context,* Ch. 31. London: RoutledgeFlamer.

Judge, T. A., LePine, J. A., & Rich, B. L. (2006). Loving yourself abundantly: Relationship of the narcissistic personality to self—and other perceptions of workplace deviance, leadership, and task and contextual performance. *Journal of Applied Psychology, 91,* 762–776.

Kaestle, C. F. (2000). The legacy of common schooling. In Roy Lowe (Ed.), *History of education: Major themes. Volume II: Education in its social context,* Ch. 35. London: RoutledgeFlamer.

Kaplan, H., Hill, K., Lancaster, J., & Hurtado, A. M. (2000). A theory of human life history evolution: Diet, intelligence, and longevity. *Evolutionary Anthropology, 9,* 156–185.

Kelly, R. I. (1995). *The foraging spectrum: Diversity in hunter-gatherer lifeways.* Washington, DC: Smithsonian Institution Press.

Kent, S. (1996). Cultural diversity among African foragers: Causes and implications. In S. Kent (Ed.), *Cultural diversity among twentieth-century foragers: An African perspective,* 1–18. Cambridge: Cambridge University Press.

King, N. R. (1982). Work and play in the classroom. *Social Education, 46,* 110–113.

Kohn, M. L. (1980). Job complexity and adult personality. In N. J. Smelser & E. H. Erikson (Eds.), *Theories of work and love in adulthood.* Cambridge, MA: Harvard University Press.

Kohn, M. L., & Slomczynski, K. M. (1990). *Social structure and self-direction: A comparative analysis of the United States and Poland.* Cambridge, MA: Basil Blackwell.

Konner, M. (1975). Relations among infants and juveniles in comparative perspective. In M. Lewis & L. A. Rosenblum (Eds.), *The origins of behavior, vol. 4: Friendship and peer relations,* 99–129. New York: Wiley.

———. (2002). *The tangled wing: Biological constraints on the human spirit,* 2nd ed. New York: Holt.

———. (2010). *The evolution of childhood.* Cambridge, MA: Harvard University Press.

Konrath, S. H., O'Brien, E. H., & Hsing, C. (2011). Changes in dispositional empathy in American college students over time: A meta-analysis. *Personality and Social Psychology Review, 15,* 180–198.

Lancy, D. F., Bock, J., & Gaskins, S. (2010). Putting learning into context. In D. F. Lancy, J. Bock, & S. Gaskins (Eds.), *The anthropology of learning in childhood,* 3–10. Lanham, MD: AltaMira Press.

Lanza, M. (2012). *Playborhood: Turn your neighborhood into a place for play.* Menlo Park, CA: Free Play Press.

LeBlanc, G., & Bearison, D. J. (2004). Teaching and learning as bi-directional activity: Investigating dyadic interactions between child teachers and child learners. *Cognitive Development, 19,* 499–515.

Lee, R. B. (1988). Reflections on primitive communism. In T. Ingold, D. Riches, & J. Woodburn (Eds.), *Hunters and gatherers 1*, 252–268. Oxford: Berg.

Lee, R. B., & DeVore, I. (1968). Problems in the study of hunters and gatherers. In R. B. Lee & I. Lee (Eds.), *Man the hunter*, 3–12. Chicago: Aldine.

Lepper, M. R., Corpus, J. H., & Iyengar, S. S. (2005). Intrinsic and extrinsic motivational orientations in the classroom: Age differences and academic correlates. *Journal of Educational Psychology, 97*, 184–196.

Lepper, M. R., Greene, D., & Nisbett, R. E. (1973). Undermining children's intrinsic interest with extrinsic reward: A test of the "overjustification" hypothesis. *Journal of Personality and Social Psychology, 28*, 129–137.

Lepper, M. R., & Henderlong, J. (2000). Turning "play" into "work" and "work" into "play": 25 years of research on intrinsic versus extrinsic motivation. In C. Sansone & J. M. Harackiewicz (Eds.), *Intrinsic and extrinsic motivation*, 257–307. San Diego, CA: Academic Press.

Leslie, A. M. (1994). Pretending and believing: Issues in the theory of ToMM. *Cognition, 50*, 211–238.

Liebenberg, L. (1990). *The art of tracking: The origin of science.* Claremont, South Africa: David Philip Publishers.

Liedloff, J. (1977). *The continuum concept*, rev. ed. New York: Knopf.

Luthar, S. S., & D'Avanzo, K. (1999). Contextual factors in substance use: A study of suburban and inner-city adolescents. *Development and Psychopathology, 11*, 845–867.

Luthar, S. S., & Latendresse, S. J. (2005). Children of the affluent: Challenges to well-being. *Current Directions in Psychological Science, 14*, 49–55.

Marshall, L. (1976). *The !Kung of Nyae Nyae.* Cambridge, MA: Harvard University Press.

Martini, M. (1994). Peer interactions in Polynesia: A view from the Marquesas. In J. L. Roopnarine, J. E. Johnson, & F. H. Hooper (Eds.), *Children's play in diverse cultures*, 73–103. Albany: State University of New York Press.

Mayes, R., Bagwell, C., & Erkulwater, J. (2009). *Medicating children: ADHD and pediatric mental health.* Cambridge, MA: Harvard University Press.

Maynard, A. E. (2002). Cultural teaching: The development of teaching skills in Maya sibling interactions. *Child Development, 73*, 969–982.

Maynard, A. E., & Tovote, K. E. (2010). Learning from other children. In D. F. Lancy, J. Bock, & S. Gaskins (Eds.), *The anthropology of learning in childhood*, 181–205. Lanham, MD: AltaMira Press.

McKinstery, J., & Topping, K. J. (2003). Cross-age peer tutoring of thinking skills in high school. *Educational Psychology in Practice, 19*, 199–217.

McLeod, L., & Lin, L. (2010). A child's power in game-play. *Computers & Education, 54*, 517–527.

McMahon, R. (2007). Everybody does it: Academic cheating is at an all-time high. *San Francisco Chronicle*, September 9.

Melton, J. V. H. (1988). *Absolutism and the eighteenth-century origins of compulsory schooling in Prussia and Austria.* Cambridge: Cambridge University Press.

Merrell, K. W., Isava, D. M., Gueldner, B. A., & Ross, S. W. (2008). How effective are school bullying intervention programs? A meta-analysis of intervention research. *School Psychology Quarterly, 23*, 26–42.

Michaels, J. W., Blommel, J. M., Brocato, R. M., Linkous, R. A., & Rowe, J. S. (1982). Social facilitation and inhibition in a natural setting. *Replications in Social Psychology, 2*, 21–24.

Miller, P. (2000). Historiography of compulsory schooling. In Roy Lowe (Ed.), *History of education: Major themes. Volume II: Education in its social context*, Ch. 38. London: RoutledgeFlamer.

Mitra, S. (2003). Minimally invasive education: A progress report on the "hole-in-the-wall" experiments. *British Journal of Educational Technology, 34*, 267–371.

———. (2004). Hole in the wall. *Dataquest (India)*, September 23. Published online at http://dqindia.ciol.commakesections.asp/04092301.asp.

———. (2005). Self-organizing systems for mass computer literacy: Findings from the "hole in the wall" experiments. *International Journal of Development Issues, 4*, 71–81.

Mitra, S., & Dangwal, R. (2010). Limits to self-organising systems of learning—the Kalikuppam experiment. *British Journal of Educational Technology, 41*, 672–688.

Mitra, S., & Rana, V. (2001). Children and the Internet: Experiments with minimally invasive education in India. *British Journal of Educational Technology, 32*, 221–232.

Mounts, N. S., & Roopnarine, J. L. (1987). Social-cognitive play patterns in same-age and mixed-age preschool classrooms. *American Educational Research Journal, 24*, 463–476.

Mulhern, J. (1959). *A history of education: A social interpretation*, 2nd ed. New York: Ronald Press.

Nauert, R. (2008). Teen suicide rates remain high. Published online at http://psychcentral.com/news/2008/09/04/teen-suicide-rates-remain-high/2874.html.

Newsom, C. R., Archer, R. P., Trumbetta, S., & I. Gottesman, I. I. (2003). Changes in adolescent response patterns on the MMPI/MMPI-A across four decades. *Journal of Personality Assessment, 81*, 74–84.

Newton, E., & Jenvey, V. (2011). Play and theory of mind: Associations with social competence in young children. *Early Child Development and Care, 181*, 761–773.

Noddings, N. (2005). *The challenge to care in the schools: An alternative approach to education*, 2nd ed. New York: Teachers College Press.

O'Brien, J., & Smith, J. (2002). Childhood transformed? Risk perceptions and the decline of free play. *British Journal of Occupational Therapy, 65*, 123–128.

Okamoto-Barth, S., Call, J., & Tomasello, M. (2007). Great apes' understanding of other individuals' line of sight. *Psychological Science, 18*, 462–468.

Oleck, J. (2008). Most high school students admit to cheating. *School Library Journal*, March 10.

Olson, C. K. (2010). Children's motivation for video game play in the context of normal development. *Review of General Psychology, 14,* 180–187.

Orme, N. (2001). *Medieval children.* New Haven, CT: Yale University Press.

Osborne, J. A., Simon, S. B., & Collins, S. (2003). Attitudes towards science: A review of the literature and its implications. *International Journal of Science Education, 25,* 1049–1079.

Ozment, K. (2011). Welcome to the age of overparenting. *Boston Magazine,* December, 88–93, 136–137.

Parten, M. (1932). Social participation among preschool children. *Journal of Abnormal and Social Psychology, 28,* 136–147.

Pastor, P. N., & Reuben, M. A. (2008). Diagnosed attention deficit hyperactivity disorder and learning disability: United States, 2004–2006. *Vital and health statistics, Series 10, #237.* Washington, DC: US Department of Health and Human Services.

Patall, E. A., Cooper, H., & Robinson, J. C. (2008). The effects of choice on intrinsic motivation and related outcomes: A meta-analysis of research findings. *Psychological Bulletin, 134,* 270–300.

Pellis, S. M., & Pellis, V. C. (2011). Rough and tumble play: Training and using the social brain. In A. D. Pellgrini (Ed.), *The Oxford handbook of the development of play,* 245–259. Oxford: Oxford University Press.

Pellis, S. M., Pellis, V. C., & Bell, H. C. (2010). The function of play in the development of the social brain. *American Journal of Play, 2,* 278–296.

Piaget, J. (1932; 1965). *The moral judgment of the child.* New York: Free Press.

Power, T. G. (2000). *Play and exploration in animals and children.* Mahwah, NJ: Lawrence Erlbaum Associates.

Przybylski, A. K., Rigby, C. S., & Ryan, R. M. (2010). A motivational model of video game engagement. *Review of General Psychology, 14,* 154–166.

Przybylski, A. K., Weinstein, N., Ryan, R. M., & Rigby, C. S. (2009). Having versus wanting to play: Background and consequences of harmonious versus obsessive engagement in video games. *CyberPsychology & Behavior, 12,* 485–492.

Pytel, B. (2007). Cheating is on the rise. Published online at www.suite101.com/content/cheating-is-on-the-rise-a31238.

Ray, B. D. (2011). Research facts on homeschooling. Salem, OR: National Home Education Research Institute. Published online at www.nheri.org.

Reaves, B., & Malone, T. W. (2007). *Leadership in games and work: Implications for the enterprise of massively multiplayer online role-playing games.* Seriosity Inc. Published online at www.seriosity.com/downloads/Leadership_In_Games_Seriosity_and_IBM.pdf.

Reich, J. W., Erdal, K. J., & Zautra, A. (1997). Beliefs about control and health behaviors. In D. S. Gochman (Ed.), *Handbook of health behavior research: I, Personal and social determinants.* New York: Plenum.

Renner, M. J. (1988). Learning during exploration: The role of behavioral topography during exploration in determining subsequent adaptive behavior. *International Journal of Comparative Psychology, 2,* 43–56.

Rheingold, H. L., Hay, D. F., & West, M. J. (1976). Sharing in the second year of life. *Child Development, 47*, 1148–1158.

Ricaurte, G. A., Mechan, A. O., Yuan, J., Hatzidimitriou, G., Xie, T., Mayne, A. H., & McCann, U. D. (2005). Amphetamine treatment similar to that used in the treatment of ADHD damages dopamine nerve endings in the striatum of adult nonhuman primates. *Journal of Pharmacology and Experimental Therapeutics, 315*, 91–98.

Richards, C. A., & Sanderson, J. A. (1999). The role of imagination in facilitating deductive reasoning in 2-, 3-, and 4-year-olds. *Cognition, 72*, 81–89.

Ridley, M. (2003). *Nature via nurture: Genes, experience, and what makes us human*. New York: HarperCollins.

Roberts, W. A., Cruz, C., & Tremblay, J. (2007). Rats take correct novel routes and shortcuts in an enclosed maze. *Journal of Experimental Psychology: Animal Behavior Processes, 33*, 79–91.

Roopnarine, J. L., Johnson, J. E., & Hooper, F. H. (Eds.). (1994). *Children's play in diverse cultures*. Albany: State University of New York Press.

Ross, E. A. (1901). *Social control: A survey of the foundations of order*. New York: Macmillan.

Rubin, K. H., Fein, G. G., & Vandenberg, B. (1983). Play. In P. H. Mussen & E. M. Hetherington (Eds.), *Handbook of child psychology, vol. 4*, 693–774. New York: Wiley.

Ruff, H. A. (1986). Components of attention during infants' manipulative exploration. *Child Development, 75*, 105–114.

———. (1989). The infant's use of visual and haptic information in the perception and recognition of objects. *Canadian Journal of Psychology, 43*, 302–319.

Sadofsky, M., Greenberg, D., & Greenberg, H. (1994). *Kingdom of childhood: Growing up at Sudbury Valley School*. Framingham, MA: Sudbury Valley School Press.

Sahlins, M. (1972). *Stone age economics*. Chicago: Aldine-Atherton.

Salamone, F. A. (1997). *The Yanomami and their interpreters: Fierce people or fierce interpreters?* Lanham, MD: University Press of America.

Saltz, E., Dixon, D., & Johnson, J. (1977). Training disadvantaged preschoolers on various fantasy activities: Effects on cognitive functioning and impulse control. *Child Development, 48*, 367–380.

Schneller, R. J. (2002). *Farragut: America's first admiral*. Dulles, VA: Brassey's.

Schonert-Reichl, K. A., Smith, V., & Zaidman-Zait, A. (2011). Effectiveness of the Roots of Empathy program in fostering social-emotional development in primary grade children. Manuscript submitted for publication.

Schulz, L. E., & Bonawitz, E. G. (2007). Serious fun: Preschoolers engage in more exploratory play when evidence is confounded. *Developmental Psychology, 43*, 1045–1050.

Schulz, L. E., Gopnik, A., & Glymour, C. (2007). Preschool children learn about causal structure from conditional interventions. *Developmental Science, 10*, 322–332.

Sherif, M., Harvey, O. J., White, B. J., Hood, W. E., & Sherif, C. S. (1961). *Intergroup conflict and cooperation: The Robbers Cave experiment.* Norman: University of Oklahoma Book Exchange.

Shostak, M. (1981) *Nisa: The life and words of a !Kung woman.* Cambridge, MA: Harvard University Press.

Silberbauer, G. (1982). Political Process in G/wi Bands. In E. Leacock & R. Lee (Eds.), *Politics and History in Band Societies,* 23–36. Cambridge: Cambridge University Press.

Skenazy, L. (2009). *Free-range kids: Giving our children the freedom we had without going nuts with worry.* San Francisco: Jossey-Bass.

Smith, H. (2000). *The scarred heart: Understanding and identifying kids who kill.* Knoxville, TN: Callisto.

Smith, J. D., Schneider, B. H., Smith, P. K., & Ananiadou, K. (2004). The effectiveness of whole-school antibullying programs: A synthesis of evaluation research. *School Psychology Review, 33,* 547–560.

Smith, P. K. (2005a). Play: Types and functions in human development. In B. J. Ellis & D. F. Bjorklund (Eds.), *Origins of the social mind.* New York: Guilford.

———. (2005b). Social and pretend play in children. In A. D. Pellegrini & P. K. Smith (Eds.), *The nature of play: Great apes and humans,* 137–212. New York: Guilford.

Spence, I., & Feng, J. (2010). Video games and spatial cognition. *Review of General Psychology, 14,* 92–104.

Spencer, V. G. (2006). Peer tutoring and students with emotional or behavioral disorders: A review of the literature. *Behavioral Disorders, 31,* 204–222.

Spinka, M., Newberry, R. C., & Bekoff, M. (2001). Mammalian play: Training for the unexpected. *Quarterly Review of Biology, 76,* 141–168.

Sudbury Valley School. (1970). *The crisis in American education: An analysis and proposal.* Framingham, MA: Sudbury Valley School Press.

Sutton-Smith, B., & Roberts, J. M. (1970). The cross-cultural and psychological study of games. In G. Lüschen (Ed.), *The cross-cultural analysis of sport and games,* 100–108. Champaign, IL: Stipes.

Sylva, K., Bruner, J., & Genova, P. (1976). The role of play in the problem solving of children 3–5 years old. In J. Bruner, A. Jolly, & K. Sylva (Eds.), *Play,* 244–257. New York: Basic Books.

Symons, D. (1978). *Play and aggression: A study of rhesus monkeys.* New York: Columbia University Press.

Thomaes, S., Bushman, B. J., DeCastro, B. O., & Stegge, H. (2009). What makes narcissists bloom? A framework for research on the etiology and development of narcissism. *Development and Psychopathology, 21,* 1233–1247.

Thomas, E. M. (1959). *The harmless people.* New York: Alfred A. Knopf.

———. (2006). *The old way.* New York: Farrar, Straus & Giroux.

Tomonaga, M. (2007). Is chimpanzee (*Pan troglodytes*) spatial attention reflexively triggered by gaze cue? *Journal of Comparative Psychology, 121,* 156–170.

Turnbull, C. M. (1961). *The forest people.* New York: Simon & Schuster.

———. (1982). The ritualization of potential conflict between the sexes among the Mbuti. In E. G. Leacock & R. B. Lee (Eds.), *Politics and history in band societies,* 133–155. Cambridge: Cambridge University Press.

Twenge, J. M. (2000). The age of anxiety? Birth cohort changes in anxiety and neuroticism, 1952–1993. *Journal of Personality and Social Psychology, 79,* 1007–1021.

Twenge, J. M., & Foster, J. D. (2010). Birth cohort increases in narcissistic personality traits among American college students, 1982–2009. *Social Psychological and Personality Science, 1,* 99–106.

Twenge, J. M., Gentile, B., DeWall, C. N., Ma, D., Lacefield, K., & Schurtz, D. R. (2010). Birth cohort increase in psychopathology among young Americans, 1938–2007: A cross-temporal meta-analysis of the MMPI. *Clinical Psychology Review, 30,* 145–154.

Twenge, J. M., Konrath, S., Foster, J. D., Campbell, W. K., & Bushman, B. J. (2008). Egos inflating over time: A cross-temporal meta-analysis of the Narcissistic Personality Inventory. *Journal of Personality, 76,* 875–901.

Twenge, J. M., Zhang, L., & Im, C. (2004). It's beyond my control: A cross-temporal meta-analysis of increasing externality in locus of control, 1960–2002. *Personality and Social Psychology Review, 8,* 308–319.

US Department of Education. (2008). National center for education, issue brief on homeschooling. Published online at http://nces.ed,gov.

Vedder-Weiss, D., & Fortus, D. (2011). Adolescents' declining motivation to learn science: Inevitable or not? *Journal of Research in Science Teaching, 48,* 199–216.

Von Drehle, D. (2010). The case against summer vacation. *Time,* August 2, 36–42.

Vygotsky, L. (1978). Interaction between learning and development. In M. Cole, V. John-Steiner, S. Scribner, and E. Souberman (Eds.), *Mind and society: The development of higher psychological processes.* Cambridge, MA: Harvard University Press.

———. (1933; 1978). The role of play in development. In M. Cole, V. John-Steiner, S. Scribner, & E. Souberman (Eds.), *Mind in society: The development of higher psychological processes,* 92–104. Cambridge, MA: Harvard University Press.

Walker, R., Hill, K., Kaplan, H., & McMillan, G. (2002). Age-dependency in hunting ability among the Aché of Eastern Paraguay. *Journal of Human Evolution, 42,* 639–657.

Wannenburgh, A. (1979). *The bushmen.* New York: Mayflower Books.

Weber, M. (1904–1905/1958). *The Protestant ethic and the spirit of capitalism.* New York: Scribner.

Weems, C. F., & Silverman, W. K. (2006). An integrative model of control: Implications for understanding emotion regulation and dysregulation in childhood anxiety. *Journal of Affective Disorders, 91,* 113–124.

Wegener-Spöhring, G. (1994). War toys and aggressive play scenes. In J. H. Goldstein (Ed.), *Toys, play, and child development,* 84–109. Cambridge: Cambridge University Press.

Whiting, B. B. (1983). The genesis of prosocial behavior. In D. L. Bridgeman (Ed.), *The nature of prosocial development: Interdisciplinary theories and strategies,* 221–242. New York: Academic Press.

Wiessner, P. (1982). Risk, reciprocity and social influences on !Kung San economics. In E. Leacock & R. Lee (Eds.), *Politics and history in band societies.* Cambridge: Cambridge University Press.

———. (1996). Leveling the Hunter: Constraints on the Status Quest in Foraging Societies. In P. Wiessner & W. Schiefenhövel (Eds.), *Food and the status quest: An interdisciplinary perspective,* 171–192.

Wood, D. J., Bruner, J. S., & Ross, G. (1976). The role of tutoring in problem solving. *Journal of Clinical Psychiatry, 17,* 89–100.

Woodburn, J. (1968). An introduction to Hazda ecology. In R. Lee & I. DeVore (Eds.), *Man the hunter.* Chicago: Aldine.

Yee, N. (2006). Motivations for play in online games. *Cyberpsychology & Behavior, 9,* 772–775.

Yogev, A., & Ronen, R. (1982). Cross-age tutoring: Effects on tutors' attitudes. *Journal of Educational Research, 75,* 261–268.

INDEX